William Graham, James Whatman

A review of ecclesiastical establishments in Europe

Containing their history and an essay tending to shew both the political and moral

necessity of abolishing exclusive establishments

William Graham, James Whatman

A review of ecclesiastical establishments in Europe
Containing their history and an essay tending to shew both the political and moral necessity of abolishing exclusive establishments

ISBN/EAN: 9783337134259

Printed in Europe, USA, Canada, Australia, Japan

Cover: Foto ©ninafisch / pixelio.de

More available books at **www.hansebooks.com**

A REVIEW

OF

ECCLESIASTICAL ESTABLISHMENTS

IN

EUROPE.

CONTAINING

Their History; with a Candid Examination of their Advantages and Disadvantages, both Civil and Religious:

An Attempt to define the Extent of Civil Legislation, respecting Ecclesiastical Objects; with

A Discussion of the Question, "Should RELIGIOUS TESTS be made a Rule of Law, in conferring Civil Rewards, or in inflicting Civil Punishments?"

AND

An ESSAY tending to shew both the Political and Moral Necessity of Abolishing exclusive Establishments, with Answers to some principal Objections.

'Η βασιλεία ή εμή εκ εστιν εκ τε κοσμε τετε. Ιωαν.

BY THE REV. MR. WILLIAM GRAHAM,

NEWCASTLE.

The Second Edition, with Alterations and Amendments.

London:

PRINTED FOR G. G. AND J. ROBINSON, PATERNOSTER-ROW; VERNOR AND HOOD, BIRCHIN-LANE; J. GRAY, GLASSHOUSE-STREET; J. COOKE, OXFORD; J. OGLE, EDINBURGH; AND D. NIVEN, GLASGOW.

M.DCC.XCVI.

TO THE

PUBLIC.

WHEN any literary work makes its first appearance, readers justly expect to be made acquainted with the reasons why it is ventured into the world. The writer of the following thoughts is aware, that they ly open not only to all that prepossession which commonly attends new publications; but, besides, that they are exposed to all those prejudices which ever haunt the minds of some readers against the works of those who dare to draw aside the mysterious veil, and attempt to expose to view the grotesque figure of certain idols. An apology is therefore necessary. Whether the following

lowing be sufficient or not, is the province of the reader to decide.

A Controversy, agitated some years ago, concerning subscription to certain articles, gave occasion to the writer to turn his thoughts to the nature and essential characters of christian churches. He was led into a train of sentiments which pleased himself:—he committed his thoughts to writing—and, upon a sixteen-years review, he flatters himself, that they are not altogether unworthy the attention of those, who, in different denominations, interest themselves in the prosperity of those sacred societies.

The evidence attending the writer's sentiments is not the only reason of their publication. The principles, commonly received upon the subject of the legal establishments of christian churches, appear to have been admitted without that degree of caution, which the seriousness of the consequences seems to demand. On that account, they call aloud for a careful review.

DISTIN-

DISTINGUISHED as this age is by a liberality of sentiment, unknown in any former period of the British history, it is not yet wholly free from some remains of that spirit of bigotry and persecution, which has ever been the disgrace of learning, and the poison of religion. Some, accustomed to associate the ideas of a christian church and of a civil exclusive establishment, cannot imagine that the first can exist without the last; and sagely conclude, that all who separate from such churches, however corrupted and tyrannical, are aliens from the common-wealth of Israel, and not many removes from a state of damnation. Others, emancipated in some degree from such uncharitable prejudices, are yet much embarrassed, when certain occasions offer to reduce their more generous principles into practice. Their good sense will not suffer them to deny the name of a christian church to any society which holds the Divine Head, though it never was, and never made any efforts to become, the object of a civil establishment. But, even these too often forget to treat the members of such christian

tian focieties according to their acknowledged character, when the church, eftablifhed by law, requires a decifive proof of their filial attachment to her fecular and feparate interefts. The intention, therefore, of the writer, is, to fuggeft fome thoughts, which, by the bleffing of God, may affift the human mind to throw off its fetters; may enable chriftians to triumph over the perfecuting fpirit of bigotry; and may render even the boafted moderation of the eighteenth century ftill more moderate,

Though thefe reafons may feem fufficient to fecure the writer of the following thoughts from the charge of arrogance in expofing them to public view, they would, probably, have been buried in everlafting filence, had not fome of his friends, to whofe judgment he thinks himfelf bound to pay the greateft deference, fuggefted a more forcible argument for their publication. It is the peculiar feafonablenefs of fuch a work. The prefent age is become remarkable for ftrange revolutions in the
fentiments

sentiments of christians, as well as in the political systems of all nations. Mankind begin to know liberty, to taste her sweets, and to aspire after a full enjoyment of that treasure which she alone can bestow. Liberality of sentiment seems, in spight of every obstruction, to force its way into parliaments and cabinets, into convocations and even conclaves. Hail, thou auspicious age! To every son of liberty, the writer begs leave to inscribe the following thoughts; and flatters himself, that they will suggest sufficient reasons for correcting and enlarging former plans of ecclesiastical reformation.

Though the writer be chiefly solicitous about the success of that cause, which this performance is intended to support; yet he dares not dissemble his anxiety about the fate of the work itself. If it meet with the approbation of some, it must be expected that it will receive the severest wounds of censure from others. It must meet its destiny. However, he hopes that it will be read with the same candour and good-nature with which it was written. His sole intention

intention of giving it to the public is, to affift the chriftian in forming juft ideas of the kingdom of Chrift; to confirm him in the principles, and to direct him in the ufe of that liberty, with which the Divine Author of the chriftian religion has ennobled all his followers; and to infpire him with a refolution to unite in his own character, the zealous and fincere difciple of Jefus, with the peaceable and induftrious citizen.

INTRODUCTION.

A Spirit of enquiry the characteristic of the age. Efforts to regain civil and religious liberty. Sentiments of parties concerning these laudable attempts. National churches have prevented their success. The question, with regard to the justice and good policy of the establishment of national churches, stated; and the signification of the terms distinctly ascertained.

A SPIRIT of disquisition is an undoubted characteristic of this enlightened age. The many bold infractions and tyrannical depredations, which had been made on the rights of conscience, from the commencement of imperial and national churches, at last roused the indignation of Europe; taught christians to set a proper value upon the rights of human nature; and inspired both princes and their subjects with the noble resolution to break that chain, which, so long, had ignominiously bound them to the papal chair. Emancipated from the yoke of popish bigotry, as well as from the heavy fetters of feudal despotism; this age is become tenacious of those rights which distinguish the subject from the slave, and of that liberty which raises the believer so much above the bigot.

The consequences are no other than were foreseen from the earliest date of the reformation. Those whose secular interest has engaged them in the defence of the throne of ignorance and imposition have always declared themselves hostile to the liberties of their fellow christians. Roused into action by their common danger, they have often sounded an alarm; and conscious of the want of better arguments to prop their falling cause, they have ever availed themselves of the secular power, the powerful avenger of national churches, to silence, to persecute, and to crush the friends of truth and freedom.

While these champions have engaged on so unequal terms, it is not surprising that the success hath borne no proportion to the merits of their respective pleas. The friends of freedom, depending on the justice of their cause, have reasonably entertained modest hopes that victory at last would have crowned their wishes and rewarded their pains. But their enemies, armed with every weapon that the well-stored arsenal of a national establishment ordinarily furnishes, and deeply intrenched in the complex political constitution of church and state, have hitherto given bold defiance even to those to whom all the world have repeatedly adjudged the victory.

Nor has the manner in which the contest has been managed, been less preposterous. Those who have exposed every scheme of ecclesiastical tyranny with the greatest force of argument, and with the greatest seeming success, have rarely failed to act over again the same tragic scenes, as soon as ever a proper opportunity has offered of availing themselves of penal statutes. On the other hand, as soon as even the most violent persecutors have felt the weight of those burthens, which they had unmercifully laid on the shoulders of others, they have at length become sensible of the justice and propriety of those

very

very arguments, which, in the hour of prosperity, they were wont to despise. They even have been champions in that very cause, for which they once imagined none but fanatics could distinguish themselves with decency of character.

While these observations expose the caprice of human nature, and prove the irresistible influence, which secular interest hath over the understandings of men; they no less demonstrate the importance of that noble cause for which all parties become strenuous advocates, when they are seen successively in such circumstances as ordinarily bring men to their senses, and oblige them to speak out the real feelings of the human heart. The great God, who dignified human nature with all its gifts and rights, is ever jealous of them, and hath, in this manner, extorted an undisguised confession of their inherent worth and consequential importance.

Though all religious denominations have thus become partisans in the cause of liberty, they have not all spoken the same language concerning the degree in which christians ought to be indulged by their civil superiors with the enjoyment of that important blessing.

Those who bask under the warm sun of a national establishment, affect to think that the cause of liberty is sufficiently guarded, and her blessings abundantly extended, when, after the public teachers of the national creed are secured in the possession of affluent livings, a partial toleration is granted to dissenters. But a toleration incumbered with limitations, and infringements on the rights of conscience, is an insult to human nature, and to him who made it. It is built upon absurdity and injustice. It supposes that all men have not an equal right to think for themselves, and to worship their common Creator and Redeemer, according to the light of their own understandings, and the dictates of their own consciences: that if some men worship God at all, they must buy their liberty to do so, at the expence of many things, to the possession of which their approved loyalty, their elevated stations, their consummate learning, and their political abilities give them the justest title in social life: and that, as the limitations of toleration are arbitrary and fluctuating, the rights of conscience must depend wholly on the caprice of government.

Though legislature have as good a right to deprive the deserving subject of the whole as of any part of his natural and religious rights, yet these gentlemen profess the most perfect acquiescence in that state of things. Guided by early prejudices, and hushed to silence by rich emoluments, they feel no check, when they subscribe a Calvinistic creed in an Arminian sense, and when they address the Supreme Being by forms, which, without a blush, they pronounce unintelligible and absurd! At the same time, they are panegyrists on the constitution, so favourable to liberty and the rights of conscience; and they even affect to wonder, that any should complain, when they must see every day the rights of conscience redeemed at whatever exorbitant and fluctuating price administration is pleased to set upon them.

The infatuation hath seized even dissenters themselves. Many of these, comparing the degree of liberty they now enjoy, with the hardships which their ancestors endured, are disposed to submit tamely to every abridgement of religious liberty, which a moderate administration may judge proper. They seem to think, that occasional conformity to rites, which their consciences condemn, is no considerable hardship, as long as a constant violation of the rights of conscience is not made indispensable to

their

their filling certain lucrative or honorary stations: and that all wishes that the rights of mankind were set on more advantageous ground are fanatical and absurd. Men of such easy principles, keep one another from blushing at their absurdity, and from remorse at their impiety. Such principles are unworthy of any above the rank of slaves and sycophants. As long as a favourite denomination enjoys alone all those privileges, which ought to be enjoyed in common by all deserving subjects, and consciencious dissenters are either robbed of their civil rights, or are obliged to redeem them at the price of daring to violate rights infinitely more precious; who, without blushing, can reckon it unreasonable to wish that liberty and right were more diffusively extended, and more firmly established?

It is plain from these and similar facts, that national churches have ever been at war, not only with the rights of mankind, but even with the spirit of christianity itself. Justice and mercy are the foundations of her throne; equity and righteousness are the pillars of her empire. National establishments therefore, are not that full, and impartial patronage of christianity, which she, by the blessings she pours down on society, ever and exclusively deserves, and which every legislature in the christian world owes her.

The proof of this assertion is intended in this work. That it may be more full and satisfactory, the question concerning the justice and propriety of national establishments must be distinctly stated; and the signification of the terms which are to be used must be clearly ascertained.

I. The question is not—Ought legislatures to interest themselves in the public profession of religion?

Some

Some deists in this, following some fanatics of the last age, have maintained the negative. Yet, the wisdom of government in all countries, and in all ages, has uniformly supported the affirmative. Convinced both by reason and experience, that the fear of God, and the love of justice are the pillars of society, legislatures have ever wisely and anxiously cherished religion, or what was accounted such, among the several classes of their subjects.

II. Nor is the question—Should christian legislatures give a legal establishment to religion, both natural and revealed?

The affirmative is not only granted, but it is the design of this work to prove it, and that national establishments are not that adequate establishment which legislatures owe to religion, both natural and revealed.

The term, *establishment*, is not without ambiguity. When it is applied to natural religion, it conveys an idea very different from what it means when it is applied to revealed religion. In order to remove ambiguity in the use and application of the term, and to disembarrass the state of the question, the following things deserve consideration.

Objects of civil legislation may be said to have received a proper establishment, when they are made, and are capable of becoming the very pillars of the political constitution;—when the native purposes of government cannot be gained, without making them the uniform and indispensable rule of all political management;—and when they and the constitution are so intimately combined, in the nature of things themselves, that they mutually establish one another, and must stand or fall together. Natural religion, in all its branches, belongs to this class of objects. But whether revealed religion is

naturally

naturally capable of *such* an establishment, may be questioned on the best grounds. Nevertheless, the public profession of it is capable of an establishment, in a sense, though different from the former, yet not less real and determinate.

Many objects may receive a proper establishment, as far as the nature of the things themselves, and the native ends of civil government can allow, even when the objects themselves *cannot* be consolidated with the political constitution, made the basis of government, and constituted the indispensable rule of administration. This description of objects obtains a proper political establishment, when the subjects, to whom these things are of importance, are legally protected and impartially rewarded, according to the degree of their political merit.

To this rank of things may be referred all branches of trade and manufacture. These are, in this manner, fully established in every nation of Europe. Legislatures, taught by the blunders of feudal ages, no more embroil themselves, and discourage national industry and enterprize, by granting precluding establishments and partial monopolies in those branches of trade, which justice and public utility require should ly open to all. To give as ample an establishment to any of these branches, as their natures admit, no wise government ever combined a system of the precepts of any art with the political constitution, in such a manner as to preclude every artisan from the common privileges of a subject, unless he brought proof of his strict attention to all the established precepts of that art.

Literature and the learned professions are established in every civilized nation. How is this done? Is a system of the art of healing, for example, so incorporated with the political constitution, that every physician who does not prescribe according

ing to the national dispensatory, shall not only be stigmatized as a quack, but precluded from the common rights of a citizen and a subject? Rather is not the profession of physic properly established, when the professors of that art are protected, patronized and rewarded according to their eminence?

Nor does the nature of the thing require a different kind of establishment to the profession of christianity. Any legislature may confer on the profession of christianity a perfect and impartial establishment, without blending a partial, imperfect, and often an erroneous system of its peculiar doctrines with the civil constitution. What legislature ever attempted to do so, even with natural religion itself? Necessary as it is to the very being of civil society, did ever any government, ancient or modern, adopt and blend with the political constitution any of those systems of moral philosophy, which have been incessantly pouring upon the world from the pens of the learned? Did they ever make Aristotle's ethics, or Puffendorf's law of nature and nations, the public creed and standard of faith concerning moral subjects? Did they ever make the doctrines of any of these often discordant writers the public rule of national manners? Did they at any time make a profession of attachment to a certain system of morals the public badge of moral orthodoxy, and the public rule of law for the distribution of rewards and punishments? Yet who, that is tolerably acquainted with the nature, genius and design of christianity, sees not, that any form the profession of it may be thrown into, in any particular creed, is incomparably less fit to be thus established, than any system of moral philosophy whatever? Let the christian subject be protected: let him be rewarded according to the degree of his political merit: let him be patronized and encouraged according to the
degree

degree of his eminence in his christian profession and deportment: and, when all this is done, the profession of christianity is **universally patronized, and impartially established.**

III. The question is not—Whether legislature, by granting a precluding patronage to one denomination of christians, does *too much?* But whether, by doing *so much* for one description of christians, civil government does not fall short of its own original purposes; and instead of establishing the church with the full and adequate profession of christianity, in her, does not in a great measure overthrow both?

There is nothing more contrary to reason as well as revelation, than to suppose that the church of Christ is confined to any one sect or description of christians. She is catholic. She comprehends, within her extensive pale, all societies, whose soundness in the faith, and whose conscientious subjection to the institutions of Christ, entitle them to the honour of being justly reckoned parts of that sacred body. When any government, therefore, grants a precluding patronage to any particular part of that body, appointing subscription to its creed the legal *condition* of enjoying the common rights of citizens and subjects; neither is the church, according to the full import of the term, established—nor does government itself act up to its original ends. It suspends the duties it owes to society, protection, patronage and encouragement, on conditions which are foreign to civil society. A particular sect alone is protected and patronized; and other subjects—other christians, equally deserving of civil society, are robbed of their property to enrich it. Such an establishment constitutes its objects a schismatical body. It puts it in their power by law, to erect a separate

separate interest from their brethren, and to pursue designs, foreign, yea, often opposite to our common christianity. It authorizes them to insult, to persecute, and to kill their fellow-christians of other denominations and of other churches, belonging to the same catholic body. It patronizes them in proudly arrogating to themselves, after the accustomed manner of all who are actuated by a schismatical spirit, the high-sounding appellation of—THE CHURCH.

IV. The state of the inquiry, therefore, is—" Whether the state of civil society, the marked character of Christ's kingdom, the law of equity, and the rights of conscience—admit that any legislature should incorporate any distinct description of christians; should dignify it with the pompous title of THE CHURCH; and should ally it to the political constitution, in such a degree of intimacy, that communion with that incorporated sect, in all the offices of religion, shall be as indispensably necessary to entitle any subject to the legal enjoyment of the common rights of men, of citizens and of christians, as his approved obedience to the common and statute law of his country?"

In fewer words, the question is—" Whether COMMUNION with the NATIONAL CHURCH OUGHT to be a RULE of LAW, in the political constitution, for conferring *civil rewards*, and inflicting *civil punishments?*

The design of the work is to shew the absurdity and injustice of that *condition* or RULE of LAW; and to attempt a proof, that in so far as it appears to be built on a supposition that the natural and civil rights of subjects depend on their religious opinions—or that according to their faith, so are their persons and their rights, in this world, as well as

in

in that which is to come;—it is more than sufficient to tear the best compacted society to pieces, and to throw all the affairs of mankind into a state of the most deplorable confusion.

To preclude all ambiguity in the use of terms and phrases, and that we may prosecute the design with all possible clearness and precision, the ideas affixed to the several terms, which are used in the state of the question, and to those synonymous phrases which occur in the body of the work, must be distinctly ascertained.

I. By *communion* with any church is meant—"The profession of an acquiescence in her peculiar creed, the public use of her ritual, subjection to her canons, and responsibility to her tribunals."

II. By the *national church* is understood—"A certain denomination of professed christians, distinguished by its peculiar creed and ritual, dignified by the legislature with the superb title of THE CHURCH, and so closely allied unto, and incorporated with the political constitution of the nation, that obedience to the common and statute law of the realm, is not a more indispensable condition, to every subject, of his fully enjoying the common rights of men, citizens and subjects, then his being a member of, and his holding communion with, that society, in all the offices of religion."

The phrases, *allied church*, *incorporated church*, and *established church*, convey the same idea.

III. The terms, *incorporation*, *alliance*, and *establishment*, mean—"That act of legislature by which it jumbles and confounds the constitution of the national church with the political frame of the nation itself, in such a way as to make it a *rule* of *law*, that communion with her shall be indispensably necessary to qualify the subject for, and non-communion shall legally disqualify and preclude him from, the full and undisturbed possession of his just rights and liberties, though in every civil and political respect, he be a loyal subject, and an useful member of society."

IV. By a *rule* of *law*, in general is meant—" A legal standard, serving to regulate and direct the executive powers, in their dispensing civil rewards and punishments:" but by that term, in this work, is specially understood, " The legal requisition of communion with the national church, as the *qualifying condition* of fully enjoying the common rights of men and subjects."

The phrases, *qualifying condition, rule of preclusion, precluding rule,* and *standard of rewards and punishments,* convey the same idea.

V. By civil rewards is uniformly meant—" The legal, full, and undisturbed enjoyment of all that a good subject merits by his obedience to the civil and municipal laws of his country, particularly the protection of his person and rights, together with a right to his just share of all honorary and lucrative employments, proportionate to his political desert, and his social qualifications."

VI. By civil punishments is understood—" All that a bad subject deserves, according to the common and statute law of his country."

CHAP.

CHAP. I.

The Origin and gradual Advances of Ecclesiastical Incorporations.

REASONING from facts and experiments is the surest and shortest road to sound knowledge. The philosopher, jealous of the fascination of an heated imagination, trusts not to any hypothesis, even though it should appear in all the charms of the highest probability. Strictly cautious, nothing is received for truth, but what is supported by well-attested facts, and confirmed by repeated experiments. The qualities of vegetables, metals and minerals are not taken on trust. Nature herself is put to the torture; nothing is neglected, in the most tedious and expensive processes, to oblige her to confess her secrets and to disclose her mysteries.

It is no small disadvantage to society, that the naturalist is seen almost alone in this safe path. The experience of ages, relating to objects which nearly concern the happiness or the misery of mankind, is too often neglected. Every new generation adopts schemes of policy as if it were the first. Surely, the world has not existed so many ages in vain. Were the lessons of experience attended to, as recorded in the historian's page, and written in the fate of societies, they would be of the same use to the politician, as the regular succession of celestial phenomena is to the astronomer. Many plans of politics, now celebrated, and almost adored, as the noblest efforts of human wisdom, would be reprobated as the greatest proofs of human folly.

Such

Such are all ecclesiastical incorporations. But before we enter on the proof of this assertion, we will inquire into their origin and gradual advances, in the nations of Europe; and make some general reflections upon their history, both ancient and modern.

SECT. I.

The Origin of Ecclesiastical Incorporations.

NONE will expect, that we should gravely open the BIBLE, in order to find the origin of incorporations among the institutions of the christian Lawgiver. Even those, who have been the most furious advocates for popery, or the grand alliance of church and state; and who, after their manner, have demonstrated the christian institution of many things which never entered into the mind of Christ himself—have never adventured to refer politico-ecclesiastical incorporations to a New Testament original.

Notwithstanding, the patrons of these alliances are loth to lose so respectable an authority as that of the inspired oracles. Though Christ and his apostles deny their suffrage, they would persuade the world that Moses is more tractable and complaisant. The Jewish lawgiver—The Jewish polity—The Jewish nation, are ever in their mouths—ever at the points of their pens.

As a presumption of the lawfulness, and even necessity of forming christian churches on the plan of the Jewish ecclesiastical nation, is one reason of that strong attachment which many have to national churches,

churches, we shall remove this stumbling-block, industriously laid in the way of many plain and pious christians.

Those writers, who ascend so high as the age of Moses to find the model of the christian church, fly higher than even human faith can follow. They are antiquarians to a dangerous excess. They are not aware, that they hurt their cause as much as the blundering Hibernian sunk the credibility of his evidence, when he swore that the duke of ———'s ancestors were the proprietors of an estate, then litigated, before the deluge. The principle cannot be admitted, till it be first demonstrated, that any thing may exist a thousand years before its own beginning. The christian church, founded on the resurrection of her own Lawgiver, was modelled by his wisdom, and established by his authority alone: were it otherwise, why are Moses and Jesus Christ so often opposed? Why is the house, in which Moses was faithful, only as a servant, opposed to that house, over which Christ, as the Lord and first-begotten among many brethren, presideth for ever?

Though some protestant writers of reputation, inadvertently copying from the champions of the popish cause, have admitted and maintained the presumption, yet it seems capable of demonstration, that no one ordinance, much less the whole pattern of the New Testament church-state, was borrowed from Moses. It is impossible. The system of ordinances, in the Old Testament, including even that which respected the incorporation of the church with the political state of the Jewish nation, was calculated to assist the faith, and to cherish the hope of a people, who, as the descendants of Abraham, were bound to live in a state of expectation of the Messiah, promised to descend from that distinguished patriarch. Now, the institutions of the gospel church-

church-state, instead of holding expectation on the rack, are formed to lead up the mind to the most perfect repose on the truth of those events and facts, so long prefigured and expected. It is therefore impossible that He who is wisdom itself, should borrow the model of his church from the Jewish lawgiver, and thus, by perpetuating a typical ordinance, betray christians, in every age, into a vain expectation of a kingdom, which hitherto has existed in its figure only.*

None ever doubted, that the supreme authority among the Jews, signified by Judah's sceptre, was typical, equally as the priesthood of Aaron. When their prefiguring purposes were accomplished in the person of Christ, who is now the " Priest upon his throne," the sceptre departed from Judah, and the mitre from Aaron at one and the same time. The political state of the nation and the peculiar frame of the church, so long typically incorporated, were destroyed together. The princes of the house of David did not derive their authority from the same sources, from which other monarchs inherit the purple. They held the sceptre, as the viceroys of the

---

* We mean not to assert, that these Old Testament ordinances were *merely* shadows. No: they only became such, when the *substance*, which they adumbrated, had actually come. Till that æra, they seemed to hold up to the church a prospective view of Messiah. Hence, the Old Testament church-state, which was made up of the several ordinances belonging to the Mosaic system, was indeed *typical*, but not *merely* such, or a shadow only without any substance. It was *real* because it was *typical*. It was calculated to assist the faith of the church to contemplate *good things to* come, which it could not have done, had it not been *typical*. Notwithstanding there never was such an object in existence as a *typical church*, as some have inconsiderately affirmed. There is an infinite difference between the *church* and her *ecclesiastical* STATE. She is the same invariably, while her *church-state* must vary according as the object of her faith is either *present* or *future*.

God

God of Israel. They were heirs to it by that typical covenant which first aggrandised the tribe of Judah, and which was afterwards appropriated to the family of David. What has been always reckoned sufficient to justify the claims of ordinary sovereigns, had no place among the Jews. None were permitted to assume judicial or regal authority, but those only whom the Supreme MONARCH of Israel honoured with a special designation, either by extraordinary inspiration, as in the case of the Judges; or by federal appointment, as in the case of the Davidic family.*

* This furnishes us with an obvious reason, why God was so displeased with the tribes, in the days of *Samuel*, when they requested a king, who might *judge them, like all the nations*. Was he displeased, that they asked a prince to judge them? No! when the sons of *Samuel*, who were their ordinary magistrates, had *turned aside after lucre*, had *taken bribes*, and had *perverted judgment*; the request was not more reasonable in itself, than we have reason to believe it was acceptable to God, who holds such magistrates in eternal abhorrence. The true reason seems to be, that the demand included in it a desire to be set on the same bottom, with regard to their magistracy, with other nations. Regardless of the *covenant* of *royalty*, or *regency*, established with the tribe of Judah, and blind to the important *intention* of that covenant; they obstinately demanded a liberty to act upon the foot of the law of nature alone, like all other nations; and to chuse a prince out of any tribe, without paying any regard to the tribe of *Judah*, or to the *typical sceptre*, with which it was honoured. This accounts for God's address to *Samuel*. *They have not rejected thee, but they have rejected me, that I should not reign over them.* "Impatient of that peculiar form of typical "government, which I have instituted among them, and by "which I have appropriated the regency of the nation to myself, "as their king; they are obstinately bent upon throwing it off, "and to become like the rest of the nations in their government; "as they have already become too like them in their worship." On the whole, it is plain, that the regal office among the Jews was a typical ordinance, which belonged to that system of figurative institutions, in which their church-state consisted, and by which their faith was instructed to look forward to the incarnation of Messiah, and to the establishment of his kingdom, not less distinguished from the former in spirituality, than in glory and extent.

It is therefore plain, that the advocates of ecclesiastic incorporations have not Moses for their patron. To establish their wild hypothesis, they must prove,—That christian princes succeed to the throne of David :—That christian nations are not under a civil government, but are cherished, like ancient Israel, under the wings of a theocracy :—That the sceptre hath not yet departed from Judah :—That christian princes are lawgivers from between his feet :—And, in short, that the Messiah is not come in the flesh ! *

* Though to attempt a proof of these propositions is a task, which will be allowed to be too hard for any christian: the abetters of exclusive charters, without giving themselves any trouble about these consequences, build their whole fabric upon an *hypothesis*, which as plainly includes them, as the number four implies twice two. To be convinced of this, one need only to peep into the controversies of the last century between the champions for the royal cause, and the parliamentary writers. It seems to have been a received principle, on both sides, that christian princes have as ample powers as ever *Solomon*, *Asa* or *Josiah* had, to reform and model the church, according to what they judge to be most agreeable to the will of heaven. The principal question, which was agitated between them, was, how far the royal authority of the Jewish kings extended ? and it is plain, that those, who most strenuously defended the noble cause of liberty against the encroachments of the court and starchamber, led away by the common presumption, even strained the point beyond the truth, when they attempted to prove, that the Jewish princes extended their authority no farther than to these limits which they were willing to set, and which reason requires to be set to christian princes, in things which are without the verge of their prerogative. Notwithstanding, should we for a moment grant the truth of that *hypothesis* which seems to have been inadvertently admitted by both sides ; one or the other of the following conclusions must be equally true. Either that christian princes are invested with their authority, in virtue of the covenant of regency among the Jews : or that there was no such covenant among that distinguished people ; and that their princes governed them upon the foot of the law of nature alone, after the manner of all other nations. Than either of these plain deductions, nothing can be imagined more absurd, antichristian and profane.

It

It cannot be objected, that as the congregation of Israel was a church, as well as a nation, combined, by the authority of God, in one mixed constitution, an alliance between the political and ecclesiastical states in christian nations can imply nothing absurd and unjust.

The analogy is so distant that it cannot support the inference. The political state of Israel was quite different from, and opposed to, that of other and ordinary nations. That people was an " holy nation" and " a kingdom of priests." It was the figure, if not the very image of the kingdom of Christ, which, like that of the Jews, is not of this world. It was no social combination, founded on the law of nature, and governed by the law of nations: It was made up of a peculiar people separated from the nations. Their social connection depended on their common relation to Abraham. Their constitution and their laws were all announced from the terrific mount of divine legislation. No argument, therefore, can be drawn from the authority which the kings of Judah claimed, and by divine right possessed. The argument can be of no force, till it be proved, that the design of God in the erection of the New Testament church, is the same with that which was in view in delivering the plan of the Jewish church to the Israelitish lawgiver :—that the throne of David was similar in all respects to that of Nebuchadnezzar, or Alexander the Great, and that the nation of the Jews was purely civil, and differed in nothing from the kingdom of Babylon, Egypt or England.*

It

---

* It follows by the justest consequence, that though those, who first laid the plan of ecclesiastical charters under the gospel, seem to have borrowed it from the Jewish polity; and though those, who have asserted their lawfulness and divine warrant, have derived all their arguments from the same source; that

boasted

It is granted, that the Jewish religion was incorporated in the political constitution of the nation. But it is refused, that it was settled there on the basis of civil authority. It leaned to a divine institution alone. Besides, the act of incorporation was not preclusive. It robbed no description of Jews, in order to enrich others. It was not artfully procured by designing men at the court of David, or of Solomon, for the purpose of depredation. It was a special effect of that authority, which the God of Israel himself exercised about a nation, which never had, and never will have, an equal upon earth. In fine, it was an immediate consequence of that unexampled THEOCRACY, to which the seed of Abraham were subjected, and which was designed to be a sacred

---

boasted example, as it was never intended to be an example, saps the enormous fabric, which it was intended to support. As the congregation of Israel was a peculiar people, separated by their laws as well as by their worship from all the nations of the world; the polity of these nations was, under the severest penalties, prohibited admission into the sacred system of their extraordinary government. When that distinguished people only wished the removal of the political discriminating badge, in the age of *Samuel*, they severely smarted for their *sacrilegious* arrogance: and when they attempted it, in the days of the latter kings, they were severely punished with devastations, not less instructive than terrible. The inference is clear. As that people, in their distinguishing typical circumstances were an instituted emblem and *hieroglyphic* of the spiritual kingdom of Christ, which is founded, as the kingdom of Israel was, on positive institution; nothing which belongs to systems of civil policy in the kingdoms of this world, ought to obtain in the kingdom of Christ. Nor is it an uninteresting observation, that christian churches, having absurdly suffered their constitutions to be blended with the civil polity of the European nations, and the authority of Christ to be supplanted by the sceptres of the princes, who have governed these kingdoms; have been severely punished, like the nation of *Israel*, by a captivity not less tremendous than theirs, and of a much longer duration, from which God hath only begun to deliver them.

figure

figure of that moſt glorious CHRISTOCRACY, under which the nations are, and without exception, ſhall be bleſſed.

By this time, it is hoped the unprejudiced are ſatisfied, that the alliance owes its exiſtence, not to divine inſtitution, but to ſome other cauſes, which we are now to enumerate.

I. Inadequate ideas of the nature, genius and ends of Chriſt's kingdom, were an early occaſion of a ſtrong deſire of the incorporation of that ſociety in the political conſtitution of earthly kingdoms.

It is plain, from the writers of the New Teſtament, that the Jews, to whom were firſt committed the deſcriptions of the Meſſiah's kingdom, had very groſs and falſe ideas of that kingdom. They always aſſociated with it the idea of an earthly monarchy. Had Herod not been perſuaded by the popular belief of the nation, that the Meſſiah was to appear in the character of a great earthly prince, and might one day dethrone him,—could he have uſed the cruel precaution to murder the infants of Bethlehem? Or, can we imagine a motive leſs ſtrong than the fear of meeting a common enemy and ſupplanter, in the perſon of the Chriſt, could have induced Herod and Pontius Pilate, intereſted enemies to one another, to quench the flames of their mutual animoſity in the blood of that divine perſon?

The diſciples of Chriſt were not at firſt more happy in their notions. Educated among their ignorant countrymen, they could not eſcape the common infection. The firſt occaſion of their ſhewing a ſtrong propenſion to an incorporation is exactly marked, and the perſon who adventured to propoſe it, is particularly named. To the reproach of the ſcheme, an ambitious old woman walks at
the

the head of all its votaries.* Fascinated with the common prejudices of an age, in which the typical signification of the Davidic covenant, throne and sceptre was in a great measure lost,—the disciples imagined; that as their master was to fill the throne of his father David, he would sway the sceptre of that victorious monarch, with a degree of splendour and earthly glory as far superior to that of David as David's Lord was exalted in dignity above Jesse's son. And no doubt, they felicitated themselves in contemplating the shining figure they would make in his court, or at the head of his armies, swimming to universal conquest in the blood of all their enemies.

Even after the resurrection of Christ, the apostles seem to have been actuated with the same spirit. This may be justly inferred from that question, which with much anxiety they put to their divine Master, at a time when no objects but those of the last importance in their view, could have employed their thoughts. Taking their leave of him, they did not judge it to be impertinent trifling to ask,—Wilt thou at this time restore the kingdom to Israel? †

Though after the effusion of the Spirit at Pentecost, the first public teachers were better instructed, the body of the Jewish converts were not so soon disengaged from their national prejudices. They continued long to think that christianity ought to be incorporated in the constitution of their nation, and wholly confined to her members. The question concerning circumcision, joined to the extraordinary acrimony with which it was long debated, fully establishes the truth of this observation. There was no extraordinary sanctity in that ordinance to conciliate a superior respect to it. But it had been

* Matth. xx. 20.   † Acts i. 6.

always

always the *gate*, by which proselytes had entered into political as well as religious connections with them. These converts were therefore aware, that if that ordinance were superseded, the whole political frame of their nation would instantly tumble down. To prevent so dreadful an event, they insisted, that all Gentile christians should become members of the Jewish nation by submitting to the discriminating rite of circumcision; and that christianity being thus allied to their nation, it might be wholly confined to it. Thus, they entertained sanguine hopes, that as christianity promised to become universal among all people, their nation would swallow up all nations on the earth, and suddenly become, in a sense agreeable to the pride of their nation, that mountain MONARCHY, spoken of by Daniel * the prophet. From his throne in heaven, the Lord beheld the rising Babel: with an indignant look, he overthrew it; and that it might become a pillar of salt, expressive, to all nations and to all ages, of his just displeasure at all attempts to blend his kingdom with those of this world, and to make christianity a tool to lust of empire, he, by one unexampled stroke of deserved vengeance, put a final period to their existence as a people; and dispersed them among all nations to tell the tidings and to proclaim the causes of the catastrophe.

Notwithstanding this example, ever present to the eyes of all christian nations, the same cause has ever been teeming with the same or similar effects. Especially since the age of Constantine, the same confusion of ideas has betrayed men, otherwise learned and pious, into the same hopeless enterprize. We say hopeless, because it is impossible to carry it into execution. Objects, naturally incapable

* Dan. ii. 44.

of mixture, cannot be incorporated. Extended and thinking substances cannot be blended. Yet, strange to behold! The enterprize is not abandoned; and in order to succeed, men plunge into practices, not only inconsistent with the genius and ends of christianity, but shocking to the feelings of humanity. Church history exhibits little besides the violent struggles of christian sects to obtain, or maintain, by the basest arts, and the most brutish cruelties, the incorporation of their respective creeds. Their pious pretences of gilded zeal could never disguise the idols of their hearts. Their violent animosities, cruel persecutions and inhuman massacres acquit christianity of all blame, and shew that these zealots had no just ideas of that holy religion.

II. Impatience of persecution, an immoderate desire to provide against it, and a violent thirst of retaliation, are one united and powerful reason, why christians have availed themselves of national establishments, as safe asylums to themselves, and engines of revenge against their enemies.

It was in the fourth century, that christians first entertained the idea of allying the profession of christianity with the constitution of the Roman empire. They viewed it as an excellent expedient, not only to entail peace on the church; but to oblige the votaries of Jupiter to become the worshippers of Jesus, on pain of having all their former cruelties returned on themselves! How delusory!—From that moment, the church's greatest woes take date. Those furies, which actuated the dragon, during the heathen persecutions, took full possession of christians. They plunged their swords into the breasts of their brethren, who, at any time, happened to dislike any article of the incorporated creed. Athanasians and Arians by turns boast of the

the alliance. Christ was supposed to preside in the court, and to govern his church by the decrees of Cæsar. The emperor's nod was sufficient to warrant them to proceed to mutual extermination. And the clergy, those ministers of the God of peace, lured by the possession, or the prospect of wealth and honours, blew the martial trumpet, and gave the signal to battle!

III. PRIDE may be assigned as another reason why christians have sought to shelter themselves under the wings of a precluding establishment.

Pride, naturally impatient of contradiction, leaves no stratagem unattempted to elude it. The man who ventures to think differently from the *great* and the *many*, tacitly arraigns the soundness of their understandings. Their pride is alarmed. Their jealousy suggests that the arrogant man is happy in thinking himself a wiser man. They are stung into resentment. They call up every angry and intolerant passion to their assistance against the imagined adversary, whom they ever view as a haughty dictator of his own opinions, and a justly hated censor of theirs. They fly to incorporations and penal laws, as the only means of accomplishing what they had attempted in vain by other methods of refutation. Like the lonely owl, they retire from the light, and seek, under the thick shade of a national establishment, a sanctuary for their pride and prejudices, which even the sacred feet of truth are forbid to approach.

But why so urgent to oppress the unfortunate dissenter? Why so forward to answer all his arguments in this summary way? Ask not a reason. It is PRIDE, which knows no reason. Nay, they reply, " Persuaded that our creed is the essence of orthodoxy, godly zeal prompts us." Well! But is not the diffenter equally pofitive concerning the foundnefs of his faith? And is it not the ftrength of his arguments in its defence, which lays him open to this mode of refutation? If confidence of orthodoxy be a fufficient reafon to juftify penal laws and perfecution, then there never was an iniquitous perfecution fince chriftianity fhot her gladdening beams on this benighted world. Zealots and cut-throats are moft confident of their own faith, and are perfectly orthodox in their belief of, at leaft, the firft and leading article of the perfecutor's creed,—"That to murder the diffenter is to do God a meritorious fervice." Such devils, with human faces, ftand acquitted of guilt, and are entitled to the character of the beft chriftians!

Let not the advocate for incorporations conceal that tyrant of the human breaft under the pretence, " that chriftianity *needs* the interpofition of civil authority for its defence." Let him be explicit. Does he mean *chriftians?* It is granted. They often need it; and, acting up to their character, they always deferve it. But do they need a power of legally invading the rights and liberties of their fellow-chriftians, and of ufurping the authority of the Almighty over the confciences of their fellow-creatures? Does he mean the *profeffion* of chriftianity? That alfo is granted. But incorporations tie up the hands of civil authority from executing that kind office to any profeffion, befides that which, being incorporated, legally devours and damns every differing profeffion of it in the world! Does he mean chriftianity itfelf? It is denied. To affirm it would betray the caufe of that holy religion to its enemies. Whether it be affirmed or denied, the neceffity of incorporations is overturned. Is it affirmed?—then chriftianity deferves no patronage, much lefs an incorporation. If it want evidence to eftablifh itfelf,

it

it deserves none from any legislature. It would be tyranny to impose, under civil pains, the belief of a creed without evidence. The human understanding is not more capable of assenting to *inevident* truths than to the most undisputed absurdities.—Is it denied?—Then why should government thrust forward its tremendous hand, and grasp that sword, which has been so often bathed in the blood of the best christians, in order to give an establishment to the self-established religion of Jesus. Let pretences be laid aside. They are dishonourable. Impartial history vouches, that the creed which has been generally most courtly, and most popular has been least allied to Christianity. Yet, the priesthood said it was Christianity: the staring multitude believed it on their ghostly testimony. Legislature found its own account in the delusion: and, as some have always been ready to ask puzzling questions, impatience of contradiction has ever directed the eyes of all parties to incorporations and to penal laws, as the most popular and powerful, if not the most convincing, arguments to silence all men, to confound dissenters, to refute heretics, and to establish the multitude in their most implicit faith.

IV. What has been just now observed serves to illustrate the truth of our last assertion,—"That a coincidence of the secular interests and views of ambitious princes and aspiring priests has been one chief cause of incorporations, and of their continuance in Europe."—Princes who modelled the several political constitutions of modern Europe; and church-men, who found ways and means to interest themselves in a business so foreign to their religious character, have always found them very subservient to their respective corrupt designs.

Though princes may justly curse the contrivers of incorporations, yet they still continue to act upon that absurd system. All the convulsions, the rebellions, and the revolutions which it has occasioned have not yet opened their eyes to its inconsistence, injustice and fatal consequences. Pressed by the hard law of necessity, they jog on in the same thorny paths which their Gothic ancestors marked out for them, while under the ghostly direction of the court of Rome. The rights of the incorporated sect must be always the first object of royal providence: and if, at any time, they be neglected, the prince, who does it, or dares to cast a favourable look upon dissenters, sooner or later has reason to repent his imprudence.

It is thus that political objects must continue as long as national churches continue according to their present constitution; and as long as the checkered administration of church and state, consolidated by incorporations, is in the hands of persons of such opposite characters, and attached to such incompatible interests. If the civil branch in the mixed administration prevail, it drags the church after its triumphal chariot, and degrades her to the humble state of an hand-maid to princely ambition. If the spiritual directors, on any lucky revolution, extend their influence over the whole, the event must be similar to those of the same kind, in the age of Hildebrand. The intrigues of churchmen will once more engage the attention of all: priests will sound the clarion, and summon the nations to croisades: priests will lead armies under the banner of the cross to exterminate heretics, and massacre whole nations: and Europe once more will see her emperors and her kings in the habiliments of penitents, soliciting forgiveness of their political sins at the levees of popes, or receiving their forfeited crowns from

from his hands. An exact equipoise never was, and never will be fixed between the prerogative of princes and the claims of dignified priests, when their ever-jarring interests are blended by incorporations. Visionaries have written about it: politicians have laboured in it; but it is all in vain. The prince or the priest must govern the whole.

SECT. II.

The Gradual Advances of Incorporations.

TO set any political object in the strongest point of view, it is necessary to mark its gradual advances, and to examine the various methods by which it has established itself in society. With this view, it is proposed to point out the more remarkable æras of ecclesiastical incorporations in the European nations, and to mark the consequences which have attended them.

The fourth century is famous for the birth of antichrist and incorporations. But the model of both existed many ages before that celebrated æra.

All, who are acquainted with the Roman history, know, that from the earliest date of Roman grandeur, certain religious rights, venerated on account of their imagined antiquity, and esteemed sacred because of their pretended mysteries, were, by authority, made the incorporated religion of the Roman republic. The gods, whom they, and their savage ancestors had worshipped, obtained a public ratification of their fancied rights to national adoration. These rights were fenced by penal laws. It was declared to be criminal, to acknowledge any new deity, till the senate had examined his pretensions,

had

had approved his credentials, and had voted him to his seat among the gods. A certain hierarchy of priests were arranged to attend in the fanes of these deities; to officiate at their altars; and to pay them those honours, in the name of the Roman people, which the supreme authority of the republic had decreed to them. Festivals were appointed. Magnificent temples were built. In short, the whole system of paganism was incorporated: and the republic had no sooner put off its ancient form, and had submitted to the government of one person, than the emperor became the head of the Roman pagan church—supreme head over all persons, and in all causes, ecclesiastical as well as civil.

From this short sketch, it is easy to see the MODEL of incorporations; and, at the same time, the MOTIVES, which prompted the christian clergy to solicit,—and the christian emperors to grant a similar alliance to christianity, in the fourth century.

Long had the children of pride, in the christian churches, beheld with wishful eyes, the distinguished honours, the immense riches, and the unrestrained pleasures, which the heathen hierarchy enjoyed by the incorporation of Roman superstition. Fastidious ambition and lust of domination had been working in the breasts of many among the ministers of Jesus, long before the celebrated triumph of the cross at the conversion of Constantine. Some of these sons of Diotrephes had obtained the designation of BISHOP, as a title of pre-eminence and domination over their brethren. They had begun to usurp on the rights, not only of their own clergy, but of the neighbouring bishops in less opulent cities. When the day at last dawned, which presented an opportunity of supplanting the heathen hierarchs, is it to be imagined, that clergymen of such a spirit, and of such a character, would suffer the golden season to pass away without

every

every effort which the lust of wealth could inspire, or the restlessness of ambition stimulate their aspiring minds unto? No: the objects were substantial, important, irresistible.

Nor had Constantine less powerful temptations. Ignorant in a great degree of the christian religion; superstitiously attached to the persons of those, who had obtained the direction of his conscience; and surrounded at all times with flatterers, who were filling his ears with lectures on the meritorious services he would do God and his church by bestowing the spoils of the merciless Egyptians on the oppressed Israelites: he would have been more than a man, had he not fallen into the snare, which was so artfully laid for secularizing christianity. More accustomed to hear the clang of arms, than to attend to the cries which violence forces from the injured; he had no time nor inclination to reflect, that even when he was laudably exerting his authority in protecting christians from persecution, and christianity from the insults of ignorance and malice; he himself would be guilty of the most flagrant violation of the laws of christianity, as well as of natural justice, if he should deprive the votaries even of a false religion of those rights to which they were entitled as subjects of the empire. A novice in christianity, he was not aware, that while he was allying it to the constitution of the empire, and secularizing its public teachers, he was laying a broad foundation for its sophistication and utter ruin. Could he have foreseen the scenes which opened on the European stage, during the middle ages, in consequence of his politics, so pious a character would have shuddered at them, and so wise a prince would have been first in reprobating them.

But Constantine was no prophet. In his circumstances, he could only reason from analogy. " Did a system of impiety, superstition and absurdity, supported only by its incorporation, not only so long triumph over the efforts of philosophy, but even resist christianity itself; shall not that heavenly religion, leaning hitherto to its own evidence only, become greatly triumphant, by possessing the throne, swaying the sceptre, and brandishing the sword of its unworthy rival?"

This was the goodly MODEL of christian incorporations! And now, christianity must change her attire, that, with dignity, she may fill the throne of her discarded rival. The ministers of the churches raise their heads; extend their views; and become lords not only over the heritage of their MASTER in heaven, but also over the dominions of their sovereign on earth. A spirit of innovation rages. Superstition opens all her tinsel treasures. Ignorance erects her ebon throne. The doctrines of christianity are adulterated. Its institutions are sophisticated. Offices, hitherto unknown in the church, are invented. And these are executed by clergymen, under characters not less foreign to christian institution than those of magician or soothsayer. Such a sudden revolution could not, indeed, have been effected but upon the plan of an incorporation already venerable and familiar to the multitude.

The political arrangement of parts in the empire was indeed another branch of the MODEL. The emperors, that they might the more firmly rivet the chains, with which they had bound the Roman world, divided it into certain districts, and these into more minute parts, over which certain civil and military officers were appointed to preside, accountable to the political head of the empire. When christianity was incorporated with the constitution of the empire, the christian church became catholic by a catholicism, *limited* by the number and extent
of

of the Roman provinces. This *catholic* church became as unwieldy as the empire, with which she was incorporated. It, therefore, became necessary to divide and subdivide her into parts, analogous and adjusted to the artificial divisions of the empire. These partitions, according to the extent of territory, and the quality of the cities in them, were to be governed by patriarchs, metropolitans, bishops, with other orders of subsidiary clergy. These, like the civil and military officers presiding in the provinces, were accountable to the emperor, in their clerical as well as in their civil character. He governed the ecclesiastical branch of the empire, as really, by the empty shadows of general councils, as he ruled the civil and military departments by the image of the ancient senate. By these means, to whatever system of religious opinions the emperor inclined, he dragged the church in imperial chains to profess an attachment to the same courtly articles, and to anathematize all the christian world beside.

Such was the beginning of imperial and national churches. But their incorporation was not yet compleat. Their advances to perfection were, perhaps, less owing to human policy than to those powerful causes, which, during many ages, agitated the empire and the church, incorporated with it, till they wholly coalited into an *aliquod tertium*, a SOMETHING, which John calls " a BEAST, with seven heads and ten horns." *

These causes may be referred to four classes,— The HERESIES which abounded from the moment incorporations commenced.—The SCHISMS, which these wild opinions occasioned.—The PERSECUTIONS which followed both.—And the POLITICAL REVOLUTIONS, or apocalyptic earthquakes which marched on, in solemn pace, in the rear.

* Rev. xvii. 3.

I. The

I. The HERESIES, joined to the part which the several emperors acted in these religious controversies, tended very much to effect a coalition.

Before the date of the first incorporation, the churches, though they had been often plagued with the absurd reveries of some lunatics, distinguished in after ages by the more respectable name of heretics, yet they had always gained an easy victory over them, by the due use of christian institutions. So long as civil authority did not officially interest itself in the sentiments of peaceable christians, that infamous generation had no opportunity to assume airs of importance; to disturb society; and by ingratiating themselves with the eunuchs and the ladies at court, to aspire after an incorporation of their opinions. Were their opinions unsupported by evidence, they were treated as they deserved. They could not engage and engross the attention of the whole world, by procuring an imperial mandate to suspend the judgment of their own church, and to refer their opinions for judgment to a council of foreign clergy, called forth to gratify female ambition, or the insufferable pride of some dreaming theologians.

How great was the change, when civil authority was prostituted to cherish, or to blast theological opinions! From that moment, there was scarcely an heretic of parts and popularity, who had it not in his power to disseminate his dreams in every province of the empire. The secular views of ecclesiastics and of state grandees were so blended, in consequence of the high station, which the incorporated sect and fashionable system had in the constitution, that no religious controversy could fall out among the first, without affecting the interests of the last, and obliging them to draw their swords against one another. Nor could any revolution

lution in political matters befal the ſtate, without nearly affecting the incorporated ſect, and giving their eccleſiaſtics an occaſion of ringing an alarm, "The church is in danger!"

Thus, the hereſies, which like noxious weeds, ſprung up in the luxuriant ſoil of an imperial church; the impolitic intromiſſions of civil authority with them; and the convulſions in both church and ſtate, which they occaſioned during a long period of three hundred years, after the date of incorporations, ſo thoroughly blended the intereſts of church-men and ſeculars, and of the eccleſiaſtic and civil branches of the empire, that they became abſolutely one in the age of Charles the Great.

II. The SCHISMS which were their inſeparable attendants, conſpired in producing the ſame effect.

Diviſions had ſometimes happened in the primitive churches; but they were either prudently cured, by the application of inſtituted remedies,—or the churches ſubmitted to them, as public trials of their faith and charity, in a chriſtian manner. Theſe churches had not yet learned to reckon numbers a chief mark of their being true churches; or that their glory conſiſted in their multitudes. When therefore any went away, in a ſchiſmatical manner, from their communion; and when all divine means had been uſed, in vain, to reclaim them: they quietly reſted in the ſatisfactory axiom of an apoſtle,—"They went out from us, but they were not of us." But when church dignitaries ſaw the ſword ready to be drawn, to tame the peeviſh ſchiſmatic, they naturally thought, that there was no reaſon to put up ſo eaſily with that perverſe generation. Whether, therefore, the ſeparatiſt was ever of the communion of the imperial church, or not,— it was all equal;—He was a ſubject of the empire, and an inhabitant in the diocess of some imperial bishop. He was suspected of derogating from the grandeur, and rending the unity of the imperial, holy, catholic church. In case, therefore, that he could not be reduced by ecclesiastical censures, the whole empire was alarmed. The emperor, sagely judging that the peace of the empire was in danger, ordinarily called the parties, heard the cause, and decided in it. If the poor schismatic remained unconvinced, and conscientiously chused to obey God rather than man, imprisonment or banishment, torture or death were the the last arguments to persuade him to return to communion with the holy catholic church. While, in this manner, schisms were the occasion of confounding the authority of the chief magistrate with that of the church;—subjects, in such cases, could not distinguish the objects of their obedience. They were taught, by the severest discipline, to blend the church and the state in their ideas; and to believe, that there were no longer distinct objects, claiming their distinct regard.

III. While heresies and schisms distracted the empire, PERSECUTION, with all its desolating train, behoved to follow: and these contributed greatly to effect a perfect coalition of church and state. Exile, torture and death are terrible objects. To elude them, men of every character looked up to incorporations, as their only refuge and protection. The dignitaries of the church, apprised of the danger, to which their opinions, and their stations exposed them, upon every new commotion, always endeavoured to secure the favour of the court. The laic grandees, on the other hand, knew the necessity of being well with the distinguished ecclesiastics, in order to succeed in their interested and sinister designs. These two ranks of men, standing equally

in

in *fear*, and in *need* of one another, were obliged to blend their interests, to conspire in their schemes, and unite their authority, in laying the inferior classes of the clergy under a necessity to teach, and the inferior ranks of the laity to profess the incorporated creed. These last, pitiable souls! unsupported by any, and oppressed by all, were obliged always to profess the most hearty attachment to the allied creed, to echo the anathemas of councils, and to execute the penal statutes of the court against all who dared to ask questions concerning any of its articles: and after all, to change their own belief upon the first hint from their superiors. It was no rare practice among them, in these ages, to procure the creed of the last council, as we do the almanack of the commencing year, that they might save their lives, by shaping their faith, according to these fleeting fugitive models. Such management could not fail to destroy all distinction of character among men, as well as between the church of Christ and the empire of Rome.

IV. The violent CONCUSSIONS, or the APOCALYPTIC EARTHQUAKES, which convulsed the Roman empire, and shook it to pieces, tended greatly to perfect the coalition of church and state.

Historians describe these concussions. It is our province to observe that they concurred with other causes to accelerate a perfect union of church and state in one huge antichristian kingdom. What the empire lost in territory by the inundation of the Gothic nations, the catholic church gained in strength and worldly grandeur. The contending princes, with hands reeking with the blood of christians, supplicated christian hierarchs for their assistance to butcher christians. Knowing the influence, which the dignitaries had obtained over
every

every rank of men, thefe royal murderers folicited them to fet the martial trumpet to their mouths, and to pronounce the curfe of Meros againft all who came not forth to the help of thefe Gothic deftroyers of the human fpecies. Ecclefiaftics, on the other hand, lying in wait for every opportunity to enlarge their power and to increafe their influence, readily affifted every Gothic invader, from whom they expected to be rewarded with the gratification of their wifhes. By fuch hopeful politics, the fecular interefts of ecclefiaftics were blended with thofe of Europe's new mafters.

Nor was this all. The imperial church herfelf was incorporated with the conftitutions of the Gothic kingdoms. Though the empire was torn into pieces, the alliance continued, and was compleated in the feveral parts, by the fame fanctified methods by which it had been effected with the whole. Though the empire feemed to have been almoft totally annihilated, yet it remained abfolutely ENTIRE, under one ecclefiaftical head, who, notwithftanding his clerical character, actually exercifed a mixed authority in, and over all its difmembered parts.

But it was not till horrid NIGHT, attended with all her train, had filled Europe with the blacknefs of darknefs, that antichrift and incorporations arrived to abfolute perfection. Though, while the Roman empire remained, the church and the political ftate were incorporated, yet the joint authority over the whole, was not exercifed by *one* and the *fame perfon*, nor by perfons of *one* and the *fame character*. But in thefe dark ages, a fovereign pontiff " oppofed and exalted himfelf above all that is called God, or is worfhipped." He affumed a mixed authority in, and over all the deranged parts of the ancient empire, both in the Eaft and Weft. While his papal influence,

influence, in every court, bound all the parts together, in one huge antichristian empire; his pontifical sanction, or at least his tacit concurrence, was held to be indispensably necessary to every law in the political, and to every canon in the ecclesiastical state of every nation, belonging to that papal empire.

Church and state being thus incorporated, the coalition continued, without any alteration, till the glorious æra of the REFORMATION. Then day poured down her golden beams on benighted Europe. The powerful charm was broken. Learning began to raise her reclining head, to throw off her monkish attire, and to extend her walks beyond the narrow confines of the cloister. Men of all ranks and of all characters, instructed by her grave lectures, became sensible of their former delusion, of their present duty, and of their future interests. Princes, opening their eyes on the liberties of civil society, as well as on the rights of sovereigns, became weary of that yoke, which had not less galled their own necks than those of their subjects. They resolved to assert the independence of their crowns and kingdoms, and to humble that absurd authority, which the Roman pontiff had so long claimed and exercised, with a high hand, over the combined state of church and commonwealth in their respective dominions. Their lay subjects, from the powerful baron to the vassal boor, feeling the cruel exactions, and illegal usurpations of the court of Rome, readily seconded the enterprize, and magnanimously risqued their all to effect a reformation. The clergy themselves, who, for so many ages, had found their account in seconding the efforts of Rome to extend her despotic sway, began at last to feel the enormous weight of papal tyranny. The prophetic beast, unnaturally cruel, devoured its own flesh. The pope had

assumed

affumed a dictatorial authority over all the churches. Their peculiar cuftoms, privileges and immunities had been treated with fovereign contempt. Even the canons of general councils, which had been held facred had been fet afide by his difpenfing power. The whole adminiftration of the churches centered in the court of Rome. All preferments ran of courfe in the fame fanctified channel. The fecular clergy, therefore, felt that there was a neceffity of limiting thefe exorbitant pretenfions. From the primate to the parifh prieft, they were convinced, that in order to effect it, it was neceffary to concur with their refpective fovereigns in promoting a reformation.

But alas! the incorporation ftill continued. The papal power was at leaft virtually affumed by the proteftant princes. The deadly wound, which the beaft had received in Peter's chair, was healed up in all the proteftant thrones. Countlefs indeed were the advantages arifing from the Reformation to both church and ftate in every proteftant nation: yet in fo far as they continued incorporated, and the firft received its form and mould from the legiflative powers of the laft, a foundation was laid, and a precedent was fixed for the exercife of the fame dictatorial powers, in acts equally derogatory to the authority of Chrift, on every future occafion. The hiftory of the feveral revolutions which have happened in all the proteftant churches, ferve to illuftrate this obfervation. Incorporated with the politic ftate of the nation, no church has ever been capable of effecting the fmalleft reformation, even in the moft palpable abfurdity, without the fanction of civil legiflature. This alone can give motion to the enormous, incorporated machine. Convocations, affemblies, and fynods have been convened: but their decrees never have been more authentic and obligatory,

tory, without the sanction of proteſtant legiſlature, than the canons of popiſh ſynods were binding without the approbation of his Holineſs. All the different revolutions and modifications which have befallen proteſtant churches, ſince the Reformation, have been only ſo many different forms, into which they have been violently forced to writhe themſelves, in order to ſuit the high or the low principles of thoſe, who governed the whole allied ſyſtem.

No proteſtant doubts the right of princes, at the Reformation, to reſume the prerogatives of their crowns; nor doubts their title to hold them, independent of their proteſtant clergy. Happy had it been for princes, as well as for the churches in their dominions, if they had ſtopt at this point! But it cannot be diſſembled, that all the reformation which many of them ever intended, was, to model the eccleſiaſtical department, in the incorporated conſtitution, into a political fitneſs and convenient ſtate of ſubordination and ſubſerviency to a proteſtant government. Finding their own crowns conſolidated with the mitre, and placed on the head of the Roman pontiff, they pulled both from his brow at once; and, without giving themſelves the trouble to ſever the unſightly maſs, they proceeded to plant it upon their own heads. Had proteſtant ſovereigns imitated the policy of Cyrus; had they proclaimed liberty to their ſubjects, who had been too long the captives of ghoſtly invaſion, and the ſlaves of prieſtly tyranny; had they reſtored to them the poſſeſſion of their unqueſtionable rights, and allowed the uſe of them, in building the temple of God, according to apoſtolic pattern, without putting a political model into their hands, and obliging them, in ſpite of their conſcientious ſcruples, to conform to it;—They would have at once provided for the peace and proſperity of their kingdoms, and for the advancement of true religion

F   among

among every clafs of their fubjects. Ignorance and bigotry, no longer encouraged by the finifter politics of courts, muft have attended the contemptible inhabitants of the cloifter, in their precipitant retreat. Superftition, with all her gaudy train, muft have retired to fome more hofpitable clime. Truth, greatly triumphant, in the fteady light of her own evidence, like the fun, would have diffipated every gloom. And chriftianity, no longer disfigured by the finical dreffes, with which the daring hands of capricious policy, or fportive fuperftition, have hid her native charms, would have " looked forth as the morning, fair as the moon, clear as the fun, and terrible, to all her enemies, as an army with banners."

It is of fmall confequence to the interefts of chriftianity and of chriftian churches, what character the man fuftains, who dares ufurp the authority of Chrift, and invade the rights of chriftians. If either an arrogant pontiff, or a proteftant prince,—a Hildebrand, or a Henry, fhall dare to mould the kingdom of Chrift into a ftate of political fitnefs and fubferviency to their refpective ends; it is vain to define, whether the authority by which it is done, is civil or ecclefiaftical; or which of the two has a preferable right. The pope, no doubt,—yea; the devil himfelf has as indifputable a right, as any proteftant prince, or any reformed convocation, to convert the kingdom of Chrift into a kingdom of this world, to rule it with defpotic fway, and to tyrannize over the underftandings and confciences of chriftians.

Though it would be ungenerous in the extreme to expofe, with wanton leer, the almoft unavoidable miftakes, either of proteftant princes, or of the celebrated reformers, yet it is a wife man's part to receive inftruction from them. We ought to know, and to avoid the rock, which has proved fo fatal to the reformed churches. Soon as they were incor-

porated

porated with the protestant state of European nations, those venerable persons, who had nobly effected a secession from the antichristian church, forsook the path of reformation. They put an almost insuperable bar in the way of succeeding generations to perfect what they had so nobly begun. Though it hath been often proved, and often confessed, that none of those religious systems, which were incorporated with the political constitutions of the protestant nations, were altogether conformable to the simple, apostolic pattern; yea, that some of them are, in the articles of worship and discipline, only a very few removes from the old popish model: yet arguments have been used in vain, either to persuade professed protestants to alter and reform them; or to engage protestant legislatures to dislodge them from their political fastness in the incorporated constitution of church and state. All future efforts to perfect the Reformation will be equally unsuccesful as the past,—till protestant princes shall entirely disengage the kingdom of Christ from its political alliance with the constitutions of their kingdoms;—till they suffer the church to stand on that foundation alone, which God hath laid in Zion;—and till they consent to her being governed by the authority of Christ alone, whose "sceptre is a sceptre of righteousness, and whose throne endureth for ever and ever."

SECT.

SECT. III.

Reflections on the Origin and Gradual Progress of Ecclesiastical Incorporations.

HAVING attempted a sketch of the early rise and gradual advances of ecclesiastical incorporations; we will conclude the chapter with a few reflections on the preceding detail of facts.

I. It is plain that ecclesiastical alliances have no foundation in any positive institution of revelation. It cannot be pretended, that the peculiar polity of the Jewish nation was ever intended to be a model, or a warrant for them: and the New Testament is quite silent on the subject. Had such a heterogeneous system been conformable to the divine will, would the apostles, who were under an infallible impulse to declare the whole counsel of God, been wholly silent about an object of so much importance both to civil and to religious society? Could they who instructed the public teachers of christianity how to behave towards the churches;—who taught fathers and masters the rules of domestic œconomy;—who even condescended to address widows,—wives,—virgins on the article of dress: could they, we say, have omitted those instructions which were to direct Constantine and his successors how to ally the imperial church with the empire;—how to convocate councils;—how to alter creeds;—how to reform books of common prayer;—and, above all, how to persecute and kill dissenters for conscience sake?

It is with pleasure allowed, that there are many predictions in the writings of the prophets, which

respect

respect the advantages which the churches shall reap under the protecting and cherishing wings of christian princes: but where is the text, which warrants any legislature, either to assume a power, or to invest others with authority, to incorporate the churches of Christ with the kingdoms of this world; to dictate despotically articles of faith, and forms of worship to the consciences of christians; and to make all obligatory by sanguinary laws and penal statutes? Let none reproach the oracles of Heaven, and blaspheme their Author, by daring to quote and to wrest any passage to support such an impious hypothesis. Jesus Christ, when his disciples gave an early specimen of that ambition, whose thirst the blood of millions has not yet quenched, struck a deadly blow at the root of all such impious schemes of policy. "Ye know that the princes of the Gentiles exercise dominion—and they who are called great exercise authority—but it shall NOT be so among you." *

Notwithstanding so express and so severe an INTERDICT, there is one text which popes and patriarchs, prelates and presbyterians, have severally chimed over in the ears of princes, when they hoped to gain their respective designs, by the help of their authority. "Kings shall be thy nursing fathers, and queens thy nursing mothers: they shall bow down unto thee with their faces to the earth, and lick up the dust of thy feet."†

It is admitted, that the churches of Christ, from this and similar prophetic passages, may warrantably expect all those blessings which civil government can confer. Their ministers have a just claim to public countenance as well as protection, from the legislative and executive powers in society, while,

enforcing,

---

* Matth. xx. 25, 26. † Isa. xlix. 23.

enforcing, among other duties of the christian life, loyalty to civil government, they approve themselves to be among the most valuable members of society. Their members have a just title to the full and undisturbed possession of all their rights, natural, civil and religious, while they support the character of good subjects. No other idea can be formed of that nutriment, which the breasts of sovereigns can furnish. Paul had no other idea of that *royal milk*. He sums up the full sense of that abused passage in LIBERTY; "Liberty," founded in the law of equity, "to lead a quiet and peaceable life in all godliness and honesty."* Isaiah himself, whose prophesies are all delivered in the figurative style, drops the soaring pinion, and resolves the sense of the text into that less poetical, though equally comfortable promise, "I will make thine officers, peace; and thine exactors, righteousness." †

It is impossible to fix a more extensive sense on that prediction, unless, intoxicated with carnal apprehensions of Christ's kingdom, men shall fancy that it is the indispensable duty of christian princes to expose christianity to contempt and execration, by incorporating one sect of christians, and giving them authority to violate the consciences, kill the bodies, and rifle the treasures of all other christians, who may be obliged conscientiously to differ from the incorporated creed. This is an authority competent to no monarch, to no mortal. It is an authority which Constantine and his successors assumed; which, from the fourth to the seventh century, they tyrannically exercised; and which they at last yielded to the prophetic whore that sitteth on many waters.‡ It is a species of authority, which the protestant princes have resumed,

by

---

* 2 Tim. ii. 2. † Isa. lx. 17. ‡ Rev. xvii. 1.

by the exercise of which, many of them have "given life to the image of the beast, and have caused as many as would not worship the image of the beast to be killed."* It is a kind of assumed power, which, instead of nourishing the churches, stands charged with the guilt of having shed the blood of millions of their children in the nations of Europe; and against which their souls are crying for adequate vengeance from beneath the altar. In one word, it is a species of power, from whose violence, if the church had not fled into the wilderness, where she has been nourished at other breasts, the name of a christian church had long ago ceased to be mentioned on the earth!

In the name of common sincerity! let the age be named, in which the churches have been suckled by such a wolf. The bellies of assuming priests have been, we own, gorged with its milk. Ambitious ecclesiastics have grown corpulent by its dainties. The interested, the haughty and the cruel, actuated by the same spirit of rapacity, have learned to smite their fellow-servants; to eat the flesh of their fellow-christians; and to drink with those, who have been drunken with the blood of the saints.

Should it be granted to the votary of incorporations, that the authority, just now mentioned, is of divine institution, and warranted by such Old Testament predictions; then let him abide by the consequences. Princes, and all whom they authorize, as nursing fathers, have a right to prescribe the articles of the church's faith, the form of her worship, and the canons of her christian conduct— That is, by divine institution, they have a divine right to supercede the divine authority in and over the consciences of christians! Besides, as the church is the object of this supposed authority; princes,

as

---

* Rev. xiii. 12—15.

as invested with it, must be a particular order of church-officers. Is it not wonderful then, that the apostles have been so disrespectful, as well as negligent, to omit this royal corps, in the list of church orders and offices?—One pious consequence more! Such detested objects as the pope, antichrist and the mother of harlots never existed! Are princes invested with this supposed authority, and shall they not have right to exercise it in that manner, and by those instruments which they judge most proper? May they not depute proper persons for their assistance in using it to the greatest possible advantage? Who are more proper than ecclesiastics? And what was all that authority which the Roman pontiff boasted of for so many ages but that which the emperors had arrogated to themselves; had exercised with an high hand; and had at last, together with their seat, bestowed on the beast?

II. We may adventure, from the foregoing detail, to fix the date of the commencement of the ANTICHRISTIAN kingdom.

From the fatal moment, in which Constantine the Great lead the way to the custom of authorizing cabals of ecclesiastics, called councils, to forge fetters for the conscience, by the imposition of creeds and canons, under civil as well as ecclesiastic penalties, we may date the beginning of popery. Should the term be taken in its greatest latitude of modern signification, as comprehending the whole MYSTERY of iniquity, the observation is not strictly just. But if it be taken strictly, for " a sovereign, dictatorial authority, assumed over the conscience," it commenced in the fourth century; and more! It is inseparable from the idea of all ecclesiastical incorporations, and now exists in the eighteenth century as certainly as it did in the eighth.

The

The assertion may probably appear strange to some. Inured to bear the yoke of protestant incorporations, at the same time that they shrink with horror from the idea of pontifical tyranny; they imagine that as popery began in the rescript of Phocas, in the seventh century, it ended in protestant nations, when their several princes were seen under the protestant banner. How great, yea, how hurtful the mistake! the quality of the character who imposes, alters not the kind, though it may greatly affect the degree and the consequences of the imposition. It is of little consequence to a person who has been robbed, whether the person, who took his money, was dressed in lace or in lawn. *Erastianism* and *popery* are but two names for one object. Ecclesiastical incorporation is the source of both.

There is indeed a vast *gradual* difference between them. Yet we have reason to insist, that incorporating establishments, even when the executive part of government is in the hands of the wisest and best prince on earth, teems with imposition, with tyranny, with popery! Yes: the best of administrations acknowledge it. How? By granting a toleration to protestant dissenters! Toleration implies, that government is sensible of the injustice of the penal laws, which guard the incorporated church, and of their incompatibility with the rights of subjects and of christians.

III. It appears, that incorporating establishments have been the teeming sources of innovation, corruption and degeneracy in the christian world.

How striking is the contrast between the primitive churches, and that church, which the imperial edict rendered catholic! Let it be viewed in a few instances.

G

1. The

1. The history of the first and purest ages of christianity furnishes accounts of churches, which were not only constituted according to the plain and simple rules of the gospel, but were governed by the laws of Christ alone. The authority of even the most venerable persons found no place in them. The apostles themselves were not LORDS over the faith of their members. They were only HELPERS of their joy. Strict regard to the laws of Christ was then equally the characteristic of the minister and the christian of every rank. There were indeed *rulers* and *ruled*. But the first were no less governed by the authority of their common master, in all their administrations, than the last, in all their ordinary acts of religion. It was then accounted necessary that the το θειον, the divine character of every office and of every institution should be ascertained and acknowledged. Without this, ministers could not conscientiously be invested with the first, nor christians regulate their actions by the last. HOLY MOTHER CHURCH had then no blind devotees.

How opposite to this happy state was the condition of the church, as soon as she became, by an incorporation, a political branch of the Roman empire! She then in a great measure ceased to depend on the authority of Christ alone. Constantine and his successors, equally weak, and more wicked, gave laws to the kingdom of Christ. How great was the change in the whole system of divine institutions! Their divine *character* was no longer respected. The το θειον of every ordinance was obliged to give place to the το πρεπον of imperial appointment. A rage for DECENCY and external pomp corrupted every thing. The churches which had been *one*, by the scriptural unity of one faith, one baptism, and the joint confession of one Lord Jesus, were constituted one imperial, organized

nized church, by a species of unity as foreign to the nature of Christ's kingdom, as to the articulation of bones in the body of an animal is to the nature of an angel. This huge body, co-extended with the empire, Roman pride pronounced *catholic*; and Roman policy adjusted to the greater or less divisions of that unwieldy community. Every such division was constituted a church, supreme or subordinate, according to the temporal dignity and precedence of the exarchate, colony, or province. Churchmen were appointed to preside in these artificial churches; were invested with new invented offices, for that end; and were distinguished by names as foreign to christian institution as the Persian appellations of *Bahaman* or *Bainmadu*. The example of the celebrated *Bereans* was exauctorated. Particular churches were prohibited from receiving a single article of faith, however plainly revealed, till a general or particular council, convocated by the emperor's authority, and directed by his influence, should stamp it with the imperial signet, and warrant its authority.

During the first years of Constantine's reign, it was his sovereign will and pleasure, that the whole catholic church should believe that Jesus Christ is God supreme. In the latter part of his reign, it is the sovereign will of the imperial court that the catholic church should anathematize her former faith, and curse her former creeds. Councils were successively called to gratify the whim of the day. Thus, the relation of the church to her divine Head was in a great measure dissolved. " All the world worshipped the beast or his image." That species of idolatry commenced with the incorporation of the church with the empire, and existed some ages before the blessed Virgin had a single statue, image or devotee.

2. These

2. These are not the only consequences. The primitive *unity* of the churches was also dissolved. During the three first centuries, that had been their *strength* and their *beauty*. They were equally ignorant of a *forced* union, depending on the rigorous execution of penal laws; and of a *catholicism*, measured by the extent of a kingdom, or even of the empire. They were not chained together, in one *catholic*, organized, imperial body, by the cumbersome links of a graduated hierarchy, terminating in one *visible* head, whether imperial or pontifical. No! They were indeed one catholic church: but they severally maintained an immediate dependence on the authority of Christ alone. Their union consisted in their being all animated by *one spirit* to make profession of *one faith*; to submit to *one baptism*; and to confess *one* GOD and FATHER, and one LORD JESUS. " Speaking the truth in love, they grew up in CHIRST in all things, who is the head; from whom the whole body, fitly joined together, and compacted by that, which every joint supplieth, according to the effectual working in the measure of every part, maketh increase of the body to the edifying of itself in love."*

The incorporation dissolved that sacred band! a mere *political union* supplied its place. Instead of mutually and willingly co-operating for their joint edification, the churches were braced together by a political chain of many links, the highest of which was first affixed to the imperial throne, and, in some ages afterward, was rivetted to the papal chair. Co-extended, with the empire in their limits, and blended with it in their constitutions, it became a matter of necessity that their union should be analogous to that of the state, in order that both might be governed by one uniform exertion of authority.

* Eph. iv. 15, 16, 17.

thority. Thus, they formed one unwieldy society, which, as it was neither purely *civil* nor purely *ecclesiastical*, merited a new name, "MYSTERY, Babylon the great, the mother of harlots, and abominations of the earth." *

Though the imperial alliance was buried in the ruins of the empire; yet its unhallowed ashes became a teeming cause of infinite divisions, and of the most irreconcilable factions, in succeeding ages. When the empire was divided into that of the East and the West, the church was divided too, and its parts naturally acted their parts in all the bloody scenes which followed. The minds of christians, in both imperial churches, were artfully whetted against one another, chiefly for the unpardonable crime of being the subjects of another monarch. Even the most trifling objects were made the means of begetting, or of perpetuating religious differences, which continue even to this day.—When that period arrived, famous for the division of the Western empire into the "ten kingdoms;" the church, which had been so long incorporated with that huge mass, out of which the modern nations of Europe where formed, was again artfully allied with their Gothic constitutions. The consequences are such as the nature of the thing might have warranted any to predict. Every national church must act a deep part in every sanguinary scene that opens. Christians must approve their loyalty, in their solemn church assemblies, by singing *te Deum*, because ten thousands of their fellow-christians are weltering in their own gore, probably in the defence of their own natural, civil and religious rights. Christian princes never go to war with one another, but after having called on the churches in their

* Rev. xvii. 5.

respective

respective dominions, under the pain of forfeiting their incorporations, to appear in the van of war; to commence hostilities at the throne of mercy and peace; and to insult Almighty God with contradictory addresses, for success to the arms of their respective sovereigns, in murdering one anothers' subjects.

In this manner, churches have been divided in their most important interests,—in the very object and acts of their worship. Divided! The term is not sufficiently expressive. "Altar hath been set up against altar." The God of peace hath been insulted. The throne of reconciliation hath been profaned. His attributes, mercy and justice, have been violated, while one church has been loyally imprecating vengeance on the same objects, for whom a sister church has been legally calling for mercy. His most sacred institutions have been prostituted legally to the lust of despotism. The kingdom of heaven hath been made a tool to advance the trade of war and murder. Did the apostles teach the churches, of their planting, to interfere with the wars of princes, and to prostitute divine ordinances to serve the ambitious views of proud men? Did any of the primitive churches leave behind them the smallest trace of their ever having done so?

Some may exclaim, Quakerism! There is, however, no cause of alarm. Christians are men and members of civil society. As such, it is incumbent on them, to defend themselves, and to fight under the banners of their own princes. Nor is it doubted, that they ought to address God for success in their lawful and necessary enterprize. But when all this is done, it is, or ought to be by society as civil,—as injured; and as appealing to Heaven, and the ways of Heaven's prescription for redress.—Be

it

it so, that the aggressors may have ultimately aimed at the invasion of religious rights. What then? Their design cannot succeed but by first invading the sacred inclosures of natural and civil right. Let these be properly defended by civil society, and the religious rights of christians and christian churches will be in perfect safe-guard.

It is therefore plain, that there is a vast difference between a necessary defence of life and property, and the practice of abusing the *peculiar* ordinances of the church to serve the secular designs of society, whether good or bad: of changing the ordinance of preaching peace to sinners into profane declamation on the necessity of war and slaughter: of converting the institution of solemn prayer, which the Saviour of sinners hath appointed to be offered up for all men, even for enemies, into an angry imprecation of death, of destruction, on brethren: of perverting the most solemn mysteries of the christian religion to the use of TESTS to government; of CONDITIONS on which civil and military offices must be enjoyed; and of OBLIGATIONS to deal devastation and death, among all the nation's enemies, real or imaginary.

3. These consequences could not have followed, without being attended with a great corruption of manners among both the clergy and the laity.

Scarcely had the alliance passed the imperial seals, when churchmen, weary of that primitive simplicity, which had been long the glory of their order, plunged themselves into all the excesses of ambition, luxury and gross ignorance. Possessed of riches formerly untasted, and of honours foreign to their character, they vied with one another only for supremacy, precedency, and a lordly dominion over their clerical as well as their lay brethren. The example of the meek and humble Jesus became obsolete.

obsolete. It was too low to be followed by men who aspired to outshine princes, and to make even emperors bend to their ambition. The simple institutions of the gospel were not sufficiently gay for gentlemen of their refined taste. No: churches must be ornamented with the ancient garniture of pagan temples. The votaries of Jove or of Woden, having become political converts to christianity, were not to be shocked with the sight of unadorned temples. Statues, images and busts of saints, of apostles, of the virgin, of angels, of Jesus Christ, and of the Eternal Father! were introduced to line the walls, to decorate the windows, and to adorn the roofs of the christian fanes.

Vice and superstition were not peculiar to the clergy. The laity, having no longer the living examples of humility, self-denial and godliness before their eyes; and beholding the church of Christ converted into a worldly kingdom, gradually declined from spirituality in their worship, and from purity in their manners. The church, secularized by incorporations, became the prophetic "court, without the temple—left out—not measured—but given to the Gentiles, who should tread under foot the holy city forty and two months*."

Besides, at this fatal æra, the pagans, lured by the alliance of christianity to the empire, rushed by thousands and ten thousands into the church, and were baptized at once in rivers. Her doors were thrown open to all; yea, her very walls were pulled down to give the more ready admission to those, whose cumbersome load of vices and impurities would not suffer them to enter any other way. Converts of this character scarcely exchanged more than the names of their gods. The good bishops, that they might invite them with success into the

* Rev. xi. 2.

communion

communion of their churches, put themselves to incredible pains, to model the christian religion after the fashion of discarded paganism. Superstition only threw away her old trinkets, that they might cram all her cabinets with new ones. Even no less a personage than the emperor's mother, moved with pious zeal to second the painful labours of the clergy, aspired to the honour of a long and dangerous voyage to the land of relicts and holy trinkets, in order that by importing a large cargo of crosses, putrid bones, and rusty nails, together with other assortments of such precious implements of superstition, nothing might be wanting either in the furniture of the temple, or in the devotional garniture of the closet.—Thus the worship of the church grew to be superstitious and carnal; and, of course, the manners of her members became corrupt and prophane.

CHAP. II.

The Impropriety of Incorporating Establishments.

WHEN any subject, claiming the reputation of being the perfection of political wisdom, falls under a review, its *propriety* or *impropriety* principally deserves a careful examination. To accomplish this, it is necessary to inquire, " Whether the natures, characters and circumstances of those objects to which such a political arrangement bears an immediate respect, do admit of that mode of management which its authors propose; and whether it be competent to them to take official cognizance of such objects?" These are the inquiries, applied to the subject of incorporated church-establishments, which we intend to make, in the following sections.

SECT. I.

A Proof attempted, " That those Objects, to which an Incorporating Establishment bears an immediate Respect, are naturally incapable of being inforced by Civil Authority."

THOUGH the protection of church-members, in the full and undisturbed possession of all their rights, natural, civil and religious, be competent to civil authority: yet incorporations extend to a variety of other objects, which are not, cannot be objects of civil legislation. Some of these we shall enumerate.

I. The first thing which is incorporated, is the national creed; or that system of doctrinal tenets, true or false, which all the subjects in the realm are bound, under certain penalties, to believe and profess.

Politicians, who ordinarily know but *one* way to attain their ends, must be at a loss to conceive how the uniform profession of faith in any system can be established among ten or twelve millions of reasoning beings, without the assistance of penal statutes. Though these means have not entirely disappointed the expectations of legislators, yet they contribute as little to the reputation of their wisdom, as they have done to the glory of the christian profession. When the characters of revealed truth are considered, the mistake of these ecclesiastical politicians immediately appears.

The most obvious character of every doctrine contained in revelation is, "the nature of its evidence." Wholly supernatural, its intrinsic evidence depends entirely on itself, and is apprehended by those only, who

who are supernaturally enlightened, and have learned of the Father. The establishment, therefore, of these doctrines cannot depend on civil authority, penal statutes and sanguinary laws. The Father of lights alone can shoot conviction into the mind, and make the understanding to see, and the conscience to feel their evidence in their importance. This conviction is their establishment. Should this be wanting, they can no more be established in any country by the utmost exertions of civil authority, than light can be arrested on the frozen mountains around the pole, when the sun is in the southern signs. Gibbets and stakes have no share in it. The spirit of truth hath challenged it as his incommunicable prerogative.*

II. The system of sacred institutions, peculiar to the christian religion, is also pretended to be established by incorporation.

The fate of christian institutions, ever since the date of incorporations, is enough to make indignation boil in the bosom of every pious christian. Since that æra, no age has passed, in which legislators have not become sick of the religious observances of their fathers; have not convocated councils to new-model the institutions of heaven, in order that they might suit the reigning taste; and have not framed new laws to establish their new dress.—After all, the institutions of the christian church are as incapable of being established by incorporations, as the marble column is of being propt up by the circumambient air; or the lofty rock of being supported by the billow which swells and breaks along its foundation. Can an authority, ever capricious, ever variable, ever sick of its exertions, give an establishment to the unalterable ordinances of the unchangeable God?

* John xvi. 13, 14.

Besides, due subjection to these institutions is not, cannot be founded on human authority. It is impossible it should be so. Its formal reason is the divine authority alone. Why should human authority, therefore, interfere? Let it be supposed, that any man is a most exact conformist to the rites of his church, not because of the authority of God appointing them, but because they are the established mode of worship in the society—He is an idolater. Worship consists not so properly in *external homage*, as in the devotion of the mind to the will and authority of its object. He therefore divides his worship between his *Maker* in heaven, and his *master* on earth; and the latter seems to have the better share!

Of this detestable idolatry, unavoidable in incorporated churches, the alliance is the principal cause. In a nation consisting of some millions of subjects, there must be many thousands, who are incapable of a just sense of the divine authority in the positive institutions of the gospel; who are still less able to see a divine warrant for rites that have none; and who at the same time, chuse not to incur the severe penalties against non-conformity. What shall such do? Conform, no doubt! yes; and "commit fornication with the kings of the earth." Obliged, independent of any conviction of their duty, to pay a forced worship to God, they perform a real devotion to their fellow-creatures.

What has been just now observed, weakens not the right of legislature to inforce, under civil penalties, the most exact obedience to the moral institutions of God. The moral law is that sceptre of righteousness, by which the Father of the universe conducteth his moral government among all nations; and as all civil policy is subordinate to it, it must be founded on, and regulated by the same eternal law. As "the work of the law is written in the heart of

every

every man, his confcience alfo bearing witnefs,*" there can be no confcientious non-conformift to that law. Nor is it to be forgotten, that civil legiflature, when it exacts obedience to that law, does not require it as an *act* of *worſhip*, due to God; but as a *debt* of *focial duty*, owing to fociety. The overt act only can be commanded, and is cognizable by human authority, as far as it ftands connected with the profit or lofs of fociety. The heart is cognizable by the fearcher of hearts alone. Hence, a man may deferve the character of a good fubject, while in the fight of God, his irreproachable obedience to the divine law, by which he ftands high in the efteem of fociety, cannot exempt him from being accounted a very bad man. Mean while, as legiflature doth not require that man's obedience as a debt due to God, but formally as due to fociety, which protects him, it fhares not in his guilt before God. It is infinitely otherwife, when government affumes an authority to command obedience to the pofitive inftitutions of gofpel worſhip, which were never appointed to be the law of civil fociety. She, as fuch, owes no obedience to them, by any law of God, natural or revealed. It is therefore plain, that as no legiflature can make that to be a rule of focial duty, which the fupreme Lawgiver hath not appointed and fitted to that end; both the legiflature commanding, and the fubject obeying muft confider that obedience, which the ftatute law ordains to the pofitive inftitutions of the gofpel, to be only a proof of devotion to God. Hence it follows, that when any obferve thefe inftitutions, if they do it without any regard to civil authority enjoining it, they contemn it, and are rebels; if they do it with a regard to civil authority enjoining it, they worſhip it, and are idolaters. And, if civil authority is neither to be regarded as the

* Rom. ii. 15.

reason, nor worshipped as the object of the subject's devotion, why should it be interposed at all?

Indeed, it is not competent to civil legislature to interpose. Is not a right of legislation common to all nations? And must not this be founded on the supposition that the rule and standard of civil legislation is, or may be known by all men. But the institutions of christianity are not, like the law of nature, engraved on the heart of every man, but are peculiar to only a very small part of the species. It is therefore plain, that they can neither be the objects nor the rule of political arrangements. The contrary hypothesis necessarily implies, either that, though the greater part of mankind, yea, all men are naturally incapable of knowing the peculiar ratio and spiritual design of gospel institutions; they are, notwithstanding, actually known and approved by all, who are capable of sustaining any character in social life! Or, that though they be foreign to civil society, they may be, nevertheless, incorporated in the political constitution, and may be made the rule of dispensing civil rewards and punishments! Than either of these conclusions, nothing can be imagined more contradictory and absurd.

After all, prejudice will still maintain, " that the church is not only capable of an establishment by incorporation; but is actually so established, in all the nations of christendom."

It is readily admitted, that ever since the court without the temple was left out of the prophetic measure, *that* which commonly is known by the name of the *church*, has been, in one form or another, so established. But let the mysterious idea, conveyed by that name, be carefully examined and analyzed. As many ideas are affixed to it as there are interests among the champions of the incorporating alliance. Sometimes it signifies the papal domination,

tion, and the pretended rights of the Romish see. At other times, it means an episcopal hierarchy, opposed to presbyterian parity. In some ages, it conveys the idea of a distinguished sect of pretended christians, empowered by authority to persecute their fellow-christians, to devour the property of their fellow-subjects, and to enjoy exclusively all the offices of honour and profit of a whole nation. But if it be understood to mean such a society as was planted, in the apostolic age, at Jerusalem, Antioch or Rome, we deny that it is capable of an incorporating establishment. It has been proved already, that neither the doctrines nor the institutions of such a society can be so established. What therefore, besides her *credenda* and her *agenda*, can be imagined? Her scriptural architype cannot be so allied. That is a positive institution of the gospel, and can no more be incorporated and made a rule of dispensing rewards and punishments than any other positive institution of gospel worship. The hand of civil authority cannot plant her, by obliging, under civil pains, the subjects of a nation to arrange themselves within her pale, and to approve her incorporated platform. It was not thus, that the first churches were planted. It is not thus, that christians are to be compelled to come in. They are a "willing people in the day," not of the magistrate's officious interference, but "of the Mediator's almighty power."*

The members of christian churches ought indeed to be protected, and their profession of christianity ought to have every possible encouragement. But the members of no one christian church, though they may have a *superior*, can have no *exclusive* claim upon government for these blessings. They can have no right to an incorporation, precluding other

* Psalm cx. 3.

churches,

churches, and their members, from the benefits of society, merely because they cannot assent to every article of their creed. When government carries its indulgence to any one church so far, it overthrows its own original design. While it pours an overplus of favours on her members, it does it at the expence of that justice which it owes others, who perhaps are equally or more deserving of society. Nay more! The penal laws, essentially necessary to every precluding incorporation, are weapons put into the hands of her members against the persons and rights of all those whom it unjustly leaves unprotected, and every moment at their mercy.

The bigot may now ask with emotion, "What! Is nothing belonging to the kingdom of Christ capable of an incorporating establishment?"

We answer; nothing: Yet we admit, that a variety of things, foreign indeed to the nature of the church, is established in incorporated churches. We shall adventure a short enumeration.

1. A species of right, which tears up the foundations of equity, is established. Equity cries aloud, "Whatsoever ye would that men should do unto you, do ye also unto them." But that incorporations tread this maxim under their feet, has been proclaimed to the world by the many persecutions, murders and massacres, that have ever walked in their suit. Who would chuse to be hanged, burnt or broken on the wheel!—especially when they are conscious, that they have not transgressed the laws, nor offended against any of the original ends of society?

2. Incorporations establish a rule of law, and a standard for the executive powers of government, in dispensing civil rewards and punishments, which oblige them to commit acts of cruel oppression, destroy the primary design of civil government, and

render

render all the rights and liberties of society precarious and unsecure.

It seems to be plain, that neither the doctrines nor the institutions of christianity can interfere with the order, laws, or fundamental rights of society: that they leave it as they found it, settled on the immutable law of righteousness: and that men may be non-conformists and worthy members of society, at the same time. Such was our blessed Lord. Such were his apostles. Such were thousands since. As soon, therefore, as any government ceases to confine itself to equity as the only rule of its administrations, and adopts what it supposes to be the doctrines and institutions of christianity as the standard of dispensing rewards and punishments, the executive powers are legally authorized, yea, officially obliged to proceed to acts of flagrant injustice toward all such worthy characters; these must be deprived of their rights; and, thus government, instead of answering its primary design, is converted into a public robber of those whom it ought to protect. If this be not the case, christians injure not a little the characters of those *worthy* magistrates, Herod, Pontius Pilate, Nero, and thousands of their brethren of pious memory, on account of what they did against the Lord of glory, his apostles and the martyrs of all ages and all churches. Their prosecutions, whatever might be pretended, were not founded on any crimes committed against the laws of civil society, but proceeded wholly on a charge of non-conformity to what they imagined to be the positive institutions of the Deity, incorporated in the political constitution and made the rule of dispensing civil rewards and punishments.

3. Incorporations, by allying one sect of christians to the political constitution, establish a pretended

tended right in it, to assume the name of the *national church*; and to claim the sole possession of all the revenues which law has annexed to it. Aided by these, and authorized by the penal laws by which she is guarded and made formidable to all her enemies, she may legally extend herself by every method that craft can contrive, or cruelty can execute. —How far such a sect may belong to the christian church, must be determined by comparing it with the authentic descriptions of particular churches in the age of the apostles. One thing, however, is certain, that those objects, which such incorporated sects believe and practise, in common with all the churches of Christ, are absolutely incapable of an incorporating establishment.

SECT. II.

The known Characters of human Authority make it incompetent to Legislatures to take official Cognizance of those Objects, which are supposed to be established in national Churches.

WHEN human authority is contemplated in the glass of history, it appears uniformly in all ages and in all countries to have been—FALLIBLE, FICKLE, FAITHLESS, and too often UNFRIENDLY to the interests of true religion.

I. FALLIBILITY is one of the most obvious characters of human authority. God alone is at an infinite remove from error. It is therefore no indignity offered to civil authority to assert, that it is infinitely unfit to give law to the consciences of millions about objects, to which infallible authority alone

lone can warrant the accountable creature to pay the smallest regard. About objects of such a nature, what can human, what can fallible authority avail? Can the wisest, can even the most pious legislature convince the understanding without evidence? Or can it bind the conscience with the cords of its own authority?

It is vain to alledge, that as some men, through inattention or prejudice, do not perceive the proper evidence of truth, legislature interposes to procure the concurrence of such persons with the national system. Can any coolly imagine that civil authority can do what God himself, in the peculiar circumstances supposed, cannot effect? Such persons may be made conformists; but they are made hypocrites too, at the same time. They cease to be, as well as to act up to the character of men. They are made objects of abhorrence to heaven; an unsupportable load on religious society on earth; and justly suspected members of the body politic, in every possible station and relation.

Meanwhile, the question of right remains to be decided.—" Is it competent to any legislature, according to the law of equity, to punish any member of society, who, though he cannot assent to the creed of the chief magistrate, acts up in every respect to the character of a good and useful subject? Sensible persons would blush for the bigot who would affirm it. Yet on this hinge all the controversy turns. What avails a precluding establishment, unless it be armed with penal statutes? Is not even the preclusion itself a punishment on the dissenter?

But whence does civil legislature derive this authority?—From God, or from men? From neither. God will not give his glory to another, by relinquishing his sovereign dominion over the conscience: and society has no right to make the surrender to

their

their governors. It must therefore be assumed. And if so, it is high time that all the nations of Europe should agree to assert a right to a general RESUMPTION.

II. When civil authority hath been stretched, at any time, beyond its proper limits, it hath always become capricious, fickle, and often inconsistent with itself. Reason affirms, and experience confirms this observation. It is therefore plain, that an authority which is fickle as well as fallible is very unfit, and very daring to pretend to give establishment to " a kingdom which *cannot* be moved." Revealed truth, like its author is without variableness or shadow of change: and like the sun, its natural emblem, establishes the belief of its own existence by the splendour of its own evidence. Incorporations serve only to eclipse it. Precluding alliances, make it like the moon, ever changing. In one age, civil authority declares one creed to be the standard of faith. In the next, the same authority, establishes another, which curses all that believe in the former. What man, having a thousand instances of this before his eye, can persuade himself that the kingdom of Christ can receive an establishment from that authority, which often sinks into the vortex of its own inconsistencies?

III. Civil legislatures have often proved FAITHLESS as well as fickle toward those objects which they have pretended to establish. To what cause can the many revolutions which happen in the church as well as in the state be assigned? Is it caprice alone? No: it becomes politically necessary to legislatures, to be faithless to creeds and rituals which they had, with every degree of solemnity, incorporated, with the political constitution, and had said and sworn
they

they would never relinquish. A change in the political state of a nation, an alteration in the political principles of the court,—the accession of a new sovereign, his family or marriage connections, —and a thousand such things may appear, and often have appeared sufficient reasons to the legislative powers to turn their backs on the allied religious system; to dislodge it from its political fastness in the constitution; and to introduce, with all the requisite solemnity of oaths, tests and penal laws, a new ecclesiastical arrangement, more suitable to the state of the nation, or to the ever variable taste of the subjects. The history of Great Britain, and of the several European nations affords a too numerous list of examples.—Having these before our eyes, may we not appeal to common sense on the question concerning the fitness of human authority to give an establishment to the kingdom of Christ?

IV. But had legislatures always approved themselves the friends of invariable truth, in these revolutions, we would have been tempted to have ascribed some right to human authority to pretend to the establishment of the church. But alas! too many examples furnish incontestable proof that, even in these vain attempts, or pretences to establish the church, it hath often acted in open hostility against the truth. How often hath it devoted all its influence to the old serpent, the devil, and to the old Roman friar, the pope, for the purpose of establishing their united kingdom? And if so, we must seek for something more stable, more trusty and more consistent with itself and with truth, to make the church of Christ that kingdom, "against which the gates of hell shall not prevail."

In fine, It is not foreign to the argument to observe, that those persons, with whom society lodges
legislative

legiflative powers, are of all men leaft qualified for the high prerogative of chufing a creed for millions of accountable beings, and of obliging them tamely to acquiefce in it.

It is vain to ftate a comparifon between the abilities of civil magiftrates, and of others, to dictate articles of faith, and to prefcribe modes and forms of worfhip for any befides themfelves. It is denied that it is, or can be, the prerogative of any man, or any clafs of men whatever, unlefs they could produce a commiffion from the SUPREME LAWGIVER to affume a lordly dominion over the underftandings and confciences of his amenable creatures; and could fatisfy the many millions concerned that their character is raifed above the poffibility of miftake in the execution of their high truft. To drop all fuch extravagant fuppofitions, all men know, that princes, courtiers and legiflators are commonly at as great a lofs, as any other clafs of men whatever, to make, even for themfelves, a wife choice in the important objects of religion. Such are their peculiar avocations, temptations and embarraffments, that were any clafs of men permitted to fatisfy themfelves with an implicit faith, they, of all men, have the beft claim to that indulgence.

It cannot be objected, that "legiflature does not make the national creed: that an ecclefiaftical convocation or council, reprefenting the national church, frame and arrange it: and that the only province which the ruling powers claim, is, to honour it with their fanction, and to inforce a general acquiefcence in its orthodoxy, by penal laws againft all who may diffent."

It may be afked, in what happy age were councils the proper reprefentatives of the church? Did ever her members elect them, inftruct them, and inveft them with powers of reprefentation? Let the creed or liturgy be named that has not been compiled by synods, convened, actuated and directed by court influence. But whoever are the compilers of the creed, legiflature both chufe and prefcribe it. It is the creed of government, chofen for, and enjoined on the whole nation. A ftatute is not lefs an act of parliament becaufe it was prepared by a counfellor, or firft framed by a felect committee. Could a creed be named, which was compiled by proper reprefentatives of the major part of the nation, and which met with their unanimous approbation; it is the creed of thofe only, who have confented to it, and approve of it in their confciences. Neither a majority, nor its rulers have a right to enforce it by penal laws, on thofe, who, to avoid being hypocrites, muft be diffenters.

CHAP. III.

The Absurdity of Ecclesiastical Incorporations.

NOTHING is more injurious to truth, than thofe falfe and abfurd ideas, which are inadvertently admitted in early years. Wifdom's moft difficult tafk is, to throw off all early prepoffeffions; to rectify firft fentiments; and to unlearn what has been acquired by much fruitlefs ftudy, during many mifpent years.

The truth of this obfervation appears in every clafs of objects, about which the human underftanding exercifes its powers; and about none more than thofe which refpect the original defign, the nature, and the diftinguifhing characters of the New Teftament church. The greateft part of chriftians, accuftomed customed from their youth, to see one sect of christians, in a nation, exclusively assuming the name of THE CHURCH, crowing over all other denominations, and incorporated with the political constitution; are taught to imagine, that a church cannot exist without an incorporating establishment. Every description of christians have betrayed such a sentiment, especially when they have had it in their power to enrich themselves with the spoils, and to stain their hands with the blood of conscientious dissenters.

Wise men ought to enquire into the cause of so cruel and so general an infatuation. Should it be found that incorporating establishments produce it, by turns, among all parties; the laws of humanity, as well as the spirit of christianity, call aloud for wiser measures. After what manner, and to what degree these establishments interest the selfish passions to commit these excesses, will be shewn in some subsequent chapters. In this their ABSURDITY shall be held up to view. To this end, a proof shall be attempted " that the Kingdom of Christ CANNOT be incorporated, in one constitution, with civil society; and that it betrays absurdity and folly to attempt it; because it is distinct in KIND from all political society; and because it even differs from those incorporated sects themselves, who assume the name of national churches."

SECT. I.

A Proof attempted, " *that the Kingdom of Chrift* CAN-
NOT *be incorporated with Civil Societies, because it
differs in* KIND *from all political Associations whatever.*

THE truth, " that the kingdom of Chrift differs in KIND from all political affociation," is fo glaring, that even the moft violent advocates for their incorporation have not yet dared to deny it, though it ftabs their idol of the alliance to the heart. We fhall therefore be the more brief in its illuftration.

All know that the kingdom of Chrift continued diftinct in its conftitution, laws and ordinances from the kingdoms of this world, during the fpace of three hundred years, immediately after its erection among the nations. And ever fince, notwithftanding all attempts to incorporate it with thefe nations, in one political conftitution, it remains diftinct ftill. Jefus Chrift, who is the truth, hath afcertained its nature, when he faid, " My kingdom is not of this world." He hath put it out of the power of all earthly authority to change its ESSENTIAL character. Can civil authority, though vefted in the perfons of the moft potent monarchs, alter the nature of things? Can it change the word of God, or the effential properties of his works? Can it tranfmute a body into a fpirit, or pebbles into pearls. No more is it capable of changing the nature of Chrift's kingdom; or of blending its conftitution with the political frame of any empire or nation. They differ abfolutely; and formally

K   agree

agree in nothing, unless in the general abstract idea of society. This will appear by an enumeration of particulars.

I. The original design of civil societies was suggested to mankind by their own necessities. In a state of solitude, the individual cannot be happy. "It is not good for man to be alone." His rights cannot be secured, nor his property defended. The law of necessity, therefore, obliges men, who dwell within convenient precincts, or who are otherwise related, to throw all their *civil* rights into one common stock; to reduce the dictates of reason and of conscience into laws; and to appoint qualified persons to execute these maxims of equity and conveniency for the common advantage of the whole.

Quite foreign to this was God's design, in erecting the New Testament church. It was not that all men might safely enjoy their rights, much less that *some men* might dictate to all, rule all, and enrich themselves by robbing the treasures of honest industry. He had sufficiently provided for the first, and armed mankind against the last, by his having instituted public order, and civil government for its protection. His design was, that " all those whom he had predestinated to the adoption of sons by Jesus Christ," * might enjoy the means of obtaining " the inheritance, which is reserved in heaven for them."† It was, that " all men might see what is the fellowship of the mystery, which, from the beginning of the world, hath been hid in God, who created all things by Jesus Christ: and that now unto the principalities and powers in heavenly places, might be known by the church, the manifold wisdom of God."‡ In fine, it was " for the

* Eph. i. 5.   † 1 Pet. i, 4.   ‡ Eph. iii. 9, 10.

perfecting

perfecting of the saints, for the edifying of the body of Christ, till they all come into the unity of the faith, and the knowledge of the Son of God, unto a perfect man, unto the measure of the stature of the fulness of Christ."*

II. The kingdoms of this world, founded on the laws of necessity, are governed by the law of nature alone. The laws of every well-governed state, are only the modifications of that law, which is written on the hearts of all men. They are the applications of nature's general law of right to the particular exigencies, and the varying circumstances of civil society. Were it otherwise, civil government could not be the common privilege of mankind.

In full contrast stands the church of Christ. Founded on the decrees of Heaven, by which "the heathen are given to the Messiah for his inheritance, and the utmost ends of the earth for his possession," she is governed by the laws and institutions of her own divine head. These, though they be not contrary to the law of nature, are quite distinct from it. This is known and understood by all men; but those being positive institutions, are found only in the scriptures, and are properly understood by those alone, upon whose renewed hearts God hath engraven his law. They are the wisdom of God in a mystery, even the hidden wisdom which God ordained before the world."†

Besides, civil legislature, as long as it regulates the exercise of its authority by reason's universal law, may frame as great a number of statutes as it may judge to be conducive to general good. But the church acknowledges but one Lawgiver, even Christ. Having furnished her with a compleat body

* Eph. iv. 12, 13.   † 1 Cor. ii. 7.

of laws, he hath left no room either for the pride of princes, or the petulance of popes. No man, no number of men, whether in councils or in conclaves, in convocations, or in synods, have authority to add one new ordinance, or to frame one new law.

III. A reciprocal obligation on the authors and objects of all civil legislation arises from their mutual relation. Government owes to the subject protection. The subject owes obedience to the laws. In case of failure, there is a forfeit of life or property, according to the demerit of the crime.

But in the kingdom of Christ, men's lives, limbs, and property, are all under the protection of the laws of the country. The salvation of men's souls, being one end of erecting that kingdom, none but madmen and persecutors will adventure to say that the destruction of men's bodies, or the seizure of their property was ordained of God to accomplish that important design. Christ never commanded church-members to pledge their lives or their fortunes to their ecclesiastical governors for their good behaviour in church society. These therefore, have no right to deliver their flocks to what was called in the days of yore, the *secular arm!* No: the kingdom of Christ indeed is not administered without penal laws; but these are of a very different nature, and the execution of them is committed to no mortal. "Fear him, who, after he hath killed, hath power to cast into hell: yea, I say unto you, FEAR HIM."*

IV. In civil society, a due respect ought to e paid to that scale of secular pre-eminence, which providence hath fixed among its members. The

* Luke xii. 5.

laws

laws of nature and of christianity require, that every man, of every station, and description in society, should " render to all their dues; tribute to whom tribute is due; custom to whom custom; fear to whom fear; honour to whom honour." *

But at the same time that Christ approves and establishes this order in civil society, he expressly prohibits all worldly pre-eminence, or even the affectation of it in his church. " The princes of the Gentiles exercise dominion,—but it shall not be so among you."† Christ himself is king alone upon his holy hill of Zion. Christians of every station in civil, and of every description in ecclesiastical society are equally bound to attend, in every thing that concerns the conscience, to the authority of Christ alone. Ecclesiastical rulers cannot govern as they ought, but by following their instructions, with a critical,— a conscientious accuracy. Even in their highest acts of government, they obey the same authority, which the lowest are bound to acknowledge. None must prescribe to others; much less presume to impose their sentiments by violence. The understanding and the conscience in all are sacred to the sceptre of Christ alone. Those who forget their immediate dependence on the Head of the Church; who overlook their obligations, arising from their character, to be servants of all; and who, intoxicated with a vain opinion of their pre-eminence, " begin to smite their fellow-servants," ought to tremble at his certification, which is dreadful,—and as its consequence, which is certain. Yes: " the Lord of these servants shall come, in a day they look not for him, and in an hour they are not aware of; and shall cut them asunder, and appoint them their portion with hypocrites: there shall be weeping, and wailing, and gnashing of teeth." ‡

* Rom. xiii. 7.   † Matth. xx. 25, 26.   ‡ Matth. xxv. 50, 51.

V. In

V. In case of either foreign invasion or civil insurrection, it is necessary that the kingdoms of this world should defend themselves by all the ways which the law of equity has pointed out to every civil society, when it is injured. Violence must be repelled by force. The injured must appeal to the God of battles. Every society is certainly bound to do to others, as it wills them to conduct themselves toward it; and is understood to have pledged the lives and property of its members to live in peace with every other independent society, as long as the same duty is discharged toward it. It is therefore equitable, that any government, in case any neighbouring society forfeit its pledge, should seize the forfeiture, and redress its own injuries as far as the laws of war allow.

The defence of the church is otherwise settled. It must be effected by methods, foreign to blood and carnage. "The weapons of her warfare are not carnal, but spiritual; and mighty, through God, to the pulling down of every strong hold," in which it is possible that her adversaries should either fortify themselves, or annoy her. No war can be carried on against that sacred society, as the church, which should make carnal weapons either necessary or useful.

It is true, she may be persecuted. Her members may be grievously injured. They may be spoiled of their property, deprived of their rights, and even their lives may become a prey to violence. All this has been but too often realized. But it ought to be considered, that as all these injuries respect the civil, not the religious character of church-members; their redress is not the object of ecclesiastical, but of civil administration. Church members are *subjects* too; and, as such, deserve both protection and redress. If government therefore, shall refuse protection

tection or redress to them; or if it invade, or authorize others to invade their natural, civil or religious rights; the laws of nature, reason, necessity and even christianity warrant them, either to withdraw from such hoards of public robbers, or to seek their redress, in those ways which the God of nature hath made expedient and just, in all such cases. Injured as men, and as deserving citizens, they may act without blame, in the same characters, in their own defence.

VI. In fine, provided that the purposes of civil society be gained, it is of no importance into what form legislatures may throw the kingdoms of this world. That mode of government which is excellent in one country, or in one age, may be scarcely tolerable in another. The God of nature, ever since the Jewish theocracy ceased, hath tied no nation to any one particular form of government. The laws of reason oblige every nation to mould itself into that form, which has the greatest probability, in its circumstances, to promote public happiness.

But neither the *fidelity* of Christ, nor the *propensity* in human nature to innovation, will suffer us to think, that the constitution, order and administration of the church is left in the same precarious situation. Political wisdom finds no scope in the kingdom of Christ. The wisdom of this world ought to be confined to the kingdoms of this world. The constitution of christian churches, together with their order and government, is planned by the unerring wisdom, and invariably fixed by the authority of their Sovereign Lord, who is " Jesus Christ, the same yesterday, and to-day, and for ever." *

On a review, it appears, that it is absurd beyond description to attempt to incorporate societies so

* Heb. xiii. 8.

essentially

essentially distinct. They agree in nothing but in the most general idea of society. Who was ever so mad as to say, that because *body* and *spirit* agree in the general, metaphysical, abstract notion of *substance*, therefore the dimensions of a soul may be ascertained by the application of a foot-rule, or the height of an angel, like that of a pyramid, may be taken by a quadrant? Or, who ever imagined that their essences may be so blended and mutually incorporated, that some *aliquod tertium*,—some strange hyperphysical compound should arise from their alliance! All efforts, which human wisdom, joined to the greatest authority on earth, to incorporate the church of Christ with the political constitutions of the kingdoms of this world, are equally ridiculous. They expose their authors to the censures of common sense. One whose instructions went no higher, describes their folly in glowing colours.

Humano capiti cervicem pictor equinam
Jungere si velit, et varias inducere plumas,
Undique collatis membris, ut turpiter atrum
Desinat in piscem, mulier formosa superne:
Spectatum admissi, risum teneatis amici?

Hor. Art. Poet.

S E C T.

SECT. II.

A Proof attempted that, " the Kingdom of Christ CANNOT *be incorporated with Civil Societies, because it differs from all incorporated Sects themselves, who assume the Name of national Churches."*

BEFORE we proceed to the proof of the proposition, "that the church of Christ differs from all incorporated sects assuming the name of national churches," we readily premise one concession,—" That the kingdom of Christ hath always subsisted in national churches, ever since the age of the first incorporation." Meanwhile, by this concession, it is only meant, that the church of Christ hath subsisted in these political churches, as a mass of oil remains in water, altogether unmixed and unincorporated with their mixed constitutions. The gospel of Christ hath been successfully preached, and the sacraments, with other institutions, have been edifyingly dispensed, in national churches. But let it be remembered, that the divine Spirit, on whose blessing alone depends the success of all ordinances, knows well how to distinguish the things of Christ from the inventions of men; and that while he blesseth the former in the experience of the saints, he anathematizes the latter in the scriptures of truth which are daily read in their assemblies. These ordinances are blessed and made the vehicles of heavenly influence, not as they are dispensed in incorporated churches, in virtue of a political appointment, by civil legislature; but in consequence of their being viewed by christians as the institutions of Christ, claiming the attention of their minds, the subjection of their consciences, and the affection of their hearts, on the ground of divine authority alone. The sacraments of the New Testament are blessed for the edification of good men, in national churches; but their establishment by law, and their legal prostitution to the use of political tests, do not entitle them to that honour!

Notwithstanding this concession, the *proposition* continues inviolate. The following considerations will illustrate its evidence.

I. The constitution of the kingdom of heaven is a grand effect of the wisdom of God, and a glorious proof of his love to men. The plan of that kingdom was "hid in God" among the other treasures of his eternal wisdom, till it was brought to view by Jesus Christ, who is "exalted to be Head over all things to the church, which is his body," and who "as a son over his own house, was faithful to him that appointed him" in founding his kingdom according to the eternal model in the divine mind.

But the constitution of national churches depends wholly on human policy, and the wisdom of this world, which is foolishness with God. Like the wisdom which plans these incorporated churches, they are always changing their constitutions and altering their forms. In some countries, and in some ages, worldly wisdom, consulting with ambition and avarice, establishes an hierarchical church, whose spire "exalteth itself above all that is called God." In other parts of the earth, the same wisdom establishes a similar hierarchical society, whose top only reaches to the monarch's throne, whom all must acknowledge as "supreme head over all persons, and in all causes civil and ecclesiastical." In some kingdoms, more happy in their ideas of liberty, the same political wisdom brings the constitution

tution of the incorporated church as near the scriptural model, as is consistent with the constitution of the nation and the genius of its civil government. Whence all this endless variety? Is it from a variety of original plans? Rather, is it not evidently owing to the policy of legislatures, who, by all this diversity, provide that the constitutions and administrations, in both departments of the incorporated system, may be consistent, and mutually subservient to one another; and may both serve the purposes of those, whether princes or priests, who sit at the helm. The truth here cannot be dissembled. Now the church is Orthodox; then Arian: now Popish, then Protestant: now Episcopalian, then Presbyterian: Why? She is a tool to ambition, avarice and political finesse, and must put on that form which will most conduce to the purposes of government, whether good or bad. If government be friendly to liberty and the rights of mankind; the national church naturally puts on a presbyterian, or a moderate episcopalian form: but as soon as the nation is cursed with an aspiring or priest-ridden prince, the national church is carried to the anvil, and is hammered into an useful engine to advance the power and prerogative of the crown, or to gratify the ambition and avarice of the hierarchy.

II. It is at least in words agreed, that the church of Christ " is built on the foundation of the apostles and prophets, Jesus Christ himself being the chief corner-stone." The sacred writings contain the plan of all her doctrines, worship and order, with a degree of precision proportionate to the importance of God's gracious design in her erection.

But national churches, as such, are built on a very different foundation. In Italy, the church, represented as a great whore, sitteth upon a scarlet-coloured

coloured beast, full of names of blasphemy, having seven heads and ten horns. In England, the national church is built on the foundation of the lords and commons, assembled in parliament; his majesty the supreme head, being the chief corner-stone. The truth cannot be disguised. Why is episcopacy the order of the church of England? Is it because that order is built on the foundation of the apostles? Pretences aside.—Is it not because it is thought to be most conducive to the political designs of government, in England? If any demur, we ask, why the same British parliament declares it to be their sovereign will and pleasure that the national church on the North side of Tweed should be of the presbyterian form? Did Christ, or any of his apostles leave it on record, that the fashion of the church in South-Britain should be episcopalian, and that the model of the Scotch church should be presbyterian? Has Christ appointed a distinct model for every country and for every clime, for every age and for every political revolution in the same age?— From the whole, it seems plain, that if different foundations infer a diversity of superstructures, the kingdom of Christ is different from all national churches, under that formal consideration.

III. Nor is the difference less remarkable in regard of the *distinct characters* which belong to their respective members. Much more is necessary to form the respectable character of a member of Christ's church, than is required to constitute that of a mere man of the world; who, in order to qualify himself for some office, in the army, navy, or excise, must become a member of the national church, must approach her most sacred mysteries, and may prosecute any minister who attempts to preclude him

on

on account of his being guilty of the trifling sins of whoredom, drunkenness and profane swearing.

The constituent members of Christ's church are credible christians: Nor is the appellation applied to them in the same latitude in which it has been used since the commencement of national churches. They profess their faith in Christ, and their obedience to him by works as well as by words. They are " faithful in Christ Jesus."* The inspired volume characterizes them—as " living stones which are built up a spiritual house;"—as " an holy priesthood, who offer up spiritual sacrifices to God, by Jesus Christ;" and as " a chosen generation, a royal priesthood, an holy nation, a peculiar people, to shew forth the praises of him, who hath called them out of darkness into his marvellous light."†

There is no historical fact more certain than that evangelical churches were originally constituted of such characters. It is therefore plain, that the character should continue the same, while we profess to adopt the same system of revelation, to acknowledge the same lawgiver, and to regulate our sentiments and conduct by the same laws.

But alas, how striking is the contrast between that character, and that of the generality of those who are members of incorporated churches! Instead of being " called out of the world," they become members of such churches, in order that they may be *of the world*, and may enjoy those emoluments in church or state, which minister to their avarice, luxury or lust. All the subjects of the nation, pious and profane, are legal members of the national church. Should any conscientious dissenter scruple communion; and should he plead, in order to be exempted from the civil penalties and ecclesiastical

---

* Eph. i. 1.   † 1 Pet. ii. 5, 9.

censures, which hang over his obnoxious head, that he is no member of the incorporated sect, because he never gave his consent to become such ;—his plea avails nothing. Though it be *logical*, it is not *legal*. It cannot divert the thunder of excommunication. He is solemnly cast out of a society, of which he never was a member; and he is fined, confined, and at last ruined, for the unpardonable sin of being a man, and asserting the rights of human nature.

Nor ought it to be overlooked in this place, that the members of national churches sustain that character formally as they are members of civil society. The reason of the assertion is obvious. In the eye of legislature, the formal reason of their membership in the national church is, its own authority ordaining and appointing them members, under civil pains. Communion, in consequence of such membership, is purely civil. It is the *legal condition* of enjoying the common rights of citizens in their full extent.

On a review, it is plain, that incorporated churches are not according to the scriptural model of the churches of Christ. Notwithstanding their ecclesiastical character, they are civil and political societies, as far as their constitutions, the designs of their erection, and the formal character of their members are all confounded with those of civil society.

CHAP.

CHAP. II.

A Proof attempted, "*That Incorporations are* HURTFUL *to the Church.*"

ASTONISHING is the power of prepossession! It is probable that European legislatures have piously imagined that they were doing the church very important service, when they were moulding her into an earthly kingdom, incorporating her with the political constitution, and authorizing one sect of christians to fatten upon the spoils of all others. Nor have the bulk of christians been of a different sentiment. Even in this age, notwithstanding the progress of liberal sentiment, an incorporation is reckoned so essential to the being of that society, which would assume the name of a church, that the historian would write in a style absolutely unintelligible, were he to describe any religious society by that designation, which had not been, at least at that time, allied to the political state of the nation. It is commonly thought, that the advantages, resulting from an incorporation, are numerous and important. The clergy are put in a state of independence on their flocks; and, at the same time, are fixed in a state of *useful dependence* on government. The people are taught by the same methods to obey their spiritual guides, by which they are obliged to honour their civil governors. An effectual bar is put in the way of all diversity of sentiment on the subject of the national creed, and of all diversity of worship, in regard to the public liturgy. In case of any religious controversies with peevish dissenters, the incorporated sect is ever sure to gain the palm, even though

though it should lose the victory. And should dissenters at any time become formidable, either on account of their arguments, or because of their numbers, the national church is always ready prepared, and legally authorized to answer all their arguments, and to lessen their numbers, by the execution of the penal statutes.

Notwithstanding these supposed conveniencies, a proof may be attempted of the following propositions.—" That an incorporation destroys the essential characters of the christian church:"—" It supplants the authority of Christ over her:"—" It spoils her members of their peculiar privileges:"—and " it tends to disappoint the very important designs of her erection."

SECT. I.

Incorporations destroy the Essential Characters of the Christian Church.

A SHORT review of some characterizing properties of Christ's kingdom will set this proposition in a just point of view.

I. The character, to which the adored Redeemer himself bare witness before the Roman governor, deserves to be first considered;—" My kingdom is NOT of this world." *

Though this character be negative, it conveys as positive an idea of that kingdom as the characters of immensity, immutability, infinity do of the Deity himself. It is such a description as serves to check all carnal notions concerning its object. That it

* John xviii. 36.

differs

differs in *kind* from every species of civil society, mixed or unmixed, is the least that seems to be imported by the terms. It must therefore follow, that incorporations destroy one of the most essential qualities of that kingdom. While they constitute the national church a department of the mixed political system, they make her what Christ testifies his church *is not*. In so far as she is incorporated with the constitution of civil society, and obtains a legal monopoly of orthodoxy, tythes and titles, she is not the church of Christ. Should even her doctrines and rites be never so pure and primitive, they belong not formally to the church of Christ. *Finis dat formam.* They are the doctrines and rites of the state. When legislature grants an incorporation, it acts with design, and with such a design as is congruous to its own nature and ends. It therefore follows, that, as its ends are and can be only civil and political, the religious system, as the incorporated system, can be viewed in no other light than as an engine of civil policy; and the society, as incorporated, can be viewed in no other point of light besides that of a society, incorporated for civil and political purposes.

Some may be disposed to object to the propriety of this reasoning; and may please themselves with the thought, that notwithstanding all that hath been adduced, " incorporations destroy not the essential character of Christ's kingdom, since the kingdom which is not of this world may, and does subsist in incorporated churches."

Though it be admitted that the *true* church of Christ may subsist in national churches, this does not prove that these, as such, are true churches. If a nation or an empire forms itself into a peculiar, mixed species of society; governs itself by a peculiar body of laws, adapted to the peculiarity of its constitution; and pursues designs quite foreign, or sometimes opposite to the noble purposes for which the kingdom of Christ was erected; it cannot be called, without a gross abuse of language, the kingdom, which is *not* of this world. If the designs of its erection, the manner of its administration, and the purposes which it pursues,—be political, it is so far a civil society to all intents and purposes. And such is every national church. The incorporating charter, on which she stands, supposes it. And the penal laws, annexed to it, are directly aimed at the *true* and *genuine* church of Christ secretly lurking in the nation, or perhaps in her communion. Yes: they mean nothing, unless they import, that no other church of Christ *subsists*, and *ought* to *subsist* in the nation, besides that society which is established by law for attaining the political ends of civil government: and that no authority, human or divine, is, or ought to be acknowledged, as obligatory on the conscience, beside that which hath bestowed the incorporated charter.

Thus are men cheated out of their religion. Religion consisteth not so much in paying a regard to the doctrines and laws of christianity, as in paying that respect *formally* on account of the authority of Christ *alone*, enjoining that respect as a proof of cordial subjection to him, as the only King of Zion, who hath, or ought to have authority in his own kingdom. But in all national churches, political authority walks forth with solemn, awful pace, and demands faith in Christ and obedience to him, as a *debt due to it*, as a proof of the subjection of the conscience to its commands, and as a *legal condition* of enjoying the common rights of men and citizens. Its language is, "To you it is commanded, O nations, people and languages, that at what time ye hear the sound of the state music, and the thunder
of

of the executive powers, ye fall down and worship the golden image which legiflature hath fet up."

Mean time, what the chriftian church gains of worldly grandeur, by incorporations, fhe lofeth of fpiritual glory. Though the moft exact uniformity fhould prevail; though the moft punctual obedience fhould be yielded to the eftablifhed fyftem; yea, though *it* were altogether unadulterated; yet there is no *visible test*, by which it can be known to MEN, whether the authority of Chrift, or of legiflature contributes moft to this uniformity;—whether fuch an ecclefiaftical nation is a fociety of idolaters and hypocrites, or of chriftians and faints. True chriftians, in fuch a fociety, are like the feven thoufand in the days of Elijah. They pay an *invisible*, though fincere regard to the authority of Chrift, amidft a countlefs crowd of idolaters, who, while profeffing the fame faith, and practifing the fame modes of worfhip, are vifibly bowing the knee to civil authority alone.

II. SPIRITUALITY is another effential property of Chrift's kingdom. This property may be juftly inferred from the former. As it is not of *this* world, it muft be *spiritual* and *heavenly*.

That the proof may be full, that this character of the chriftian church is overthrown by incorporations, we muft lay it down in various points of view. The church may be confidered,—in her relation to her divine Head and Lawgiver;—In regard of her conftituent members;—as fhe is governed by her own peculiar laws;—And as fhe is conftituted to anfwer ends, wholly foreign to thefe of civil fociety.

1. As the chriftian church ftands related to the Mediatorial character of Chrift, which is wholly fpiritual, fhe alfo muft be characterized by the fame property. It requires no extraordinary degree of penetration,

penetration, to perceive from the nature of Chrift's character, that he is not invefted with it, that he may be qualified to govern an earthly kingdom, either by the exertion of his own authority, or by that of his fubftitutes.

It hath been proved already, that chriftian churches are formally diftinct from incorporated churches; and that thefe laft, however they may be denominated, through the abufe of language, are, as fuch, focieties purely political. It follows therefore, that, if Chrift have no other kingdom, he muft either renounce his *spiritual* character, or abdicate his *political* kingdom. There is no medium. His Mediatorial offices, calculated for fpiritual and heavenly purpofes only, are infinitely difproportionate to the nature and purpofes of incorporated churches, viewed as political focieties. Were it true what incorporations fuppofe, that Chrift hath no other church in the nation, befide the incorporated fociety, the confequences would be fhocking. The wifdom of God in invefting Chrift with royal, fpiritual titles muft be accounted folly: as the Mediator's offices have no vifible correlates, they muft be abfolutely unneceffary: and as every government makes it criminal by the penal laws, connected with the act of incorporation, to acknowledge any other church, as a true church of Chrift, befides the national church, which, by its incorporation, becomes a political fociety; Chrift is robbed of his kingdom, in every nation where incorporations takes place; and at the fame time, and by the fame rafh interference of civil authority, his kingdom is divefted of one of its chief excellencies.

2. The fpiritual character of all Chrift's fubjects infers the fpirituality of his kingdom. They, as fubjects of that kingdom, are "*not* of the world." It is true, they are members of civil fociety: but in
their

their religious character, and as related to the church of Christ, they are not to be viewed as combining in civil association, and as prosecuting its peculiar designs. They are viewed as *credible saints*, called to fellowship with Christ, and with one another in a peculiar kind of society, wholly distinct from civil association. Whatever some eminent persons may have written in favour of promiscuous admission to communion, it seems plain that this is the character of all such as ought to be admitted to the christian mysteries. Can any indeed be accounted members of any free society, who refuse to obey its laws, and conform to its maxims? Can those be accounted the subjects of Christ, who visibly contemn his authority; openly bid defiance to his laws; and practically declare, that they neither know the Lord, nor will obey his voice?

Incorporations destroy the spirituality of Christ's kingdom, while they secularize the character of its subjects. The members of national churches, instead of being called out of the world, are no other than the men of the world. Every national church considers all the subjects of the prince as her members *de jure*; and, on that principle, claims a civil right to excommunicate those, who, *de facto*, were never of her communion. The same law of necessity, which obliges them to be members of the commonwealth, constitutes them members of the church. Thus, their religious character is swallowed up in their political relation to civil authority. They have but *one* character. They are, in every respect, subject to political authority, presiding over both departments of the heterogeneous constitution. How different is the character of Christ's subjects! They are "*called* to be saints;" They are not born such. They are " a willing people ;" not pressed into Christ's service. They are " redeemed out of every
kindred,

kindred, tribe and nation;" not every one of every nation.

From this contrast, it appears, that as far as incorporated churches secularize the character of their members, they are not these societies to which as such, the spiritual character of the Redeemer bears the most distant analogy.

Nor is this the only branch of the christian's character which incorporations tend to annihilate. The subjects of Christ's kingdom, having dedicated themselves, to their divine Lawgiver, profess a resolution to sacrifice every earthly interest to their loyalty. " Raised up together with Christ," they profess " to seek those things which are above," where He sits enthroned on the right-hand of God. Renewed in the spirit of their minds, they " set their affection on things above," and not on earthly objects. How ruining to this temper are incorporations! By them, every man is entitled to the character of a good subject, and of a good christian, (churchman) in proportion as he falls out with his own conscience, by contemning the authority of Christ in those doctrines and institutions, which legislature may have thought proper to discard, or to adulterate in the incorporated system. They are legally accounted good christians, in proportion as their hearts are warmly engaged in the pursuits of ambition, and are resolved to sacrifice every object that is sacred, at the shrines of conformity and preferment.

There is nothing more obvious from experience than that incorporations tend to make this character universal. Should it even be supposed that the national system is agreeable to the sentiments of conformists; yet these, exempted from the cross, tempted by the charms of ease and affluence, and seduced from the disagreeable paths of mortification

and

and animated piety; become carnal, sensual, and a reproach to the christian profession. On the other hand, the baits of riches, honours and preferments, and the horrors of disgrace, poverty and ruin, are held up to allure, or to affright the scrupulous to purchase the fashionable and lucrative character of good churchmen at the expence of their christianity. When national churches are generally constituted of such members, are they not carnal and worldly? Is not their spiritual character, as parts of Christ's spiritual kingdom, in a great measure annihilated? If the christian church were made up of such societies only, as her component parts, no man could believe her to be that society which our Lord intended to describe, when he said, " My kingdom is not of *this* world." Yet incorporations make it penal to acknowledge any other churches on earth!

3. The nature of those laws by which the kingdom of Christ is governed serves to demonstrate the spirituality of that kingdom. Such as the laws of any society are, such are the nature and character of that society. Laws cannot answer their end, if there be no political fitness in them to the nature of the society, to the general character of its members, and to the peculiar designs of its institution. But who knows not that the laws of Christ's kingdom are entirely spiritual? To suppose, therefore, that the church is capable of being governed by civil or statute law, would at once impeach the wisdom of her Lawgiver, and annihilate one of her essential characters.

All this is more than supposed in national churches. A certain sect obtains a precluding incorporation. A peculiar creed is authorized. A certain liturgy is canonized. By what authority? Is it not by that of legislature? Must not then those doctrines and modes of worship, which receive the

form

form and *force* of law from the national legiflature, be viewed by them, and all the world, as *statute law?* And fince *civil* legiflature cannot legiflate for any fociety but what is civil, and of which it is the proper reprefentative; does it not follow, that legiflature, when legiflating for the national church, in legitimating her creed and ritual, confiders her merely as a civil fociety, and as a fociety of which it is the proper reprefentative, and in which, on that account, it has a right of civil legiflation? If all this be juft, is it not plain, that the inftitutions of chriftianity, as they are bound upon incorporated churches, by civil authority, are no longer fpiritual, but are ftatute law; that thefe churches are confidered by legiflature in no other point of view than in that of civil focieties; and that if Chrift have no other kingdom on earth befides thefe, he hath none at all, which anfwers to his own defcription of it?

It is in vain to reply, "that though the inftitutions of chriftianity, as they are enforced by civil authority, may be viewed as ftatute law; yet, being ftill divine inftitutions, they may, and ought to bind the confciences of all chriftians, as the inftitutions of the chriftian lawgiver. True! but the objection implies an acknowledgment of the juftice and propriety of the above reafoning. And if fo, then Chrift can have no kingdom at all that correfponds to the defcription which he himfelf gives of it. Not that which is the object of civil legiflation, becaufe it is conceded, that this is civil and of *this* world. Nor any other, in the eye of the law; both becaufe government refufes to acknowledge any other befides that which it eftablifhes by a precluding incorporation; and becaufe the penal ftatutes, annexed to the act of incorporation, neceffarily imply a denial that there *is,* or *ought* to be an acknowledgment of

any

any other church of Chrift in exiftence, within the limits of the legiflature's influence and authority.

Befides, it is denied, that the peculiar doctrines and inftitutions of Chrift can become the matter of ftatute law to any fociety whatever, over which civil legiflature hath a right of legiflation. They have no affinity with the law of nature, which, being alone univerfal, is, according to its various applications, the only ftandard of civil actions, and the only univerfal rule in the difpenfing of civil rewards and punifhments. As thefe doctrines and inftitutions have an immediate and primary refpect to the underftanding and the confcience, which are neceffarily exempted from all *human*, not to fay civil jurifdiction, and are fubject to God only; they cannot become matter of ftatute law, nor be enforced by civil authority, appearing with even all its attending lures and chains. The confcience is naturally incapable of feeling the force of *human*, authority, or even the *pains* of penal ftatutes.

4. The fpiritual purpofes for which the kingdom of Chrift was erected, ferve to demonftrate its fpirituality. If the defigns of erecting incorporated churches be foreign and oppofite to thofe for which Chrift erected his kingdom, it will follow, that incorporations, in fo far as they fubvert the ends of the erection of Chrift's kingdom, deftroy its fpirituality. A contraft of thefe defigns will fet the fubject in a proper point of view.

The purpofe of Chrift in the erection of his church was, that in and by ordinances of his own inftitution only, in her, the adored perfons and perfections of the GODHEAD might be illuftrioufly difplayed, and for ever glorified in the final falvation of all, who, by a divine faith, approve, receive and fubmit to him as their compleat Saviour.

But is this, or any thing analogous to this, the

design of erecting incorporated churches? Is it not rather, that the incorporated sect may legally arrogate to itself the pompous title of THE CHURCH; that its public teachers may enjoy all those dignities, preferments and riches, which legislature hath pinned to the national profession; and that its laity *alone* may legally possess an exclusive title to every station of honour, profit and ease in the civil branch of the mixed administration? Whatever may have been, in some ages, the pious design of some legislatures, the uniform history of incorporations proves, that this has been their ultimate aim and constant result. It follows, therefore, that as the spiritual design of that society is exchanged for those which are entirely at war with christianity, and plainly inconsistent with the laws of justice and natural equity; if the precluding incorporation imply that the national church is the only church to be acknowledged in the nation, it imports, at the same time, that Christ hath no church at all within its boundaries.

III. Another essential quality of Christ's kingdom, to which incorporations are hostile, is, its immediate DEPENDENCE on the authority of Christ alone. Christian churches are built on his person, as their only foundation; are related to him, as their spiritual Sovereign; and are accountable to him, as their final Judge. They sing, "The Lord is our Judge, the Lord is our Lawgiver, the Lord is our King, he will save us."*

Though this principle be generally acknowledged, yet incorporations overthrow it. They create a civil relation between legislature and the members of national churches, as such, which subverts the relation between Christ and them, as members of *his* church. Let it be supposed that the national church

* Isa. xxxiii. 22.

is the most orthodox on earth; yet the penal laws, inseparable from the act of incorporation, supplant the authority of Christ, and make the conformity of church-members to the national system, *visibly* to hang on the authority of legislature. I say, *visibly*, for though charity may suppose that they are sincerely attached, their conformity is no *proof* that they are so. It does not glorify God. It only glorifies the mighty power of legislature. True christians act, in all religious concerns, solely from a sense of the divine authority. And if this be the case, where is the necessity of legislature's interference? Could any human law, armed with tortures and all the terrors of death, have made the apostle Paul a more orthodox believer of the doctrines he taught? All truth must stand upon evidence; not upon *human* authority. And, if evidence has already procured the assent of the understanding, the authority of all the legislatures on earth cannot add a grain to its effect on the mind. Would an act of parliament have made Sir Isaac Newton a more confirmed believer of his own demonstrations? It will be answered, no: "But such laws influence the conformity of those who have no sense of Christ's authority." But we may ask—May not these laws also greatly injure those, who, because they have the most tender sense of Christ's authority, dare not conform? Besides, are these political conformists made christians? Are they not made vile hypocrites? Such policy is a most wonderful effort to make every man's religion independent of his understanding, of his will, of his conscience, of himself, and as convenient to him as his cloak. It is an attempt to put the human species on a level with baboons; and to increase the number of their more irrational and mischievous brethren,—the atheists!

IV. Once more; incorporations tend to destroy the *unity* of the church, to circumscribe her *catholicism*, and to hurt her *identity*.

1. Scripture bears ample testimony to the *unity* of the church: and experience bears no less ample witness, that incorporations are very hostile to it. This will fully appear, when it is considered in what her unity consisteth.

The unanimous concurrence of church-members, in the profession of their faith, enters into the idea of her unity.

Though the christian faith hath been fixed in scripture, with a degree of precision, which should have exempted it from corruption, yet how is it varied, distorted, mangled and adulterated in almost all national churches! and how much more among them all! Christians, according to the country in which they were born, and the nature of its political constitution, are forcibly divided into political, schismatical sects, every one of which has a faith, stamped like the coin of the country, with the image of that authority, which gives it its national currency. Their faith is not the faith of the church catholic. To every national creed, legislature ever finds it politically necessary to add, or cause to be added, some discriminating shibboleth, from which the incorporated faith derives a *characteristical speciality*, by which it is not only politically differenced from the ONE common faith of the universal church, but also, in like manner, from similar differencing *notas* in other incorporated churches. Thus, the dialect of the first schismatics is revived and perpetuated. One saith, I am of the church of England; another, I am of the church of Scotland; another, I am of the church of France, &c. If you ask, why?——It is answered, they breathe in these countries; and unless they were willing to forfeit their civil rights, perhaps
their

their lives, they must profess themselves members of these churches.

Farther, the unity of the church consists in a voluntary and harmonious regard among their members to the institutions of Christ. Instead of being made the subjects of Christ by the iron hand of secular authority, they are drawn by the silken cords of gratitude. Actuated by the same principle, governed by the same laws, and prompted by the same motives, they pursue the same spiritual designs, with a degree of unanimity which shews that they are under the influence of one Spirit.

No room seems left for any part of this description in incorporated churches. At the time when the incorporation is to be made, legislature calls a synod; commands it to sit till it shall have framed a number of canons, sufficient to answer the ends of the interested, and to cramp the liberty and enslave the consciences of christians; and finally appoints the ghostly assembly to prefer this their book of canons for a parliamentary revisal. It is corrected and approved. And now it is the only standard of religious uniformity. Thus, instead of an unity and uniformity founded on a joint sense of Christ's supreme authority, a political *likeness*, unallied to union, is established and enforced by the fear of the magistrate's sword, which, concerning objects of this kind, he seldom bears in vain.

Nor is it less plain that incorporations destroy the union of churches. This must be the case, while there are more national churches than one on the earth. The rule of uniformity differs in every nation from that of all others. It becomes therefore impossible, that the union of churches can subsist. The ministers of the church of Scotland are no ministers in the eye of the church of England, because their ordination is not episcopal, agreeable to the incor-

porated

porated canons of that church. Nay the Scotch are no chriftians in England, becaufe, happening to have been baptized by minifters, who are no minifters in the eye of the Englifh book of canons, their baptifm is not canonical, and confequently not valid!

We muft not forget the true fpring of confent in the faith, and harmony of worfhip. It is the " unity of the Spirit."* Endued with the fame holy difpofitions, " chriftians walk by the fame rule, and they mind the fame things ".†

But incorporations fuperfede the unity of the Spirit. A conftrained conjunction of men, actuated by the moft oppofite fprings of action, is accounted ecclefiaftical unity. It is of no importance to legiflature, whether they be actuated by the Spirit of God, or influenced by the devil. Hence, in fuch focieties, it is not lefs common than fhocking to fee whoremongers, drunkards, extortioners and—faints —all good, legal chriftians, approaching the awful myfteries, and profeffing, at that facred table, that they are *one body*, and *one bread!* Can that be accounted the "*unity* of the Spirit" where the fons of God and the children of Belial are violently driven together, by the fword of the magiftrate, into church communion, and are legally authorized to prophane the moft tremendous myfteries!

2. The CATHOLICISM of the church is not in lefs danger from incorporations than her unity.

Whatever caufe is capable of crumbling the church into independent pieces, militates againft that article of the ancient creed, " I believe the holy catholic church." Incorporations, by authorizing national fhibboleths, make every national church an independent part, which can have no communion with other parts of the fame body. Incorporations

* 1 Cor. xii. 13.   † Philip iii. 16.

imply

imply that no other church is, or ought to be acknowlegded by its members. Gold, the moment it receives the ftamp of any country upon it, is no more of univerfal currency. In other countries, it is eftimated only at its intrinfic worth. Had the Judaizing teachers fucceeded in their defign of making circumcifion the *test* to Gentile converts of their becoming members of their commonwealth, the chriftian church, however extenfive fhe might have been, inftead of being catholic, muft have been entirely national and particular. The cafe is fimilar in all national churches. They ceafe to be parts of the one catholic church, fince their incorporations, eftablifhing their refpective fhibboleths, oblige the members of all, refpectively, to renounce the communion of each other, and to hold their own church as the only church of Chrift with which they legally can have communion on earth. It follows, therefore, by the jufteft confequence, that fince this is the cafe of all incorporated churches, if thefe be the only churches of Chrift, there is no fuch fociety as the one catholic church upon earth.

Some may alledge, " that feeing different churches, even in the primitive ages, had different ufages, the chriftian church was never univerfal in the above fenfe." We anfwer, they had different cuftoms, and even different fentiments about fome things; but did any of thefe primitive focieties make their peculiar cuftoms and fentiments dividing *tests* of fchifmatical parties? If any did, they ftood reproved.—" Who art thou that judgeft another man's fervant? To his own Mafter he ftandeth or falleth. Let us not judge one another; but judge this rather that no man put a ftumbling block in his brother's way." * Chriftians, in thefe early ages, had no temptation to incur that reproof to which incorpo-

* Rom. xiv. 4, 13.

rations

rations have exposed their interested and schismatical votaries.—Laudable, especially instituted customs are to be maintained; truth, at all hazards, must be avowed; but neither is it to be imposed. Separation from any church is never lawful till she becomes an imposing society, with whom communion cannot be maintained without falling out with conscience. And in this case, the separatist is no schismatic. He only separates from a society, become schismatical by tyrannic imposition, that he may cleave to such churches, as keep the unity of the Spirit in the bond of peace, and hold themselves parts of the catholic church, by frankly and faithfully avowing what they believe to be truth, without daring to impose their creed, or ritual, on other churches, or any new doctrine, or rite, on their own members. Were incorporations annihilated, impositions would in a great measure cease; schism would be much more rare; and lawful separation, of course, could scarce ever exist. Christians would then see the propriety and universal applicability of that inspired canon, "Whereunto we have already attained, let us walk by the same rule, let us mind the same things: and if in any thing ye be otherwise minded, God shall reveal even this unto you." *

3. Incorporations are not less hurtful to the IDENTITY of the church than to her unity and catholicism.

It is plain from the scriptures, that the gospel church-state is absolutely invariable. It is "a kingdom which *cannot* be moved." It is superior to the influence of sublunary causes. It leans "on the Rock of ages," and its "foundations are in the holy mountains." Its order and mode of administration are immutable as the Divine Person who has fixed them, and on whose shoulder the government is

* Philip. iii. 15, 16.

laid.

laid. Men have in vain ſtrained every nerve to change them. They are ſo congenial to the nature of the church, that no other order and mode of government can ſuit it. When any other have been attempted, a correſponding change on the characters of the members of the church behoved to be introduced, in order that they might become *fit* objects for them. The church behoved to be ſecularized; and her members conſidered upon a level with thoſe of ſociety, purely civil. It is impoſſible that the church can ſubmit unto any other mode of government, in her own real character. She muſt borrow one. She muſt become a civil and ſecular ſociety in order to be governed by regulations which originate only from civil legiſlature.

It is hence eaſy to ſee how incorporations hurt the ſameneſs of the church. From the moment a church is allied and blended with the conſtitution of a nation, ſhe becomes ſubject to all the confuſions and convulſions of that nation. Every alteration in the mode of civil government introduces a proportionable change in the mode of governing the church incorporated with the conſtitution. What ſtrange alterations has the kingdom of Chriſt, or what is preſumed to be ſuch, undergone from the policy or caprice of princes! May we not make a ſhrewd gueſs concerning the ſyſtem of politics, or the peculiar humour of any prince, from the mode of worſhip, or the form of eccleſiaſtical government, which he chuſed to introduce into the incorporated church? Who ſees not the *gay*, the *haughty* and the politic queen in the hierarchy and the liturgy of queen *Elizabeth?* Who, at firſt view, is not ſenſible of the weakneſs and caprice of *James* I. in the religious changes which he attempted in his *gude* kingdom of Scotland? Who can be ignorant of the reigning politics in *Charles* the I. court, when he conſiders the ecclesiastical alterations which he intended? Even in one short reign, the contrary humours of one prince have been exposed to view in the incorporated church. In the first years of queen *Ann*'s reign, every thing in the British churches wore the face of liberty; but in the latter part of the same reign, all know how much the complex constitution of church and state was changed. And had not divine providence, ever watchful over the interests of Great Britain, put a surprising stop to the execution of some designs, none can tell how far the protestant interest might have been hurt, and the protestant succession, in the present illustrious royal family, been prevented, by the folly and caprice of one woman.

Can it be imagined, that societies, necessarily subject to such constant change, are that kingdom which *cannot* be moved? It is impossible. The model of that kingdom is fixed for ever, and superior to change. The despised few, both within and without the pale of national churches, who, in every age, and in every nation, without regard to the rescripts of emperors, and the sovereign mandates of mighty monarchs, have realized the authority of Christ in the important doctrines and plain institutions of christianity, and have walked together in a voluntary and harmonious regard to them, in their several churches;—are justly intitled to the exclusive character of subjects in Christ's kingdom; and constitute that church against which the gates of hell shall never finally prevail.

SECT.

SECT. II.

Incorporations tend to supplant the Authority of Christ, in National Churches.

IT cannot be consistently controverted among protestants, "that Christ is the only Sovereign in his own kingdom." The Father hath set him on his holy hill of Zion; and all her daughters shout their cordial *Amen* — " The Lord is our Judge, the Lord is our Lawgiver, the Lord is our King; he will save us."

Meanwhile, incorporations are hostile to the regal office of Christ, while they supplant this authority in his own kingdom. In incorporated churches, civil authority boldly steps forth and assumes the despotic control and direction of the understandings and consciences of their members. This cannot be attempted without a direct invasion of the Redeemer's prerogatives. Why have protestants applied the title of antichrist to the Bishop of Rome? Is it not because, by his assuming the direction of the conscience, he, as God, sitteth in the temple of God, shewing himself that he is God? Is not conscience the proper seat of God's authority? And can any legislature, whether at Rome or at London, assume the direction and control of that power, sacred to God alone, without usurping upon the prerogative of the Almighty, and entailing on itself the guilt of " opposing and exalting itself above all that is called God, or is worshipped."

When legislature incorporates any creed, making it criminal, and of consequence punishable in any subject not to profess it before both God and man, as his creed; it must view itself either as fallible, or as infallible. Though all dominion over the conscience must be founded on a supposition that he who claims it is infallible; yet no civil legislature has ever *directly* arrogated that extraordinary gift; and every protestant legislature, from a just abhorrence of popish arrogance, openly disclaims it. How inconsistent, therefore, must it be, for any protestant legislature, disclaiming infallibility, to dictate to the understandings and control the consciences of all its subjects? These powers are the eyes of human nature. Incorporations are an attempt to extinguish them. They cannot be controuled by fallible authority. The arrogant claims of a Roman pontiff are not so inconsistent as these of a civil legislature, owning itself to be fallible, yet acting as if it were infallible, by dictating articles of faith, to millions of their fellow creatures. The pretended vicar of Christ, affirms that he hath both an authentic commission, and proper qualifications for an universal dictator. He is the vicegerent of Christ, and altogether infallible. But protestant legislatures frankly acknowledge, that they are neither; and yet they arrogate a right to act, as if they were both!

If civil legislatures can pretend to no commission, nor any qualifications from Christ, to legislate for the understandings and consciences of his subjects; it does not appear, that ever civil society could invest them with any such powers. By what original contract, explicit or virtual, did civil society confer them? Is it to be imagined that rational and accountable creatures, uniting in society for the express purpose of more effectually securing their rights and liberties, could, without the most gross impiety, make a present of their understandings and consciences to their civil governors; could put off, at pleasure, and with impunity, the chief characteristics of human nature; and, renouncing those very

rights

rights and liberties, which they had proposed to put under a guard, by entering into society, associate themselves with the browsing herds, by giving up their moral nature, with all of man but the human shape? If not; what right hath civil government to assume what never was, and never could be, ceded to it?——Is it not hence plain, that incorporations supercede the authority of Christ in the conscience; and are founded on an assumption of power, neither granted by God, nor ceded by society?

There is no room to object, " that this reasoning, by proving too much, proves nothing: that it implies, that legislatures ought not to inforce, by civil pains, the observation of moral precepts, lest the authority of God in them should be supplanted: and that, therefore, it is hostile to all order and equity in society."

It is answered, that none of these consequences follow. There is a vast difference between the *moral government* of God in the world, and the *mediatorial government* of Christ in his peculiar kingdom. As the moral law, written in the hearts of all men, is the rule of that moral government which God maintains among the nations, so magistrates are God's vicegerents to execute that law. The authority of every lawful magistrate is no other beside the authority of the Supreme Legislator himself. " Whoever resisteth the power, resisteth the ordinance of God."[*] But in the mediatorial kingdom, Christ hath appointed no vicegerent, hath substituted no vicar, hath committed the reins to no creature. He is the only Sovereign, and the sole legislator in his own kingdom. No magistrate can produce letters of deputation from Christ. As he never gave a commission to any without giving, at the same time, adequate qualifications for the discharge of it; had

[*] Rom. xiii. 2.

he

he bestowed any such deputation on earthly princes, to see and to think for his subjects, he would have bestowed on them a gem infinitely more brilliant than any that shone in the crown of Constantine or Charlemagne. The nature of their trust would have made it necessary, that MOST INFALLIBLE should have stood before *most potent*, in the list of royal titles.

SECT. III.

Incorporations tend to rob Church-members of their peculiar Privileges.

RELIGIOUS freedom is as much an unalienable privilege of every church-member in the kingdom of Christ, as civil liberty is the birth-right of every subject in a free state. Liberty to serve God, with a *reasonable* and *willing* service, is, indeed, the capital privilege of that society. To purchase it, her Redeemer died; and to secure it, he took and maintains his station " on the right-hand of the Majesty on high." All the names by which the church is characterized suggest the idea of liberty, and prove that it is the rightful inheritance of every person who has the honour of membership in her. She is a family; and liberty constitutes the difference between sons and slaves. She is a city,— the New Jerusalem, in which every credible professor is " a fellow citizen with the saints." She is a kingdom, the idea of which is inconsistent with that of dependence on a foreign yoke. In fine, she is the kingdom of heaven, which, as it is not of this world, must be independent of the kingdoms of it.

Let

[111]

Let none surmise, that christian liberty is inconsistent with loyalty. There is nothing more friendly to civil society, to the authority of legislatures, and to all the just rights of princes. It implies " a power to chuse judiciously and to observe conscientiously the articles of the christian faith, and the institutions of gospel worship, according as they are produced to view, in the holy scriptures." A power this, which is not only founded in reason, and necessarily connected with every other distinguishing excellence of human nature; but is essentially necessary to qualify mankind for the right discharge of every duty in social life. As the Supreme Father of men has bestowed reason and the power of moral perception on them, it is absurd to suppose that these important gifts disqualify them from discharging the duties of society; and that he hath prohibited their use, or authorized their fellow-creatures to debar them from exercising them, under pretence that they are inimical to the prerogatives of princes.

Though the attempt be impiously rash, yet incorporations annul that right of human nature. By a legal anticipation of rational choice, every man is obliged under severe penalties, to dismiss his reason, in regard to those very objects, for the investigation and choice of which, reason was principally given; and to acquiesce tamely in the political choice of his superiors. This shall be illustrated by a few instances.

I. Incorporations preclude freedom of choice in regard of church-membership and communion. Nothing is more plain than that churches are, or ought to be free societies. Spontaneous consent is necessary to constitute any a member in such societies. But church-membership in national churches is independent of any rational and free choice. Every
subject

subject of the state *must* be a member of the national church, unless he resolve to forego many of the common privileges of society, and incur the penalties annexed to the act of incorporation. Churches, so constituted, lose the nature of free societies; and, were it not for the abuse of language,—would lose the very name of churches. It is certain, that they are very different from the churches of Christ, whose members are "a WILLING people in the day of the Redeemer's power."

The primitive churches were such. No compulsive means were used, either to drive men into their communion, or to keep them in blind subjection to their spiritual guides. The gospel alone was the approved mean. It was then, and ought to be reckoned still " the power of God unto salvation." The apostles knew not the more expeditious arts of founding churches. They did not attempt to persuade the Romans to incorporate the christian relegion with the constitution of the empire. Nay; when the Jews violently set themselves to attempt such an incorporation with their commonwealth, the apostles unanimously opposed the scheme. Had laborious Paul been as sagacious as some of his pretended successors, how had he saved himself much fatigue, danger and persecution! By one slight manœuvre of human policy, he might have filled the world with christian churches. No more was necessary, than to have humoured his countrymen in incorporating christianity with the political state of the Jewish nation, by allowing circumcision, or some such rite, to be the door of admission to Gentile converts, and the test of their being one with the Jewish people. But he had not so learned Christ; and he knew the nature of the gospel church-state better than to attempt any such schemes of fleshly wisdom!

II. Incorpo-

II. Incorporations preclude church-members the liberty of chufing the articles of their own faith and the manner of their own worfhip. Though poffeffed of thinking and reflecting powers, they muft not think for themfelves. Though accountable to God for what they believe, as well as for what they do, they are not permitted to examine the national faith for themfelves, and to reject thofe articles, which, for want of evidence, they dare not profefs to believe. Though they have the oracles of God among their hands, they muft not ufe them but to vouch the articles of the allied creed. They muft not imitate the noble example of the Bereans, who fearched the fcriptures for themfelves, and even dared to try the doctrines of apoftles by them.

III. It is not lefs plain, that incorporations deprive chriftians, in national churches, of a right to chufe their own teachers. A privilege this, of the greateft importance to the edification of the church, and nearly connected with the honour of her divine Head. If churches be free focieties, they have an undoubted right to chufe their own officers. To deprive them, therefore, of this privilege, is to fix a mark of flavery upon them; and to commit one of the greateft acts of injuftice towards their members.

But incorporations make this politically neceffary! Yes; as foon as a church is incorporated, fhe becomes a branch of the *one* conftitution of church and ftate. Government cannot be faithful to its truft, if it do not extend its legiflative power and its political adminiftration to both branches of the conftitution, if it be neceffary that government fhould appoint its own officers and agents in the feveral departments of the ftate, it may nominate, prefent, and inftal, or caufe to be inftalled. If, at

P   any

any time, it hath yielded the reins of ecclefiaftical adminiftration into the hands of others, it hath always had reafon to repent its impolitic indulgence. Ever fince the commencement of incorporations, when princes permitted national churches to be governed by men, who afpired to be independent of their lawful fovereigns, under a pretence of fanctity of character, their kingdoms have been theatres of confufion, rebellion, and the moft unnatural wars. The recovery of the right of nomination and prefentation to ecclefiaftical benefices, and of invefture, has coft the feveral fovereigns in Europe, in certain periods, more blood and treafure than was ever expended for the fafety of all their other prerogatives. As long as incorporations fubfift, were government to remit of its vigilance about the ecclefiaftical branch of the mixed conftitution, a repetition of the fame tragic fcenes would foon enfue. The allurements of honour and rich emoluments would foon draw forth Guelphs and Gibbelines in abundance upon the European ftage, and Chriftendom would once more fee their Henrys and their Johns at the feet of proud ecclefiaftics. But modern policy, become wife by the leffons which the twelfth and thirteenth centuries abundantly afforded, is not like to fall into that error foon. Government, authorized by incorporations to afcertain what the church is to believe, as well as to fix what taxes the fubject is to pay, will, in every nation, confider itfelf as equally intitled to appoint the teachers of the national faith, as well as the collectors of the national treafure.

Thus, though Chrift hath appointed churches to chufe their own officers; though this is an effential privilege of every free fociety; and notwithftanding this privilege was claimed and enjoyed by the primitive churches, during near fix centuries;—it is
a pri-

a privilege which national churches cannot poſſeſs, without throwing civil ſociety into confuſion and blood; without bringing once more the dignity of princes into a ſtate of the moſt abject dependence on the arrogance of an ambitious prieſthood; and without unhinging the whole ſyſtem of modern policy, in the ſeveral nations of Europe.

SECT. IV.

Incorporations tend to fruſtrate the Designs of God, in the Erection of the Christian Church.

HAVING diſcourſed already, in the firſt ſection, concerning ſome of thoſe important deſigns of God, in the erection of his church; we ſhall be more brief in the illuſtration of this title. Two ends only ſhall be mentioned, which incorporations in a great degree eminently fruſtrate.

I. The chriſtian church was erected, in order to diſplay the tranſcendent glory of Chriſt's mediatorial character, as her prophet, prieſt and king; that all the ends of the earth, beholding it in the glaſs of her doctrines and inſtitutions, might believe on it, and be ſaved by it. For this end ſhe has been ſurprizingly preſerved, as the buſh, unconſumed in the midſt of devouring flames. The church is " a peculiar people, who ſhew forth the *virtues* of him who hath called them."

But when ſubmiſſion to the laws and inſtitutions of Chriſt is effected by coaction, violence, and penal laws, the divine virtues of the Redeemer's character and grace are obſcured, and the rod of the Mediator's power is evidently declared to be ineffectual for accomplishing its own ends. That the Mahumedan imposture could not obtain in the world by its own evidence, but that it behoved to be propagated by violence and supported by force, is an unanswerable argument, that it is a vile lie! and that its prophet neither had a divine commission, nor supernatural powers to effect its establishment. In full contrast stands the christian religion. Supported by its own evidence, and recommended by its own excellence, it not only gained an entrance, but it maintained its ground against all the fury of the dragon, and against all the united force of the Roman empire. This is justly accounted as strong a proof of the truth of the christian religion, as the manner in which the Eastern imposture was propagated is of its falshood.

But since the date of incorporations, when the maxims of christian sects have been propagated for christianity, by the same means by which the Turkish superstition triumphed, we may ask, Where is the glory of that supernatural evidence, by which christianity once conquered the nations? Where is the glory of that sceptre, under which kingdoms bowed with willing submission? ICHABOD! It is departed, christians are now sent to church by the same rough hand, which sends the mussulman to the mosque.

II. Another important design of erecting the church was, that the thick shades of mental darkness might be dispelled, by the triumphant entrance of the " day-spring from on high." On this account she is characterized " the pillar and ground of truth;" and her members are said to be " brought out of darkness into his marvellous light." As long as the christian system continued free from the fetters of an incorporation, this end was rapidly gained. The darkness passed in these first and
brightest

brightest days of christianity, and the true light shone out in all its divine splendour. Then, truth proved its own excellence, by its own evidence and enrapturing beauty; and even now, she asks no more but the removal of political obstructions, to procure her a triumph over the darkest regions of error and superstition.

I say, truth asks no more to procure her a triumph, but the removal of political obstructions; and incorporations are a principal obstruction! As soon as legislature, finding the religious system of some sect conducive to the political designs of government, gives it an incorporation; every absurdity, every foolery, every mistake in that system, obtains a safe and permanent lodgement behind the rampart of the constitution. Being part of that incorporated system, by which the national clergy enjoy their honours and wealth, these errors will never want zealous, because interested, advocates. Every way, by which the truth and common sense may enter, will be industriously blocked up. Truth shines in all her native charms; but it is as light shines upon a dungeon, where thick walls and iron gates preclude its entrance. Day pours down his gladdening beams; but midnight darkness still maintains her sway, and fills her ebon throne. The consequences are direful. Christians must either stain their consciences with the guilt of hypocrisy, while they profess to believe articles against which their understandings revolt; or they must incur the imputation of disaffection to government, to the constitution, and to christianity itself, together with its numerous train of consequences on their persons, estates and families. In such a case, to what straits must men of understanding, integrity and spirit, be reduced! Incorporations answer no ends so effectually as to afford a safe retreat for error and superstition; to

preclude

preclude the influence of truth; and to banish religion, honesty and every virtue out of the world. Atheists and hypocrites have the only chance to rise in the church as well as in the state. To what a miserable condition must a nation, must a church be reduced, when men of such a character, or even suspected of such a character, are called forth to take the helm, and to fill the chief places in the temple of the living God!

Would the European governments disengage their respective political constitutions from all improper connections with ecclesiastical sects:—would they put it out of the power of one religious denomination to ride down their fellow subjects; to fatten upon the spoils of their fellow-christians; and to persecute all who question their right to do so:—would they clear the stage of all political lumber, that divine truth might once more look her antagonist in the face on equal terms:—would they impartially keep the peace among those who differ in their religious sentiments:—would they religiously guard every man's life, liberty and property, as long as by his innocence, usefulness and loyalty he deserves it :—and would they, judging only for themselves, countenance and encourage that profession of christianity chiefly, which appears to them most agreeable to the holy scriptures, and consequently most conducive to the welfare of society, without allowing even those of that profession to injure others, by claiming any part of their property, as a reward of their own orthodoxy:—would they take such steps as these, to reform their respective constitutions, christianity would appear once more in all its original beauty and excellence; a laudable ambition would warm every heart and prompt every endeavour to excel in religion, loyalty and public spirit, and contentment would regale every mind, and smile in every countenance.

CHAP.

CHAP. V.

A brief View of the absurd Principles on which exclusive Establishments of Churches appear to be founded.

AMONGST all the various methods of reasoning concerning political systems, there seems to be none more safe, than that, which consists in an impartial and accurate inquiry into the principles on which they are founded. They are ordinarily advantageous or hurtful to religious as well as to civil society, in an exact proportion to the *quantum* of good or evil, of truth or falsehood, in the political foundations, on which they are built. Their effects bear a good or an evil aspect on the rights and liberties of all ranks of men concerned in them, according as the materials of these political structures are naturally more or less proper, to be intimately combined with one another and with the foundation.

God's moral government is excellent beyond all possible description. The reason is obvious. It rests on principles, which are not only congruous to the several parts of the system itself, but besides, are naturally fit to promote, in an infallible manner, the wise designs, for which it is established.

In like manner, systems of political government are more or less perfect, according as the principles on which they rest are more or less agreeable to the nature and designs of civil policy. While the principles and maxims of eternal equity are religiously attended to and supposed in any plan of political government, it is impossible to suppose that it can be wrong, or that any bad consequence can result from it. On the other hand, when any system of

civil

civil policy is eſtabliſhed, in which theſe maxims are diſregarded;—in which government is not conſtituted an equal debtor to every equally well-deſerving member of civil ſociety;—in which the lives and properties of ſubjects are ſuſpended on *iniquitous* or *impossible* conditions;—in which legiſlature puts it in the power of one part of civil ſociety to rob the other part of their rights and liberties;—it is morally impoſſible that it can be attended with any conſequences, but ſuch as are, in the higheſt degree baneful to civil as well as to religious ſociety.

Such a political ſyſtem is that, in which the conſtitution of the church is blended with the political frame of earthly kingdoms. We have already ſhewn, that it is baneful to religious ſociety. We intend to ſhew, that it is no leſs hurtful to civil ſociety. But before we proceed, we ſhall offer to view ſome of the erroneous and pernicious principles on which it is founded, from which it may appear, with the greater evidence, that none but the moſt fatal conſequences can attend it.

SECT. I.

Exclusive Establishments of Churches are built on the the Principle, that the Kingdom of Christ is a Society of the SAME NATURE *and* PROPERTIES *with the Kingdoms of this World.*

THOUGH this propoſition muſt appear abſurd, in the higheſt degree, to thoſe, who have conſidered, without prepoſſeſſion, the teſtimony of the FAITHFUL WITNESS concerning his own kingdom; it appears to be the original foundation, on which the GRAND ALLIANCE between church and state hath been always built. How is it possible to conceive, that men, endued with reason and discernment, could ever have made an attempt to blend the constitutions of societies so infinitely distinct, unless they had first admitted its truth in its fullest extent? Mixtures of every kind must be made up of diverse ingredients, which, though they may differ in some particular qualities, must agree in some common essential property. No abstract, metaphysical notion can become a foundation of an alliance, or of an union between opposite extremes. Though *body* and *spirit* agree in the abstract generical notion of existence; possessed of properties not only distinct, but infinitely opposite, they are intirely incapable of being blended in one compounded medley.

The case is exactly similar in regard of the kingdom of Christ, and the nations of this world. Though they agree in the common and abstract notion of SOCIETY, a mixture is impossible, on account of the opposition between their real, specific properties. The first is *heavenly, spiritual* and *unchanging*. The latter are *earthly, secular,* and subjected to *constant vicissitude*.

Notwithstanding the obvious distinction between these societies, the original projectors of the miscellaneous system, not attending to the incompatibility of their respective characters, must have admitted the principle of an antecedent possibility of mixture, before they could have entertained the thought, that it was in their power to accomplish it. Nor have its advocates in every age, founded their plea on a different *hypothesis*. Blind, or at least affecting to be blind, to the spiritual character of Christ's kingdom; the obvious foundation on which their mighty piles have been built, is, that the church is so similar, and naturally so nearly allied to the state, that it is

Q   absurd

absurd and fanatical to suppose, that she is capable of being governed by a system of laws, foreign to those of civil society;—that she is subject to the legislative power of Christ alone;—and that she is wholly exempted from all human jurisdiction.

In reasoning concerning objects of this kind, it is safest to appeal to facts. The faithful annals of the church bear witness to the following truth, viz. That the zeal of those, who have, in every age, approved themselves willing advocates for the alliance of church and state, hath flamed and blazed, in exact proportion as ignorance concerning the nature of Christ's kingdom, and inattention to the civil and religious rights of mankind have taken possession of their minds.

Who, and of what character, were the first projectors of the grand alliance between the catholic church and the Roman empire? Were they men, who were mortified to the world, with all its pomp, profits and pleasures? Were they governed by the same spirit, which actuated christians in the first and second ages of christianity? Did they live in an age, when the rights of human nature, civil and religious, were justly understood? Their character was, indeed, the strongest contrast to every thing connected with liberal sentiment, and the unalienable rights of human nature. As they had lost just apprehensions concerning the *capital character* of Christ's kingdom, they devoted their attention to the vindication of their own secular honour, and to the security of their temporal grandeur. Prepossessed in favour of their own religious usages, especially on account of the intimate connection between them and the smile of the court, they became impatient of contradiction; intolerant of every different religious practice, however indifferent or innocent; and viperous persecutors of all, who dared to think for themselves.

themselves, or to worship God according to his own laws and institutions.

Nor were those, who during the middle ages, have been the most celebrated patrons of the miscellaneous system, of a different character. Were they such as *prophesied in sackcloth, during the apocalyptic period of one thousand two hundred and sixty years?* * Were they those, who maintained the purity of the christian faith, in the wilderness, while all the world wondered after and worshipped the beast? No! It cannot be denied, that the most celebrated champions for the infernal claims of the Romish See, have ever shewn the greatest zeal, and have always acquitted themselves with greatest care, consistency and decency in the important cause. They have sufficiently proved their attachment to it, by all the murders and massacres, with which the church of Rome stands so justly charged.

The reformed churches furnish not an exception to the general maxim. It cannot be dissembled, that those in their communion who have shewn the greatest warmness for exclusive establishments, and the execution of penal laws against dissenters, instead of having being blessed with clear and just ideas concerning the nature and rights of the christian church, have demonstrated themselves to have been ignorant of human nature, and of its unquestionable rights and sacred liberties. The pompous liturgies, together with the books of canons, which they introduced, clearly shew, with what spirit they were actuated. These trammels, which they made for themselves and others, sufficiently prove, that they neither consulted the happiness and prosperity of civil society, nor cared to provide for the protection of that liberty, with which Christ hath made all his servants free. It is a truth wholly

* Rev. xi. 3.

unqueſtionable, that thoſe princes, of infamous memory, who were the greateſt zealots for a violent uniformity, for confounding every eccleſiaſtical object with the affairs of the ſtate, and for ſuſpending every man's ſocial rights on his creed and mode of religious worſhip—were the avowed enemies of human nature, public robbers of their own ſubjects, and ſupplanters of Chriſt's authority in the conſciences of upright and conſcientious chriſtians. Nor is it leſs notorious, that the dignified hierarchs, who were moſt active, during theſe reigns, for perfecting the alliance between church and ſtate, were not only blind, in a great degree, to objects of eternal importance, but attended to nothing ſo much as the hoarding of wealth, and accumulating honours, till they became an offence to every ſenſible man, even of their own principles.

We are, meanwhile, far from affirming that no good man ever abetted the alliance between the church and ſtate. We frankly own, that the beſt of men may, through miſtake, engage in a bad cauſe. Periods can be mentioned, in which the zeal of the moſt upright champions for reformation and religious liberty, hath taken a wrong direction, and hath flamed out for an excluſive eſtabliſhment, with ſuch extravagance, as to throw the iſland of Great Britain into much confuſion and blood-ſhed. But when?—It cannot be denied, that it hath fallen out only at ſuch times as have been immediately preceded by the triumphs of cruelty, tyranny, and wanton barbarity. It hath only happened, when the courſes of a contrary party, fierce for domination, have forced them on meaſures, which their peculiar circumſtances only can excuſe or extenuate; and which they themſelves, on cool reflection, have generouſly condemned. As their natural and religious rights had been wreſted from them by the

the mercilefs grafp of gigantic tyranny, maddened and enraged by clerical influence, they bravely engaged in the vindication of thefe objects, to which God hath given every man an indifputable title. Their only miftake confifted, in their not duly confidering, that a juft and effectual vindication of their natural rights, as men, and of their civil liberties as citizens, was a fufficient fecurity and guard to their religious rights, as chriftians, without their impofing, in their turn, a contrary fyftem of religion on the authors of their former mifery. The infernal intrigues of their mercilefs perfecutors had forced them to admit it as a maxim, that the moft effectual method to fecure to themfelves the invaluable poffeffion of their natural rights and religious liberties, was to fupercede the claims, and to make reprifals on the natural rights of thofe, whom their cruelties had declared to be unworthy of fuch favours. This was their miftake. A very pardonable one! Every one muft fee, that there is an infinite difference between what thefe worthy men did, only for a fhort time, and in the hurry of the jufteft refentment for the vileft encroachment, not only on the natural and religious rights of mankind, but on the authority of Jefus Chrift, their divine Sovereign, —and what princes, popes and politicians have done, in all ages, againft the liberties of mankind and the peculiar privileges of the church. Their invafions have been cooly contrived and wantonly executed. Inftead of meeting with any juft provocation, they have never attempted thefe facred inclofures of eternal right, but with a deliberate defign to fwell the *prerogative* of the *prince*, and to glut the *avarice* and *ambition* of the *hierarchy* at the expence of every thing dear to human nature.

Though we have admitted the fact, that the moft worthy characters may have, in fome periods, and
in

in peculiar circumstances, become flaming advocates for some favourite establishment, this militates nothing against the truth of our maxim. We hesitate not to affirm, that even these worthy persons, in common with all other abettors of the unnatural alliance, were inattentive to the spirituality of Christ's kingdom, when they attempted to give it an exclusive establishment in the political constitution of the state. Every advocate for that alliance, must first have supposed a near likeness between the church and state before he could reconcile his reason to the idea of their alliance in one political system. We have already attempted a proof from the testimony of Christ himself, concerning his kingdom, that it cannot be blended with the constitution of any kingdom on earth. It must, therefore, follow, that it must be *something besides* the kingdom of Christ, that is the object of mens attention, in the political frame of earthly kingdoms, under the designation of the established church. It must be something distinct from the kingdom of Christ. It must be something *earthly* and *secular* in its nature, and disposed by the policy of men into a due subordination to the earthly and secular purposes of civil government. On examination, this will be found to be the justest notion of every established church, as such, on earth. A few considerations will make this assertion abundantly evident.

I. God, having appointed men to social happiness in this world, hath instituted civil government, as the mean of conferring it. Careful, as the indulgent parent of mankind, of the means as well as of the end, he hath wisely provided for both in the frame of human nature. While every man is urged on toward social happiness, by desire; he is made capable

capable of securing the means of attaining it, by the principles of natural religion, which constitute him a subject of civil, as well as of moral government. Every human form is as capable of civil government as he is of social happiness. As these principles of natural religion are sufficiently established in the hearts of all men, all that the Sovereign Rector of the universe hath appointed his deputies to do, is, to cultivate these natural principles implanted in the hearts of their subjects, and to govern them according to their genuine import. It is not the province of any civil legislature, because it is beyond their power, to superinduce other principles into the bosoms of their subjects,—principles foreign to the light and law of reason, and to attempt to govern them by laws, which have no relation to the original principles of human nature.

II. Notwithstanding this obvious truth, civil legislators have seldom been content, in any age, with the foundation of God's moral government for the basis of their deputed regency. Too often intent on the prosecution of schemes wholly inconsistent with the original designs of civil government, they have either added to, or have diminished from the principles of natural religion, according as they have found the objects of their policy to suit with their absurd designs. This is one of the principal sources of the political encouragement, which superstition has ever received from the courts of princes, and accounts for its establishment in the political constitution of almost every nation in the world. Ambitious princes have always found, that the more effectually the spark of natural religion could be raked up among the ashes of superstition, the more it was in their power to sway an absolute sceptre, and to sacrifice all that is valuable in human nature to their pride and luft of arbitrary power. It was thus, in all the monarchies, kingdoms and republics which are famous in ancient hiftory. Their fuperftitions and vile idolatories were introduced, under the notion of their being *improvements* on the law of nature, and *new revelations* of what was well-pleafing in the fight of God.

III. Accordingly, when the TRUE REVELATION dawned among the nations, and became not lefs popular than univerfal, it was eagerly feized and forcibly treated in the fame manner. It was fuppofed to be an addition to the law of nature, and a mere improvement on natural religion. It was deemed capable of becoming, after a few political improvements on it, a powerful engine to keep people in all due fubjection to their political oppreffors. With this view, all pains were taken, in a fucceffion of feveral ages, to model it, by a thoufand additions and adulterations, into an exact fubferviency to the political purpofes of governors; and to combine it, in that corrupt ftate, with the conftitutions of their refpective nations.

Meanwhile, it is obvious, that neither chriftianity, nor the church of Chrift were, in any proper fenfe, eftablifhed. The object of thefe exclufive patents was, and continues to be fomething fubordinate to the political defigns of civil government. A priefthood is eftablifhed, which hath fome diftant likenefs, in their defignations to the minifters of JESUS. An hierarchy, adjufted to a political fcale of fubordination to the fupreme civil magiftrate, is fupported at an immenfe expence, to affift in putting out the eye of reafon, and in plunging people into an abyfs of fuperftition and idolatry. Religious fyftems have alfo received a political and exclufive eftablifhment, which vary, in every age, according to the

exigencies

exigencies of civil government.——Syſtems theſe, which, as they depend on civil authority, as their *basis* and *bond* of obligation, muſt be accounted *formally* civil and political. In one word, whatever is eſtabliſhed, it is ſomething miſtaken for the church of Chriſt:—ſomething homogeneous with theſe kingdoms, with whoſe conſtitutions it is induſtriouſly blended, which frequently lies in direct ſubordination to the worſt deſigns of political adminiſtration in them.

A political ſyſtem, thus founded, muſt be of the moſt pernicious tendency, eſpecially to the cauſe of chriſtianity. It has been, and it muſt continue to be fatal to its intereſts, in the ſeveral nations of Europe. Princes, and dignified prieſts will always be tempted to do as they have done. They will always be tempted to ſurcharge the chriſtian religion with additions and ſuperſtitious obſervances, in order to make the favourite ſyſtem more palatable to the vitiated taſte of men, and more ſtupifying to their ſenſes, that they may rule over them in the moſt arbitrary manner with applauſe, or at leaſt with impunity. Heatheniſm itſelf was overcharged with fooleries. Nor would the original projectors of the popiſh ſyſtem have been without ſurpriſe, had they lived to ſee the glorious improvements, which were afterwards made on their plan, by the politicians of after ages, for the purpoſes of civil,—rather *tyrannical* government in the European nations.

While the ſincere friends of the chriſtian religion mourn over this execrable abuſe, infidels triumph, as if they had fully eſtabliſhed their *hypotheſis*. A little acquaintance with the writings of theſe modern *Porphyries* will convince any, that the political abuſes that have been made of the chriſtian ſyſtem, have furniſhed them with their moſt plauſible arguments againſt that divine ſcheme. They take it for granted;

R

ed; and law supports their hypothesis, that these are the *only* churches of Christ which are established by law; and that national creeds and liturgies, blended with the political states of Europe, and made engines of civil government in them, furnish the *only authentic scheme* of the christian religion. The consequence, which men of that complexion ordinarily draw, is too well known to need explication; and too shocking to pious ears to be mentioned. Having seen heathenism used in the same manner, and for the same purposes, for which they daily behold the christian religion abused; and being ascertained from history, that civil policy hath been brought to as great perfection under the influence of the first, as of the last; they are tempted to believe, or at least to feign a persuasion, that the former is as conducive to all the purposes of political government as the latter; and that it is an object of absolute indifference, which of the two is blended with the constitutions of civil societies. To be short, what can they, who are willingly blind to the internal and supernatural evidence of the christian religion, imagine that divine scheme to be, when they behold it supplying the place of pagan or of popish superstition in the European systems of policy? Can they—will they pronounce it to be any thing but a *political institution*, or a *system* of *priestcraft?*

Nor will the more daring stop at this goal. The absurd principle on which the political alliance between church and state is founded, will tempt them to carry the matter one step higher. While the deist, for the reason already suggested, pronounces the christian religion a political fable; the more intrepid, blind to the distinction between natural religion, the only *basis* of civil government, and those
supplements

supplements which princes and priests have made to it from revealed religion, whether real or feigned,—will daringly pronounce even NATURAL RELIGION itself—a system founded only in the POLITICAL FITNESS of things?

SECT. II.

Exclusive Establishments of Churches are founded on the no less pernicious than absurd Principle,—that the Legislative, as well as the Executive Power of Government, with WHOMSOEVER *it is intrusted, is founded on, and derived from, the* AUTHORITY *of* CHRIST, *as He is the divine Mediator and Head of the Church: or that civil Government, instead of being founded in the Law of Nature, is entirely derived from* GRACE.

THOUGH this *hypothesis* must appear to be extravagantly *wild* to all, who have acquainted themselves with the origin, the nature, and the ends of civil government,—the most cursory reflection on the subject must convince every unprejudiced person, that it is a principal part of that foundation, on which the combination of church and state, in one mixed system, has been, and continues to be built. During several ages, it was an *orthodox article* in the creed of all christian nations. Nor is it probable, that it would have so soon fallen into discredit, any more than some articles, yet in vogue, though not less absurd, had not the court of Rome, imagining that it was a solid foundation for their most

extravagant

extravagant claims, to the prejudice of royalty,— carried their arrogance a little too far, in attempting to dethrone princes, and to difpofe of kingdoms, at their fovereign pleafure.

Notwithftanding it hath been almoft univerfally difcarded in *theory*; as long as the *alliance* between church and ftate, in one mixed conftitution, remains approved, it muft be *practically* adopted by all the abettors of that fyftem, as one of the chief pillars to which it leans. It is an obvious truth, that in the political adminiftration of fuch a combined fyftem, the fupreme authority muft be lodged with the officers, either of the *fpiritual*, or of the *civil* department. As it is abfolutely impoffible, that it can eminently refide in both, at one and the fame time; it muft be exercifed moft confpicuoufly, either by him, who, claiming the honour of an immediate deputation from Chrift, fills the papal chair; or by thofe, who, though anciently doomed by fovereign pontiffs, of infamous memory, to the drudgery of blindly executing papal decrees, now hold the fecular fcepters of the European nations, in juft contempt of papal arrogance.

Should we fuppofe the *firſt*; the fecular powers muft be wholly under papal controul, efpecially in all bufinefs belonging to the ecclefiaftical branch of the alliance. If the papal court defines; royal authority muft add the civil fanction to its ghoftly definitions: if the former makes canons, the latter muft ratify them: if holy mother fhall excommunicate her children; princes, that they may not fall under her difpleafure, muft fay, Amen; and if fhe fhall condemn haplefs heretics to the flames; her royal fons muft furnifh faggots and an executioner. Now, as, in all thefe inftances, the church is the object of magiftratical authority; unlefs the exercife of it fhall be accounted a violent intromiffion, it muft must be derived, one way or another, from him, whom all christians compliment with the honour of sovereignty in his own kingdom. And as that authority is exercised, under spiritual directors, who challenge the honour of an immediate deputation from Christ, it must be considered, in no other point of view, than as derived through them from that divine person. The authority of princes is immediately in the arrogant priest, who struts under the triple crown. As Heaven's vicegerent, he derives it primarily from *Jesus Christ*; and it is only exercised by the secular powers, in the same manner, as the executive power of the *British* SOVEREIGN is exercised by the *sheriffs* of the several counties.

On the other hand, should we suppose the last, as is happily the case, in all protestant countries; as civil authority is exercised in no other manner, in enforcing articles of faith on the understandings and the consciences of the subjects, than in laying taxes on their estates; it must follow, that the exercise of that authority either is a prophane imposition on the conscience, or is derived from the Lord of the conscience. It avails nothing to say, that it is only in so far as the civil magistrate interferes with the affairs of the church, that his authority is derived from the Head of the church. We are bold to affirm, that, on the present *hypothesis*, all his authority, even about secular objects, must be conveyed to him from the same source. Is it not the *same* kingly authority which ratifies a *creed* or a *liturgy*, that confirms a *money-bill* in parliament, or authorizes a levy on the subject? The prince does both, as the sovereign over, not one branch, but the whole complex system. If he is deputed at all by Christ, as his authority is *one*, and of *one kind*, his deputation must respect his *whole character*,

racter, and the whole of his office-power over one branch, as well as the other of the political alliance. Should it even be allowed, that it is only in so far as the prince interposes in ecclesiastical business, that his authority is conveyed to him by the Sovereign of the church; may it not be asked with propriety, of *what kind* is that authority, which is so conveyed? Is it *civil*, or is it *ecclesiastical?* If the first; CHRIST must be a *civil Sovereign;* his church must be a *civil society*; and mankind are imposed on, when they are told, that his *kingdom is not of this world*. If the last;—the supreme magistrate is the primate of all his dominions by christian institution: his ecclesiastical authority extends to every capital object in the kingdom of Christ: he sovereignly prescribes to the understandings of the whole nation: he binds the church to worship God according to the precise method which he, by his episcopal wisdom, thinks proper: he obliges her to acknowledge such offices, and such officers over her, as he judges to be most subservient to political purposes, in civil administration: and he, as supreme dignitary, measures out the district for every inferior hierarch, saying to him, *Hitherto shalt thou come and no farther, and here shall thy* haughty rule *be stayed*.

It is a diversion, senseless as it is groundless, which some have attempted, by distinguishing between civil authority as it is conversant *circa sacra*, and as it is exercised *in sacris*. The last they pretend to refuse to the princes of the world. The clergy, possessed of spiritual authority, must approach holy things. But the first, they compliment to the prince, alledging that it is no more, than what is competent to him, as a *christian* magistrate. We believe, that this hackneyed distinction had some important meaning, at the time it was first luckily
thought

thought of—when scarcely any more was permitted to even the most active monarchs, than to execute implicitly the sentences of holy mother-church. But it is wholly obsolete, and without any meaning now, at least, in protestant nations. In all countries where the *alliance* subsists, and where the balance of authority over the complex medley inclines to the officers of the civil department, the supreme council, or the supreme magistrate employs his authority no less *in sacris*, than he does *circa sacra*. Though the prince ascends not the pulpit, nor dispenses the sacred mysteries at the altar, those who do both derive all their authority from him. Notwithstanding they are ordained by the *Bishop*, or by the *Presbytery*, it is by virtue of civil authority, bestowing its sanction on such a *particular mode* of creating church-officers, that they are made and reputed to be the officers of the church. If this is not a just account of the derivation of office-power to the ministers of chartered churches, we would ask, why those who are ordained by the *Presbytery* cannot be reputed ministers of the chartered church in *South Britain*; and why those who are ordained by the *Bishop* cannot be esteemed ministers in the religious department of *North Britain*? Must not their office-power, in their respective churches, depend wholly on the political constitution and particular laws of the countries in which they officiate? If this is a just account, then it will not only unavoidably follow, that the authority of the civil magistrate is conversant *in sacris*, as much as if he dispensed the christian mysteries with his own hands; but that every ecclesiastical officer, from the *primate* to the *parson*, derives his spiritual powers from his authority. If therefore the church-power of ministers in chartered churches be from Christ, as the Head of the church, the power of the

the civil magistrate must flow from the same sacred source, seeing all the power of the former, is derived to them through the channel of that power, which the latter immediately claims.

Though every sober christian must shudder at this plain deduction, it is not only the real foundation, on which the famous combination of church and state is built, but it has been acknowledged to be such, ever since the commencement of that alliance.

Constantine the Great received it as the most indisputable *axiom*, when he established the church imperial. He was made to believe, that he was possessed of the most ample, delegated authority to model the kingdom of Christ according to the plan of political government in the empire. This he accomplished with the loudest acclamations of the clergy, who were his ghostly directors, and with the strained panegyrics of all their successors. It was from a persuasion of his being honoured with these powers, that he, exulting in his new authority, addressed the dignitaries of the church—*vos estote episcopi intra ecclesiam ; ego ero foras*. A sentence highly applauded, as well as carefully retailed by all church historians, since *Eusebius* wrote.

When the civil authority devolved, in a great measure, on the bishop of Rome; did he not pretend, that he had derived his whole authority, from Christ, his pretended constituent? Did he not openly declare, that government is founded in grace; and that the kings of the earth held their crowns of him, as the delegated head of the church? Was not that principle, the very foundation on which he adventured to dethrone princes, and to dispose of kingdoms? Could politicians, in these dark ages, judge, that the foundation of civil government was laid on any other *hypothesis*, when a mere contravening the sovereign

vereign pleasure of holy mother church, in even the most contemptible trifles, was the only alledged reason for such audacious impertinence?

Since the glorious *æra* of Reformation, the same *hypothesis* is invariably maintained, even in protestant countries, and by protestant churches. It must make every sensible person both merry and sad, to behold how even the most pious and learned writers of the protestant denomination are puzzled to remove, with decency, this foundation, and, in the mean time, to support the important alliance. How are their tongues divided! Into what confusion and absurdity have they been cast! All agree that the *hypothesis* is grosly absurd; but they have found that it is impossible to remove it effectually without pulling down the whole FABRIC OF CONFUSION.

But why should we speak of particular writers? The principle is accounted an *axiom* in the protestant political constitution of Great Britain. In England, his majesty is *supreme* over all persons, and in ALL CAUSES, ecclesiastical as well as civil. The very *being*, as well as the *peculiar mould* of the English church, hangs on the *supremacy*. The *hierarchy* grows out of the princely *primacy* of the sovereign. Whence have their GRACES their *office*, together with their *right* to exercise it? Does not his majesty bestow, or, at least, authorize the collation of both? Whence have *the thirty-nine articles* their sanction? Do they derive it from their intrinsic evidence? for the same reason, they ought to be the articles of the catholic church? Rather, is it not from the civil authority of legislature? Whence is this authority over the church, and over the understandings and consciences of so many millions of christians in the British dominions? No one who attends to what he says, can assert, that it is derived from, or is founded on the law of nature, which sets all men on
a level,

a level, as to the objects of pure understanding and conscience. It must therefore be supposed, that it is immediately derived from Christ, as the Head of the church; that every crowned head is his vicegerent; and that, as christians are bound to give up the direction of their consciences to him, with implicit acquiescence in his infallible oracles, his royal vicegerent may lawfully claim the same devotion from them.

The like is not only exacted, but is tamely yielded in Scotland. Whence is it, that the *Westminster* Confession of Faith is the established creed, in that country? Is it on account of the excellence of its composition, and of the divine *character* of these doctrines, which are methodized in it? No! Though it seems to deserve, that it should be received on these accounts, before any composition of the kind, its *national profession* depends wholly on the authority of the parliament, and of the prince.

It is a trifling evasion, to alledge, it became the confession of the Scotch church, not as it was authorized by king William III. and the Scotch parliament, or as it was made fundamental in the union of the two nations; but as it was found agreeable to the scriptures by the church herself, in her general assemblies. We would ask whence had the General Assembly that power to make it the creed of all congregations, and of all persons, ONLY *on the north of the Tweed?* Was it not from the national legislature, who gave the church a *presbyterian* mould; who conferred legal powers on her judicatories; and who assigned, with minute exactness, the extent and boundaries of their ecclesiastical authority? Ingeniously! Would the act of the General Assembly, without the civil sanction annexed, have been sufficient to have constituted it, the standard creed of the established church of Scotland, as such? No!

No! The changes which have been introduced by civil authority, without afking, at leaft, without waiting the confent of her judicatories, are a fufficient proof, that her intrinfic power, as an eftablifhed church, is a mere *bawble* in law: and that government hath always confidered itfelf, as fully *impowered* to introduce fuch changes in the church.— And by whom *impowered?* Not by the nation. She, as fuch, has no right to interpofe her authority about ecclefiaftical objects: and to impower agents for a fociety effentially diftinct from herfelf. Not by the church. A parliament, or a fovereign prince can be no reprefentative of the kingdom of Chrift. The church can confer no powers on princes, unlefs her fupremacy over kings once more becomes orthodox doctrine. It remains then, that government muft poffefs the power of moulding the church by an inherent and original title. If fo, this title muft have been originally conferred, either by the God of nature, on the foundation of the law of nature; or by the Mediator, on the footing of grace. Was the *first* fuppofed, it would unavoidably follow, that Chrift hath no proper kingdom: that the church muft be effentially one with civil fociety: and muft be fubject to the deputies of the God of nature alone: and that the INSCRIPTION on the MEDIATOR'S *vesture* and *thigh* fhould be entirely without a meaning—KING *of* KINGS, *and* LORD *of lords*. The *last*, therefore, can only be fuppofed with decency and propriety. Sovereign princes muft poffefs an original right from Chrift as his fubftitutes, on the foundation of grace, to turn his kingdom upfide down, at their fovereign pleafure.

The pernicious confequences, which attend this, and the foregoing baneful principle, fhall be confidered in the following chapter.

CHAP.

CHAP. VI.

A concise View of the PERNICIOUS EFFECTS, *which teem from an* ALLIANCE *between Church and State, in one political Constitution, as it is* FOUNDED *on the* BANEFUL PRINCIPLES *already considered.*

THAT a political syſtem, founded in miſtake, error and abſurdity, muſt be fraught with the worſt conſequences, and muſt produce the worſt effects on every perſon, and on every thing concerned in it, can be denied by none. Such is a political combination of church and ſtate, in one miſcellaneous ſyſtem. Its effects on the *thrones* of *princes,* on *social happiness,* and on the *characters* of men in every rank of life, muſt have a degree of malignity in them, proportionate to the abſurdity and impiety of thoſe principles, on which we have ſhewn it to be founded. This we ſhall attempt to prove, in the enſuing ſections.

SECT. I.

An ALLIANCE *between the Church and State, so founded, is ruinous to the* SOVEREIGNTY *of Princes, and to the* STABILITY *of their Thrones.*

ACCORDING to ſuch a political ſyſtem, the thrones of princes, removed from their *true* foundation, are ſettled on a *mere quick-sand.* It is ſuppoſed, that the law of nature and of neceſſity is

not

not a foundation sufficiently broad, on which civil government might rest; but that, in so far as the church, incorporated with the state, is the object of administration, it is founded on the Mediatorial authority of Christ. Thrones, so established have not only been miserably shaken, but have often tumbled down, and buried the sovereignty of the monarchs who filled them, in their extensive ruins.

The experience of Christendom, during these last thirteen hundred years, confirms the observation, that there hath not been a revolution of any importance in Europe, but has arisen in a great measure from those absurd maxims, on which princes have judged it good policy to build their thrones. Not content with the *law* of *nature*, as the *original foundation*, and as the *only rule* of civil policy; and attempting to extend their royal authority to the kingdom of Christ; they have uniformly built their title to this last branch of their prerogative, either on the impious maxim, *that the kingdom of Christ is homogeneal with their own*; or on the absurd *hypothesis, that, if the church differs in any respect from the kingdoms of this world, they are possessed of a deputation from Christ, to take the burthen of its government on their own shoulders.* What hath been the uniform consequence? Their thrones have lost of stability, what they seemed to gain of grandeur; and have tumbled down from beneath them. The part of the political edifice, which had been constructed on the solid base, connected with that which leaned to the absurd foundation, hath always shared in the common ruin. The alliance between the church and state in one mixed constitution, hath always produced an alliance between the *rightful sovereign* and the *usurper*, in *one mixed character*; and hath frequently precipitated the unhappy monarch to his ruin.

To

To what cause shall we ascribe the final ruin of the Roman empire. Though the *Augustan splendour* of that monarchy had greatly declined before the date of the *imperial alliance*, it must be confessed, that had the Roman emperor continued to govern according to the original laws of society; had he not extended civil administration to a manifest vicegerency under *Christ*, the *King* of *Zion*; and had he not admitted priests to his council, the imperial throne had probably remained possessed of a considerable degree of *eclat* to this day. But, alas! as soon as the Roman emperor became Christ's vicegerent, it was very natural, and it became highly necessary, to admit the dignitaries of the church to court, as prime ministers in the ecclesiastic department of government, as the Roman fathers had been, in the civil allotment, from the commencement of the Roman grandeur. These, after some centuries, having views and interests to pursue, which were not only foreign to, but were inconsistent with the rights of sovereigns, and the privileges of civil society, found ways and means to engross the whole administration. The emperor, reduced to the necessity of providing for his own safety, was obliged to trim to ecclesiastical factions, till at last, like a charioteer thrown from his seat, he resigned the reins. The Roman pontiff instantly ascended; and, seizing the golden opportunity, translated the empire to his faithful ally, CHARLES *the* GREAT.

Let us look back to the revolutions, which have fallen out in our own island, especially since the Reformation. They have neither been few, nor of obscure birth. The impolitic alliance between the *British churches*, and the civil constitutions of the *British nations*, will be found, on an impartial review, to have been the fatal source, and the only adequate cause.

What made the throne of Mary, queen of Scots, to shake, during the whole time she ingloriously filled it? The infirm foundation, on which it stood, is, without doubt, the only cause, which can be assigned with justice and propriety.

The queen, born the rightful sovereign of Scotland; educated in all the errors, absurdities and superstitions of popery; and finding, that the frame of the Romish church, of which she was a zealous member, had been long allied to, and blended with the political constitution of her kingdom; judged, as other sovereigns before and since have done, that her royal authority extended to the whole complex system of church and state: that, in her circumstances, she could neither answer it to her understanding, to her conscience, nor to the miscellaneous constitution of the church and nation, to permit the sworn enemies of that very church, which was, during so many ages, engrossed in the political constitution, to tear her from her ancient ally: and that, though her barons, zealous for new-modelling the constitution, possessed a large share in the legislative power of the nation, they had no right, without her consent, to overthrow the ancient constitution; much less to force her into their measures against the maxims of her understanding, the dictates of her conscience, and her obligations to the church of Rome.

On the other hand, a large majority of the lords, together with the commons of all classes, justly jealous for the natural rights of free-born subjects—instructed in the reformed religion, and legally possessed of an important share in legislature;—judged, on the same common prepossession concerning the necessity of a charter of exclusive, civil privilege, or of an alliance of some religious system with the political constitution,—that truth hath always a preferable
right

right to error and abfurdity: that they could not be refponfible to God, who had beftowed on them fo great a fhare of the *nomothetic* power, to fuffer a fyftem of error and fuperftition to fill the throne of truth, in the conftitution: and that the queen, a fingle woman, weak as well as young, infeparably attached to the execrable houfe of *Guise*, and zealoufly devoted to popery, had no right to force, not only the commons, but even the body of the nobility, to lend their authority for the fupport of a religon, which they were rationally convinced was falfe, and for the overthrow of a fyftem, which they were fure was according to godlinefs.

In this manner, the queen and her barons, equally perfuaded that the conftitution of the church behoved to be blended with that of the nation, and that thofe who hold the reins of government cannot difcharge their duty to God, to the Head of the church, or to the mixed conftitution, without making every effort in their power, to have the ecclefiaftical, as well as the civil branch of the conftitution thrown into the mould, that is moft agreeable to their own underftandings and their own confciences, went confcientioufly by the ears; deluged the nation in blood: and entailed on the Scots Reformation the reproach of diforder, cruelty and rebellion. In vain have partial hiftorians endeavoured to throw the *odium* on the obftinacy of the queen, or on the intemperate zeal of the barons, while, according to the principle, on which both acted, neither the queen could have been confiftently lefs firm in defence of the old religion, nor the nobility lefs ftrenuous in defence of the new. If the maxim was juft, they were both in the right. As the dictates of even an erring confcience are obligatory on the unhappy being, who is under its government they attempted nothing but what thofe, who have

been

been accounted the beſt men, have done with applauſe. Though they were ſo unfortunate as to oppoſe one another, in all the horrors of a civil war, they only endeavoured to eſtabliſh that religious ſyſtem in the conſtitution, which was moſt agreeable to their jarring underſtandings, and to their diverſly perſuaded conſciences.—But if the principle is falſe, it accounts for every improper thing which theſe famous litigants attempted againſt one another, and which the advocates of either party produce, as a ground of accuſation againſt the cauſe, which they have reſolved to condemn. The neceſſity of an alliance between church and ſtate, which both injudiciouſly allowed, together with the abſurd foundations on which we have ſhewed the common prejudice to be founded, introduced all that confuſion, blood-ſhed and murder, with which the enemies of the Scotch Reformation have endeavoured to ſtain its glory. Had both parties deliberately conſidered the abſurdity of the alliance, together with the impiety of theſe principles to which it leans; had they liſtened with an unbiaſſed ear to the plaineſt of declarations,—*My kingdom is not of this world*; had they ſeen the glaring inconſiſtency of attempting to give the *authority* of CHRIST an *additional force* in the conſcience by *ſtatute law*; had they amicably agreed to allow the kingdom of Chriſt to ſtand on its own baſe, and to be governed by HIM on whoſe *ſhoulder the government is laid*; and had they both concurred in what both in general agreed to be their intereſt, as well as their duty,—in aſſerting the rights of her majeſty's crown againſt *all foreign* powers and claims, and in ſecuring the rights and liberties of every claſs of ſubjects;—the church would have been reformed without any noiſe; the *Romiſh* as well as the *French* yoke would have been wholly ſhaken off; the barons would have had their rights ſecured to them: the

T   queen

queen would have enjoyed her crown, her prerogative and her life; nor would she have left to her royal descendants an example of prejudice, of obstinacy and of bigotry, which, as it has proved fatal to the whole race, was copied, with a scrupulous exactness, by king CHARLES I. to his own destruction, and the ruin of many thousands of his innocent subjects.

That unfortunate prince, having been trained up by his royal father of sage memory! in the most extravagant notions of prerogative, and of the matchless utility of the ecclesiastical dignitaries to support its most exhorbitant claims; having ascended the *British* thrones in a critical moment, when ambition and bigotry conspired to call him to the execution of schemes for making the *British* sceptre to vie with that of *France* in tyranny and oppression,—schemes, which, though long meditated, the timidity and caprice of his royal parent had hitherto rendered abortive; and finding himself to be *constitutionally* the HEAD of the *church* as well as of the *state*, by virtue of the constitutional alliance, and ready to be supported by her clergy in his most extraordinary claims, in return for his royal indulgence;—resolved to reign without his parliaments; to erect courts of high-commission and of star-chamber in their room; and to extend the prerogative to every object, by laying intolerable and countless burdens both on the purses and on the consciences of his subjects, in the most arbitrary manner. In this way, he, with a degree of sagacity equal to that which governed all the actions of his father, judged that he had a *divine* right to extend his royal care to both branches in the combined constitution, as the *supreme head* over all persons, and in *all causes, ecclesiastical* as well as civil.

The nations beheld, with infinite concern, the
hasty

hasty steps which his majesty was taking to eastern despotism. They saw prerogative extending its claims to the whole of the legislative power in both nations, in which parliaments, according to the most ancient records, and even according to the *genius* of the feudal system, had ever claimed and possessed a large share. They were justly alarmed; they loudly complained; they humbly petitioned his majesty; they boldly remonstrated against the ministers and the measures of government; and they strenuously refused to comply with the royal exactions; till they should once more see their supreme assemblies convened by royal authority. His majesty, though he had been long deaf to the cries of his injured subjects, was at last roused to anxious concern about his own interests, by the hollow sound of his empty coffers, and by its faithful *echo* among his hungry courtiers. The parliaments were summoned. These august assemblies, constitutionally entitled to their proportion in the legislative power over church and state in one mixed constitution, — resolved to assert their own privileges, together with the rights of the injured kingdoms which they legally represented; to set boundaries to the prerogative; and, as they had found that the frame of the church, in her courts, and in her hierarchy, had been a fatal engine for the crown against the interests of both nations, to exert their authority in her reformation. Charles, soon apprized of the designs, which his parliaments had formed, openly struck out against their authority; declared war against his own subjects; and shed their blood by an army of Irish banditti; which he ingloriously hired for that cruel purpose. The forces, however, which the parliaments raised for the defence of these rights, which they had determined to assert, prevailed; and the tragedy ended in the ignominious and untimely death of the monarch.

From this review of a reign fo inaufpicious, we fhall make the following obfervations.

I. The *genius* of the political fyftem fully acquits the unfortunate monarch, who fovereignly prefided in its adminiftration, of every charge which has been brought againſt him. Perfuaded that the epifcopal model of the church was of apoftolical inftitution; finding himſelf a rightful fovereign over nations, in which church and ftate were allowed by all parties to be ftrictly allied, and in which his *supremacy* over all perſons, and in *all causes*, civil and ecclefiaftical, was allowed in law; and bound by the ties of his coronation oaths, as well as by the fetters of his own prejudices, to exert the fovereign authority with which he was invefted for both branches of the mixed conftitution, according to the beft of his royal wifdom,—and not to betray either into the hands of any, nor even of thofe who fhared the legiflative power with him;—in what manner, different from that in which he acted, could he have acquitted himfelf, in his peculiar circumftances? The church, in her epifcopal drefs, incorporated with the conftitutions of the Britiſh nations, was the peculiar object of his royal care. Who, on the *hypothesis*—that the alliance is lawful and neceffary, can impute it to him as a crime, that he, who, according to the principles on which the alliance is founded, and according to the laws of his own realms, accounted himſelf Chrift's vicegerent and the head of the church, fhould ftep forth a zealous patron of that fociety; that he, who, as the patron and the head of Chrift's kingdom, was only accountable to his heavenly conftituent, fhould follow the dictates of his own princely underftanding, in all his fovereign adminiftration about ecclefiaftical objects; and that he, who, though he fhared the legiflative authority of his kingdoms with his parliaments,

ments, enjoyed alone the honour of being SUPREME IN ALL CAUSES-ECCLESIASTICAL, should not permit these assemblies to encroach on his divine and incommunicable prerogative, and to pull down that church, which his coronation oaths, his fidelity to Christ, and his attachment to the objects of his own ambition, bound him to support?

II. Nor does it appear to have been possible, on the same principles, that the parliaments could have conducted themselves towards his majesty, in any other manner than they did. The alliance, together with the principles, on which it was founded, seems to have forcibly hurried them along, in every step which they took. The members of both upper and lower houses, in these assemblies had been long the mournful spectators of the arbitrary measures, and of the despotic designs of the court, in all things which concerned the civil and religious parts of the united system. Constitutionally convened in parliament, they well knew, that, notwithstanding they had no share in the *idol* of the prince, —the *abused prerogative*, they possessed an important allotment in legislature ; and that, notwithstanding the church, in her *hierarchical* form, was blended with the political constitution, they, as legislators, had a right, no less devine than that of his majesty, to reform the constitution,—at least, to purge it from the innovations, which an ambitious monarch, by the baneful advice of a crafty arch-prelate, had illegally introduced. They were very sensible, that, though his majesty intended that the nations should be the slaves of prerogative, the victims of his idol, and the dupes of superstition, they should be wanting no less to themselves, than to those whom they represented, should they permit even the chief pilot himself, when drunk with enthusiasm, ambition and whim,

whim, to steer directly on a rock so tremendous and fatal. They found, that he was not only resolutely averse to their measures, but was determined to pursue his own, with a firmness not to be shaken by petitions, by remonstrances, or even by any other submissive method of application to the throne; and to force them into a tame acquiescence, by all the terrors of the high-commission, massacre and civil war. In these circumstances, would it have been either prudent, or pious, to have resigned the reins of government entirely into his hands? Would they not have betrayed the trust reposed in them, and have acted in a perfidious manner, not only towards their constituents on earth, but to the prejudice of Christ's kingdom, and to the dishonour of its divine Sovereign, who, according to the maxim, on which the alliance is built, had invested them with legislative authority in and over his church, blended with the constitutions of the *British* nations?

III. When the unhappy contests, between his majesty and his parliaments, had come to all the extremities of a civil war, it was an event, which any might have foreseen, without the help of prophetic impulse, that the *weight*, not to say the *right* of government, would devolve on the party, or on the most eminent person of the party, who had the longest sword, or the greatest interest in the parliament's army. This was the case. OLIVER CROMWELL, having had the address to secure to himself the leading of the army, mustered under the banner of the English parliament; and finding himself in possession of the executive authority of that assembly, yea, of a power to model it according to *his own ideas* of *right*, or of political fitness; resolved to employ his interest for the good of the whole, according to the dictates of his own cloudy understanding.—But he
was

was an USURPER! Be it fo—notwithstanding, on the
supposition that a political combination of church
and state is lawful and necessary, we assert, that, in
so far, at least, as the kingdom of Christ was concerned in his administration, he was a *lawful magistrate*, as well as a BRAVE *man!* Did not the
parliament of England invest him with his military
character, and put it in *his power* to act in that
character, in so far at least as religion was concerned, according to the best dictates of his own
understanding? and as every man is to do all in the
cause of religion he *can*; and to follow no man's
direction against the maxims of his own reason and
conscience, in any part of his conduct, which re-
lates to objects so momentous; was not the GENE-
RALISSIMO of the English forces, and the LORD
PROTECTOR of the nation bound in conscience, to
do all that was in *his power* for the kingdom of
Christ, incorporated with the constitution of that
society, which his oaths had bound him to protect,
according to his own religious maxims? This was
no more than what king Charles claimed a right to
do, in his turn; what the parliaments asserted a
title to do, in their turn; and what every man,
unless he shall act in a manner unworthy of an
accountable being, must do on the present *hypothesis*,
when the Supreme Disposer of all events puts it in
the power of his hand.

IV. Nor need any to account it either a paradox
or an absurdity, should we assert, that, supposing
the legitimacy of the political alliance so often
mentioned, together with the absurd maxims, on
which it is built,--there is no crime either in the
most cruel persecution, or in the most unnatural
rebellion on account of religion, since the commencement of that political system.

Persecution,

Persecution, for conscience sake, is no object of blame in any country, in which the church is blended in one constitution with the state political. The prince, who fills the throne and presides over the constitution, as its guardian, has as good a right, in virtue of his *primacy* and *vicegerency*, over both departments of the united system, to punish the conscientious dissenter as the mutinous rebel. They are equally enemies to the constitution, which his coronation oaths bind him to protect inviolable: and his more sacred obligations to Christ as his vicegerent, and the head of his chruch, make it necessarily incumbent on him to mark the former with a brand of greater infamy than the latter. He cannot answer it to his divine constituent, to suffer one rebel to Him in his dominions; and unless he shall give himself up implicitly to the directions of a pope, or a ghostly council, and obsequiously burn all whom they may brand with heresy, he must depend on the maxims of his own judgment in the determination of the important question,—who are, or who are not rebels to Christ's authority. Having satisfied his princely conscience in that important business, he must persecute, even unto death, the unhappy objects of his religious fury.

Nor is *rebellion*, on account of religion, a crime, since the date of *Constantine*'s famous edict. It is supposed, as above, that the sovereign, though he may be accountable to society in all things which respect its civil interests, is responsible to Christ alone for his princely administration of his kingdom, and governs according to his own royal sentiments, without any regard to the consciences of his subjects. But should it fall out, that these last should judge, that the religious commands of their sovereign on earth are contrary to the more sacred institutions of the Sovereigns in heaven;

as

as they are likewife unaccountable to CHRIST,— nothing is left to them but to rebel; and, as it is always *better to obey* GOD *than men*, in fuch circumftances, their rebellion is fo far from being a *crime*, that it is a *virtue*, and an *indifpenfible duty!* Yea, if it is in their power, it becomes neceffary to tumble the monarch from his throne. Though according to the dictates of his own mind, he is zealoufly difcharging the duties of CHRIST's *vicegerent*; according to their fentiments, he is abufing his deputation, and is prefenting them with an opportunity of approving their affectionate loyalty to that fame divine perfon, by driving even the lawful monarch from his throne, and by fetting up the kingdom of CHRIST, in the political conftitution, according to the plan, which is moft agreeable to their own confciences, and which, whether right or wrong, they muft judge to be according to the fyftem of its heavenly Lawgiver. In this manner, the *political alliance*, under confideration, will juftify all the perfecutions, rebellions, affaffinations, murders, maffacres, confpiracies, plots and treafons, which have been perpetrated in the caufe of religion fince its fatal commencement.

SECT. II.

The Alliance between Church and State is the Bane of social Happiness.

EVER fince a political combination of the church with the kingdoms of this world prefented princes with an opportunity, and *species* of RIGHT, to model the kingdom of Chrift at pleafure, and to claim the direction of their fubjects confciences,

ences, as an essential branch of prerogative,— *lamentation, mourning* and *woe* have filled the nations of Europe. If thrones, established on that foundation, have tumbled down, ruins so enormous could not but pour destruction on the unhappy nations, which dwelt under their shadow. If, on the other hand, some princes have successfully reigned in the genuine spirit of that system, and have finally triumphed over the laudable struggles of the oppressed, their populous and opulent kingdoms have been converted into deserts, and climes where liberty guarded every cottage, as well as every castle, and gladdened every countenance, have been changed into the regions of haggart tyranny and of horrid slavery. Those sons of liberty, who, having fled to the wildernesses of *America*, as an *asylum* from oppression, first peopled these inhospitable deserts, could have well told, how such a system, under the administration of ambitious, arbitrary or priest-ridden princes, suits with the sacred rights and liberties of mankind. But we shall attempt a more particular proof of the assertion.

It hath been shewn already, that the objects of pure understanding and conscience are foreign to the cognizance of those who preside in civil society: that no man can pledge more to civil society than what is capable of protection and of forfeiture: and that as the *moral arbiter* in the bosom, is subject to GOD only; and cannot be put under the controul of any other, without throwing off all moral dependence on the DEITY; government can neither lawfully abridge its liberty, in any thing, in which the genuine interests of civil society are not concerned; nor justly inflict punishments on those, who, while they use that liberty in its fullest extent, approve themselves peaceable members of civil society.

Though

Though these are *axioms* of *eternal truth* and *justice*; the political system under review, establishes a plan of political administration, which lies in direct contradiction to them, and introduces scenes of persecution and misery into every country where it is adopted. According to the true spirit of *alliance*, every deflection from the chartered standard of thinking and of worshipping God must be reckoned, by government, to be a plain and dangerous infraction on the constitution. Should administration overlook it, they must be unfaithful not only to the political system, of which it is the guardian, but even to Jesus Christ, who hath constituted it the patron of his kingdom. Should government punish it;—they instantly usurp on the incommunicable prerogative of GOD, who claims an exclusive right to dictate to, and to controul the conscience; they let loose persecution on mankind, with all her infernal train; they seize on the lives and properties of the best members of society, before they are forfeited by any crime, which falls under the cognizance of civil judicature; and they make a booty of all, which the eternal law of equity binds them to protect. Thus, civil government, which GOD appointed as a *blessing* to society, becomes its heaviest *curse*; and the security, which men have, by that institution of the DEITY, of their lives, rights and liberties, is entirely unhinged.

Administration, conducted according to the true spirit of the alliance, must be in the hands of those, who are either the *dupes* of *designing ecclesiastics*, or the *slaves* of their own *boundless ambition*. They must be actuated either by the lust of spiritual domination, or by a wild desire of secular despotism. —The system is, indeed, equally subservient to both designs.

Should we suppose the *first*; the dignitary governs all,

all, even the prince himself. He dictates in the cabinet and controuls at the council-table. The sovereign thus tutored, claims a civil supremacy over the consciences of his subjects, and deprives them of their natural right to think, to believe, and to worship God according to those institutions, which they are assured are of divine appointment. As he supercedes the authority of God over their moral powers, and annuls their moral obligations as accountable beings, he converts them into beasts, *which have no understanding,* or, at least, *no right* to use it, even in their most important interests. Do they refuse submit?—And who, unless he is either an *atheist* or an *ideot,* can submit over the belly of his own understanding and conscience?— Civil liberty, property and life itself ly at stake. In this manner, civil authority, by extending itself beyond its own boundaries, becomes a *public robber:* It siezes with equal degrees of violence and injustice, these very objects, which, according to the original reason of social combination, it is bound to protect: robbery, rapine and murder are established and perpetrated by law : civil society degenerates into a den of thieves : civil authority is changed into a licence to break down all the inclosures of eternal equity: and magistrates, whom God hath appointed to be *as the light of a morning, without clouds,* to society, become *licensced pillagers, and authorized murderers.* It is easy to guess what must be the fatal consequences in society. Government is drowned in confusion: thrones are cast down; peace and social happiness take wings to themselves, and fly to some more happy climes, where the rights of mankind and of society are better understood and preserved: society is dissolved: and the land of peace is turned into ACELDAMA.

If we shall suppose the *last* ;—as aspiring princes commonly

commonly find it neceffary to hire the ecclefiaftical dignitaries to fecond their ambitious defigns, by putting it in the power of the eftablifhed clergy to enflave the confciences of their fellow-fubjects, the fituation of fociety differs very little from that, which has been already fuppofed. Only, in the former cafe fubjects ly at the mercy of the fuperftitious prince; but, in this latter ftate of things, ecclefiaftics are hired with the wages of unrighteoufnefs, to affift the prince in robbing and in plundering at difcretion, even when there is not the fmalleft appearance of a fault againft the laws of civil fociety. Though all this is fhocking in the laft degree, to common fenfe and to common equity, it becomes *legal* on the footing of the political fyftem under confideration. The fovereign, who prefides over it, is bound to protect and to cherifh the church blended with the ftate in one political conftitution, according to his own ideas of her interefts; and, as her *champion*, to crown her with victory over all her enemies.—How ready muft he be to atchieve all this, when it fo much befriends his *lust* of *despotism* !

But, is human nature capable to fubmit to fuch a yoke? Impoffible ! It cannot furvive its moral obligations to the author of its being. Subjects, unlefs they fhall tamely confent to lofe all of man but the human figure, muft *rebel*. Rebel, did we fay? A juft vindication of thefe rights and dignities, by which men are diftinguifhed from the brutal tribes, cannot be called by that hated name. Meanwhile, even this cannot be done without deluging fociety in confufion and blood.

But, whether the former or the latter cafe obtains, civil government, proftituted to the vile defigns of ambitious princes and of afpiring priefts, cannot anfwer the important ends of its inftitution in fociety. Can profperity fpread her cherifhing wing; or

peace,

peace, with her lovely train, dwell in that nation, in which one half of the wretched inhabitants transform themselves into *devils,* that they may effectually metamorphose the other half into *beasts?* Can life, liberty, or property, be relished in society, when they can only be enjoyed in their full extent at the expence of throwing off all dependence on the moral government of God, and all regard to the authority of our LORD JESUS CHRIST? No! men, when deprived of all that is dear in social life, will rather choose to adventure their lives, in a just and laudable attempt to regain the possession of blessings so valuable, than to live in slavery without them.

Nor are the cases, which we have supposed, to be reckoned uncommon. What nation in Europe has not, at some time or another, been a wretched example of both? *Fatal alliance!* Thou teeming source of imposition, desolation, and woe! How hast thou *destroyed empires* and *kingdoms! Their memorials are perished with them! When shall destructions,* effectuated by thy baneful influence, *come to a perpetual end!*—BRITAIN! Thou canst too well attest the dismal truth. Thy annals are one uninterrupted history of the terrible effects, which that system hath had on the estates and the lives of thy sons. The blood of thy *saints* and of thy *heroes,* which hath been shed in the defence of their obligations to GOD and to society, loudly calls for vengeance on that political institution, which, till the glorious æra of the last revolution, which it occasioned, made it to run, like water, in the streets of thy cities and in thy solitary deserts! Nor art thou alone. *Every nation* in *Europe* hath answered THEE with sigh for sigh, and with groan for groan, ever since that *common pest* shed its pernicious effects on civil, as well as religious society!

SECT.

The Political System, wherein the Church and State are blended in one Constitution, tends to TARNISH *the* CHARACTERS *of Men, in every Rank of Life, from the august* MONARCH *to the humble* PEASANT.

IT will be readily allowed, that whatever injures the religious character, muſt ſully the civil reputation. Regard to the DEITY is granted by all men, to be the *foundation* of morality, and of every ſocial duty. An *atheist* and an *hypocrite*, a *tyrant* and a *rebel* are characters deteſted even among heathens. What law can reſtrain the monſter, whether he be the monarch or the meaneſt of his ſubjects, who hath renounced his allegiance to his MAKER, and hath acquired an habit of trifling with his conſcience?

Nevertheleſs, the political ſyſtem under conſideration forcibly plunges men into the guilt of both. It throws men into the afflicting *dilemma*, either to renounce all regard to the ſovereign dictates of conſcience, and to every moral obligation, or to maintain the rights of human nature at the expence of becoming firebrands in ſociety. It is true, that, in this lukewarm age, notwithſtanding the political ſyſtem is adopted in all the *European* nations, there is no perſecution in any proteſtant country. Sovereigns and ſubjects, bleſſed be God! enjoy profound peace, in ſo far as religious objects are concerned. Why!—This ſtrange *phænomenon* cannot be rationally accounted for on any other ground, than the ſurprizing prevalence of *infidelity* and of *practical atheism*. Men of all degrees, attached to

their

their secular interests, cultivate social tranquillity, even while, according to the *genius* of the constitution of every *European* nation, they are rebels to the authority of their own consciences, and to GOD who is greater than their consciences. During many ages, while men acted up to the *spirit* of the system, and so long as princes and people made their *oaths* of fidelity to it, a point both of honour and of conscience; nothing could be heard in courts but the sanguinary laws of inhuman tyrants; and in the most thinly inhabited countries, as well as in the most populace cities—nothing but the mournful cries and the dying groans of the oppressed, persecuted and murdered. But in this age, not so famous for liberal sentiment, as for licentious manners, sincerity seems to be banished, in a great measure, from the societies of men, by their equally strong attachment to a system of persecution, and to the practice of moderation. Is there any thing more common, than to see men of every rank binding their consciences, by *oaths* and *vows* of *eternal attachment*, to church and state combined in one system, while, notwithstanding, they are of the most moderate principles towards dissenters; or while probably, they are dissenters themselves? Need we say more? Though the man, who by profaning oaths, sacraments and every solemn tie, can thus set his GOD and his conscience at defiance, deserves no *regard*, much less any *trust* in society; he who would act up to the *genuine spirit* of that execrable alliance, which he swears to maintain, deserves to be put from the society of the human species, as an *animal* more noxious than the *lion* or the *tyger*.

How hath this chequered system, *tarnished* the *characters*, *vitiated* the *principles*, and *branded* the *reigns* of even the *best princes!* Their administrations have been one series either of tyranny or of deceit;
and

and their otherwife amiable characters have been blackened in the records of time, with the guilt either of inhuman barbarity, or of deteftable prevarication.

During that long and uninterrupted fpace of a thoufand years, preceding the date of the glorious Reformation, when fuperftition, attended with all her gaudy train, had enthroned herfelf in the confciences of princes, as well as of priefts, what fovereign is not in the roll of tyrants? Was it, that they had natures lefs tractable, or difpofitions lefs happy than thofe, who have worn the purple fince that dreary period? No! Many of them were the greateft of men, and the moft amiable of princes. But their coronation oaths, by which they were folemnly bound to be the patrons of the church eftablifhed by law, to tyrannize over the confciences of their fubjects, and to revenge holy mother on all her difobedient children, by the blind execution of penal ftatutes, made them to exceed all the tyrants of antiquity, even a *Procrustes* himfelf, in execrable cruelty.

Nor were thefe ages, famous for the reign of ignorance, the only period which teemed with fuch monfters. The fame caufe muft always produce fimilar effects, when government attends to thefe obligations, which naturally arife out of the alliance between the church and the ftate in one chequered conftitution. Even fince the date of Reformation, the beft of proteftant princes have been *metamorphosed*, by *these ties*, into formidable enemies to the real happinefs of the nations, which *these same oaths* bound them to cherifh under their royal wings. Shall we mention queen ELIZABETH of England? Making neceffary allowances for fome few defects, —was there ever a greater princefs? Neverthelefs, how cruel was her adminiftration, in fo far as religion was concerned! How were the natural rights, together with the civil property of her beft proteſtant ſubjects invaded, becauſe they would not put out their own eyes, offer violence to their own conſciences, and renounce their allegiance to GOD, by complying with the popiſh rites, which ſhe judged proper to retain and to eſtabliſh in the Engliſh conſtitution! The *ghoſts* of thoſe, who periſhed in their *precipitant flight* to the wilderneſſes, of *America*, from the cruel execution of penal laws, bear awful witneſs, *from beneath the altar!* Who, or what was to be blamed Not ſo much the illuſtrious princeſs, as the *genius* of the *alliance*. It conſtituted her the HEAD and the PATRONESS of the church; and that *character*, together with her *oaths*, to defend and to proſecute the ends of that unnatural combination, bound her to do all that was in her power, according to her own underſtanding, for that ſociety, even though it had been at the expence of all that was dear, both to herſelf and to her ſubjects.

Though, in theſe happier days, the rights of human nature and of civil ſociety, have been both better underſtood, and more attended to by princes, the remarkable *contraſt* between their *laudable attachment* to the *maxims* of *moderation*, and their *coronation vows* to maintain the conſtitution, or the alliance of church and ſtate, by the execution of theſe laws, by which it is fenced,—brands their *characters* with *prevarication*, and their *reigns* with a *prophane neglect* of the moſt ſacred obligations. Since the Revolution, the *Britiſh monarchs* have been renowned for thoſe god-like excellences—*moderation, clemency,* and *love to mankind.* But how much is the luſtre of theſe royal virtues tarniſhed, when, according to the *genuine ſpirit* of the *alliance* in the Britiſh conſtitution, which our ſovereigns are bound to maintain, they muſt be regarded by poſterity

as

as a *flagrant violation* of public faith! Let us inftance king WILLIAM IIId. of precious memory. Poffeffed of every virtue in an eminent degree, generoufly attached to the caufe of liberty, and nobly bent on promoting the happinefs of every denomination of proteftants in the *British* empire; he repreffed the infolent fury of high-church; he exercifed the utmoft clemency to proteftant diffenters; and, with courage that defied danger, refolutely tied up the hands of thefe, who gladly would have cut the throats of thofe men, to whom, a little before, they had made the moft humble fuit. Meanwhile, all this was a *virtual violation* of his coronation oaths. Having fworn to maintain epifcopacy in England againft prefbyterians, and prefbytery in Scotland againft the fury of epifcoparians, he bound his confcience to exercife the royal authority both according to, and againft the fentiments of his own underftanding, and the dictates of his confcience! Churches, which differed fo very widely, that a minifter in one of them could not be reckoned a minifter at all by the other, on account of the manner in which he was ordained to the office, could not both be conftituted according to the *infallible rule,* or even according to his MAJESTY's *ideas* of that rule. Muft we condemn that excellent prince, as a *profane* and *determined violator* of the moft facred ties? No: rather let us deteft the *policy* which obliged him firft to afcend the *British* thrones by fettering himfelf with thefe contradictory obligations, and then to break through them, that he might not be guilty of cutting the throats of one half of his proteftant fubjects. Let us abhor a fyftem, which neceffitates the *British monarchs* either to prevaricate, or to perfecute: which fubjects them to the abfurdity of proftituting their royal authority to maintain and to fupport two churches in their dominions,

dominions, as both agreeable to one divine rule, even while they stand in hostile array against one another: and which as it fixes them in a condition infinitely worse than that of any class of their subjects, makes them pitiable examples and proofs of the TRUTH, which *Sophocles* sings in the person of *Agamemnon**—*Princes will always find it to be a difficulty almost insurmountable, to sway the sceptre of the monarch, and at the same time, to approve themselves religiously obedient to the sceptre of the King of the Monarchs.*†

Inferior *magistrates*, together with *officers*, in the army and in the navy, in the customs and in the excise, are in the same uneasy circumstances. It is impossible, according to the *genius* of the alliance, that any magistrate; or any officer whatever, in the executive department of government, whose sentiments differ from the chartered creed, can be invested with his office, without virtually renouncing the character of an honest man. He must profess, by partaking of the most sacred mysteries, that he is *one body* and *one bread* with the chartered church, notwithstanding he has openly renounced all membership with her, and is a stated member in some other religious society. Can sincerity and truth dwell in such, as tamper, in this manner, with GOD, as well as with their own consciences? Is it reasonable to expect, that the *magistrate* will rule *justly*, or that the *officer* will act *faithfully*, who
dares

* Τόν τοι τύραννον εὐσεβεῖν ὀ ῥᾴδιον.

† How pernicious to the *morals* of a nation must such examples prove!

———*Componitur orbis*
Regis ad exemplum; nec sic inflectere sensus
Humanos edicta valent, ut vita regentis.

CLAUDIAN.

dares to play with oaths, sacraments and tests? Absurd policy! Heathens and the votaries of *Mahumed* fear an oath, and even tremble to falsify their word, while the system of policy adopted among christian nations *obliges* christian magistrates, either to violate the most solemn pledges, or to forfeit those offices of trust and honour, to which they are entitled by their birth and station.

Nor are those, who ought to be possessed of the most irreproachable characters, exempted from sharing in the pernicious effects of that system. We mean the *ministers* of the chartered church. These, though convinced that the *patent creed* and *liturgy* are blended with revery and superstition, must subscribe these systems of absurdity, as a condition of investiture in sacred offices.—It is true, that none are forced into holy functions by pecuniary mulcts, or by any positive pains. But it is as true, that the provision which government makes for the patent public teachers, in the chartered society, are *lures*, equally powerful and irresistible, as any objects whatever, by which government may work on the passion of fear. It seems to be a matter of pure indifference, by what passion men are actuated, when they are powerfully dragged along to sacrifice the maxims of their own understandings about religious objects, to their own temporal interest and emolument. Nor is that policy less blameable, which presents to view the *objects* of *desire*, than that which *menaces* by the *objects* of *aversion*, in order to draw men into absurd or sinful measures. Whatever summons expectation, and calls forth hope, forceth, with as much propriety of expression, every agent, who is capable of being actuated by these passions, to defile his conscience, for gain, as the flattering lips of the harlot forceth the young man to pollute his body, for the enjoyment of animal

mal gratification. Experience proves it. Nor does it weaken the argument, whether men are *led* or *driven* to proftitute their confciences, and to pollute their characters. It is done. Clergymen, led or driven, fubfcribe, even though they have probably written volumes againft the tenets, which they fubfcribe. All the world fee, deteft and execrate the infincerity of the practice, contemn thofe who are guilty of it, and curfe thofe who defend it. This is indeed one of the principal fources of that *contempt* of the *clerical character*, which has become almoft univerfal, and from which minifters of the moft unexceptionable deportment are fcarcely exempted. Who muft bear the blame?—The bold men, who dare their God, mock the church, and flight their own confciences!—But, is it not fome alleviation of their crime, that they were tempted, yea, even *forced* by the *genius* of the political conftitution?

Men in public characters are not the only fufferers. Every clafs of men labour under embarraffments equally grievous. Should any differ, in their religious fentiments, from the eftablifhed ftandard of thinking; it feems impoffible, that they can preferve both on *untarnifhed character* and the *poffeffion* of their *civil property*. Every man is *bound* to make profeffion of his faith, efpecially when he is commanded to go contrary to the *maxims* of his own underftanding and confcience. As foon as he approves himfelf fo faithful to God, and to his own confcience, he muft become obnoxious to government, as a perfon difaffected to the chequered conftitution; he commences a rebel in the eye of the executive powers; and he forfeits all the civil privileges, to which his birth, ftation and loyalty had entitled him. But fhould thefe powerful objects, which government holds forth to the hopes and

fears

fears of men, in order to allure or to affright them into compliance with the chartered fyftem, prevail with any to diffemble their religious fentiments; they purchafe the enjoyment of their civil privileges with the lofs of their natural rights, of a good confcience, and of the integrity of their characters, as honeft and good men.

The time has been, when men refufed, with generous difdain, to buy their civil privileges at fuch a dear market. Animated by a courage fuperior to the terrors, as well as the allurements of every earthly object, they confidered themfelves under indiffoluble obligations, by the very law of nature, to vindicate their natural rights, at the expence of every object, that was dear to them in focial life. Hard cafe!—But now, alas, few, very few hefitate one moment to facrifice *loyalty* to their GOD, the peace of their confciences, and the integrity of their characters at the altars of fecular intereft; while the fmall number, who account it an object worthy of their attention, to *maintain a confcience void of offence toward* GOD, *and toward all men*, are hooted at, as men of narrow principles and of unfafhionable practices! In this manner, men, in every fphere of life, gradually fink into *infidelity* as well as into a *bafe neglect* of every thing that is valuable in human nature, and fhould be dear to the human fpecies. The multitudes who conform notwithftanding their declared fentiments, keep one another in countenance and make example to become irrefiftible. In vain is the *irreligion* of the age lamented, while thofe who affect to do it, in the moft pathetic ftrains, fhut their eyes on the teeming caufe.

During the inaufpicious reigns of the STUARTS, the *Puritans*, thofe venerable pillars of *British* liberty, were willing to fell all, in order to purchafe
a good

a good conscience, more valuable than the *sapphire* or the *onyx*. But since the important *arcanum* of *occasional conformity* was luckily found out, *pure religion and undefiled*, which consisteth in *keeping the conscience unspotted from the world*, hath bidden *adieu* to the *British* island, in a degree that hath alarmed all men of serious reflection. Protestant dissenters in *England*, and Scotch presbyterians, residing in that part of the island, seldom refuse to conform to the most idle superstitions, and boldly bid defiance to their own declared religious maxims. It is true, that they *ought* not to do so; but legislature, ever attentive to the honour of the chartered faith, and of the patent superstitions, obliges them under the penalty of being exposed to hardships, which those only, who are possessed of the most uncommon virtue will submit to undergo. Besides the countless injuries, to which men in peculiar stations are laid open, we shall adduce a few instances, under which subjects in every rank of life have too just reason to be uneasy.

Notwithstanding a *young gentleman* shall have given all reasonable satisfaction to government of his loyalty, and of his inviolable attachment to the interests of his country, by taking all the necessary oaths of fidelity? and notwithstanding he has given away his whole fortune to purchase a commission under the crown; government, in compliance with the *genius* of the political system under consideration, obliges him to throw away his conscience, after his patrimony, annually, by taking the *sacramental test*. This is an insufferable hardship on all, who understand the nature of the *Lord's supper*, and who are, indeed, the only fit persons to receive the communion of the BODY and BLOOD of CHRIST. They must either forfeit their commissions, or pollute their consciences, by concurring in the prostitution

tution of the moft auguft ordinance of the chriftian church, and by conforming to all the monkifh rites, which are added to that facred inftitution. What young gentleman can be expected, in thefe circumftances, to withftand the powerful temptation! Though the mifcellaneous conftitution cannot wholly excufe fuch profane facrifices; that, however, together with the famous *test and corporation acts*, are the teeming fources of fuch infernal profanation. The *Lord's supper* is ordained for thofe, who are faints by profeffion and by practice. But even *charity* herfelf, that *believeth all things*, will not eafily be perfuaded that all the commiffioned gentlemen, in the Britifh army, and navy, and in his majefty's cuftom-houfes are of that holy fraternity. If we miftake, we fhall gladly hail the arrival of the *Millennium!* Notwithftanding his prefent majefty, as well as his two royal predeceffors of the fame illuftrious family, difpenfes with the feverity of the law towards fome, the argument is not weakened by this neceffary exercife of clemency. It declares that he is not blind to the abfurdity of that political fyftem, which required that legiflature fhould eftablifh fuch a teft; and proclaims as loudly his royal mercy, as that law betrays plainly the perfecuting principles of thofe, who were moft active in forging that chain.

Nor are civil and military offices the only objects about which fubjects find themfelves wretchedly embarraffed, in confequence of the political jumble under confideration. No diffenter can enjoy the common privileges of nature, without going over the belly of his religious profeffion, by conforming to the moft ludicrous rites of that church, from which he has feparated. Though, for inftance, the GOD *of nature* hath ordained the inftitution of *marriage* to be a common bleffing to mankind, without exception; legiflature, the watchful guardian of the

alliance,

alliance, hath wholly confined that bleffing, in England, to the members of the chartered church in that part of the *Britifh* Ifle, or, at leaft, to thofe who conform to her rites, as if *these only (Quakers* excepted) had a *right* to enter into wedlock. Every proteftant diffenter muft pollute his confcience, before he can enjoy the means of avoiding fornication : he muft receive his bride, through a *consecrated ring*, from the hand of the *established patentee* of holy offices : he muft be betrothed to her by nearly the fame *bastard sacrament*, which unites the *sons* of *holy mother* with their fpoufes : he muft be received into the holy ftate of matrimony, in almoft the fame form of words, by which the chriftian Lawgiver hath appointed the ordinance of *admission* to communion in his body to be adminiftered : and he muft be made *one flefh* with his wife, in the name of the Father, and of the Son, and of the Holy Ghoft ! Thus, he muft either fit down with the lofs of his natural right to the happinefs of the married ftate; or he muft pollute his confcience by conforming to thefe very fuperftitions, on account of which he had found it neceffary to feparate from the communion of the chartered church. It avails nothing to alledge, that as marriage is a *civil* tranfaction, and on that account, is wholly under the cognizance of the magiftrate, government may lawfully appoint it to be celebrated with fuch ceremonies as it judges to be proper. We deny that marriage is either a *civil* or a *christian* inftitution. All civil appointments prefuppofe the actual exiftence of fociety, and chiefly the connection of the fexes, as one of the principal cements of civil fociety. Though civil legiflature hath always found it neceffary to make proper regulations concerning that inftitution, it never carried its claims fo high, as to arrogate the honour of its appointment. It is an inftitution which

which originally belongs to the *law* of nature, and cannot be the object of any civil regulations, but such as evidently tend to promote, and effectually to secure its original design. All regulations, therefore, which suppose it to be either a *civil* or an *ecclesiastical* institution, and tend to deprive any class of men whatever of the benefit of that appointment, on any civil or religious pretence, are bold attempts to supersede the very laws of nature, are mischievous efforts against the happiness of civil society, and are cruel violations of the rights of human nature. We own, that among the political regulations, which legislature may lawfully make about that ancient institution, it may appoint certain rites to be used in its celebration. But let them be such as are of divine appointment, or are, at least, merely indifferent, *prior* to their becoming obligatory by civil authority. They must neither be absurd imitations of *pagan superstitions*, nor the profane mimicry of *christian institutions*. Government defeats its own design, when it authorizes rites, which are evidently calculated to make one half of a nation either *bachelors* or *hypocrites*.

We shall only add another instance of those intolerable hardships, which the political alliance lays on the shoulders of all protestant dissenters.—A grievance which must plunge every dissenter either in *guilt* or in *ruin*. It is the MODE of *swearing*, which is established in all courts of judicature, whether civil or ecclesiastical, on the south side of the *Tweed*.

It was in the darkest hour of that long night, during which popery overwhelmed all the *European* nations, in profound ignorance and wretched superstition, that the idolatrous MODE of *kissing* the gospels was introduced into their constitutions, and was made the only *canonical* and *legal* method of appealing

appealing to the Deity, by oath, in every court. *Custom*, which gives authenticity to every thing, which wants a better foundation, gave it such credit in England, that it maintained its seat in the political system at the Reformation: and even to this day, the civil as well as the ecclesiastic department of government insist peremptorily on the use of the same *mode* of appeal to HEAVEN. Hence, it becomes absolutely impossible, that any *protestant dissenter*, or any *Scotch presbyterian*, who professes to believe, that the *second precept* of the *decalogue* prohibits him from attempting to worship God in methods, which are not authenticated by his word; who condemns the use of the cross in baptism; and who refuses to kneel at the communion-table;—can carry on any branch of lawful business; recover a just debt; or can enjoy any place in the army or navy, in the custom or excise, with a *safe conscience* and with a *consistent character*.*

Few scruple to comply!—So much the more pity, as imposition hath made men to bury these scruples and their consciences together in a hopeless despondency of redress, a general compliance, instead of rendering the grievance more tolerable, makes it more shocking. Neither the authority, nor the inattention of men diminishes from the absurdity of professing and practising contraries. It only shews, that the system, which forceth them, to adventure on such absurdity, is infinitely *baneful* to their *morals*, as well as to the integrity of their characters. From the *peer* to the *peasant*, none can sustain and act their part in civil society, unless he shall commit a
species

---

* As the mode of swearing by *kissing* the gospels is derived from the same source, from which every other idle superstition has ever teemed,—the wild imaginations of daring enthusiasts; it seems to be a species of prevarication too gross, tamely and for worldly advantages to comply with the *former*, while they continue to exclaim with justice against the *latter*.

[173]

species of idolatry, similar to that of *Jeroboam*, the son of *Nebat*, who made *Israel* to sin. This political institution tends to destroy all just *sense* of an oath from their consciences, seeing their consciences must be *debauched*, before they can submit to the *mode* of its administration. We are bold to say, that the protestant dissenter, together with the Scotch presbyterian, who shall tamely submit to that idolatrous mode of solemn appeal, ought to be accounted legally incapable of feeling the obligation of an oath. Either he must be grossly ignorant of his own religious principles, or his conscience must be miserably debauched. In either case, he ought not to be allowed to make an appeal to *heaven*, while *heaven's vicegerent*, in his own bosom, has him so little under its check.

Should any ask, in what the idolatry of that mode consisteth?—The putting such a question shews, that will-worship, once tampered with, stupifies the understanding, as well as all the moral feelings in the human breast. Why are the sign of the cross, and kneeling at the communion accounted unlawful and superstitious by every denomination of protestant dissenters? *These* are not commanded in the gospel! Neither is *kissing* the gospels.—But *these* owe their original to that *forge* of modern idolatry,—the church of *Rome!*—From the same source is this derived. But kneeling at the altar smells strong of *transubstantiation*, and of the *corporal presence!*— And is not kissing the gospels too like to the worship of *Jeroboam's cherubim*; or to the worship of the sun and moon, which *Job* has mentioned with religious contempt? The latter are as capable of being the *object*, or the *means* of divine worship as the former. As the *Deity* hath revealed his perfections by both, he is as really in the *last* as in the *first*. If there is therefore any appeal to GOD

in

in the action of *kissing* the holy gospels, it must be addressed to him, as speaking, and as revealing himself by these inspired books. And, pray, does not he as really, though not so explicitly, speak to mankind by the *the sun when he shineth*, and *by the moon when she walketh in her brightness?* The whole difference consisteth in the degree and manner of revelation. Wherefore, if it would be, without question, accounted idolatry, to worship the Maker of heaven and earth, by *kissing* the *hand* to these *natural emblems* of DEITY, which preside over day and night; it must be reckoned impious and daring superstition to appear before the JUDGE *of all the earth*, and to appeal to his dread tribunal, not only in a manner not authorized by himself, but in the use of rites, which are *marked* with *ignominy* and *divine contempt* in *these very books*, which are thus profaned.

On the whole, as this piece of superstitious worship was imported into our island, in consequence of the execrable alliance, between the *English* constitution and the *Romish* church, to which it owes its detested birth; as it is still retained by the force of inveterate custom, as a branch of the chartered system of religion, now blended with the same constitution; and as no protestant dissenter, without becoming *Felo de se*, can comply with it:—The unprejudiced must account it intolerably grievous and unjust, especially since the *union*, by which a free communication in commerce was opened between the *south* and *north* divisions of *Great Britain*, that *compliance* with that detestable rite should be made an *indispensable condition*, on which all subjects, *Quakers* only excepted, can have liberty to *buy* or *sell*, to *recover* a debt, to *enjoy* an office, or even to *bear witness* to the truth, in order to save the innocent from an halter. It seems to have a striking resemblance to the *conditio sine qua non* of the *apocalyptic*

lyptic writings, called the MARK *in the right-hands, or in the foreheads of those, who worship the image of the beast*, without which no man could become a *denizen* and free trader in the *apocalyptical Babylon*.

CHAP. VII.

An Attempt to evince the REASONABLENESS *to urge the* NECESSITY, *and to shew the* POSSIBILITY *of abolishing Ecclesiastical Patents.*

THE arguments, which have been discussed in the preceding chapters of this work, may perhaps be considered by the intelligent reader, in no other point of view, than as so many substantial reasons for the total annihilation of that scheme of policy, according to which, the kingdom of CHRIST is consolidated with the kingdoms of this world. They at least seem, to plead strongly, for bringing that *political system* under a serious *review*; for providing effectually against its pernicious consequences; and for adjusting it to the original, unadulterated designs of society, civil and religious. That this cannot be effectuated without a *total abolition* of religious patents, shall be shewn in the ensuing sections.

SECT. I.

The TOTAL ANNIHILATION *of religious Monopolies is proved to be* REASONABLE.

WERE not charters of exclusive civil privilege, sovereignly conferred on one religious denomination of christians, to the manifest prejudice
of

of all others, familiar to mankind, the very recital of such grants would throw them into astonishment at their absurdity and injustice. Should an historian gravely inform his readers, that in a nation, celebrated for wisdom and good policy, a royal patent passed the seals, in favour of all men, who were *six feet high*, impowering them, by an *exclusive grant*, to possess all the rights of free-men, and to treat every man of a *more diminutive* stature, as unworthy to enjoy the common privileges of society; would not the absurdity of the fact justly bring the *veracity* of the *trifler* into question, and his story into contempt? Notwithstanding, religious monopolies, granted on account of qualifications, which are as *foreign* to the advantage or to the hurt of civil society, and are as little under the *direction of their wills*, as the *gauge* of their stature, are equally absurd, and were they not common and familiar, are equally incredible. *Reason, religion* and the *maxims* of *true policy*, conspire to demand the *abolition* of the *latter*, with equal propriety, as they would have persuaded the annihilation of the *former*, were it possible that such flagrant injustice had ever found place among civilized nations. The justice of this assertion will appear, with convincing evidence from the following observations.

I. It seems to be not only an *universal maxim* with mankind, but one of the *first* and most *genuine shoots* of reason, that religionists who attempt to establish their creed on the ruin of social happiness, or on manifest violations of justice toward individuals, whom society is bound to protect, are unreasonable; that society is bound to use all lawful means to baulk the designs of such madmen; and that, should they persevere in their absurd designs,

government

government is under obligations to treat them as the enemies of mankind.

From this plain maxim, the reader, awake to reflection, will see the *absurdity* of every *religious monopoly*, and the *propriety* of *abolishing* every charter of *exclusive privilege*, founded on objects foreign to the nature of civil society. If it is reasonable to prevent monopolies which would be prejudicial to society; if it is incumbent on government to defend the rights of individuals against the furious efforts of enthusiasts, who would establish their creed by violence and injustice; and if all men, in all ages, have agreed in their declared sentiments, and have conspired in their uniform practice, to reckon it agreeable to eternal reason, that the creed which teaches its votaries rebellion, injustice and murder, deserves no place in any political constitution; then, as no religious system whatever can be advanced to that throne, or can be maintained in it, without the most flagrant violations of justice, and intolerable encroachments on the natural and religious rights of mankind, it is less impolitical to suffer any creed to *enjoy* a civil patent, than it is unreasonable to allow the votaries of a religious system, to *aspire* after its establishment *on the ruins* of a former. The *malignant influence* of *creeds*, on the lives and liberties of mankind, arises not from their *heterodoxy*, but from their *exclusive establishment*, and from the *penal laws*, by which they are made objects of terror, and engines of cruelty against every man, who dares to use his own understanding. Nor are their effects less baneful, when they have reached the *meridian* of an *exclusive settlement*, than during the *shock of competition* with rival systems for the legal pre-eminence.

Notwithstanding *actual possession* seems to plead in favour of a chartered creed, the question is, by

Z what

what means did it attain it, and by what juſt claim doth it hold that favour? No religious ſyſtem ever travelled up to the honour of a ſeat, in the *conſtitution* of any empire or of any nation, but in *red apparel*, and with *garments died in blood*. Nor has any creed maintained its throne, but either by the iron rod of the oppreſſor, by the dagger of the aſſaſſin, or by the ſword of the perſecutor. An unjuſt poſſeſſor ought to be ejected. The law of equity, which warrants any man to repel an unjuſt attempt to ſeize his property, makes it his duty to wreſt from the villain the poſſeſſion of the ſeizure.

There is no ſtrength in the popular objection, which has been uſed indifferently againſt every effort for reformation, and as an unanſwerable argument for every creed, when it had the honour of being eſtabliſhed by law—" The chartered ſyſtem is *so* good, *so* orthodox, *so* apoſtolical, *so* ſeraphical,—*so every thing* that is a topic for panegyric, that no man can *reaſonably* diſſent from it, and thereby expoſe himſelf to the civil pains, which law provides againſt heretics and non-conformiſts." The abſurdity of ſuch declamations will appear from the following remarks.

1. Though we readily grant that *some* creeds are infinitely ſuperior to others; all, neither are, nor can be *superexcellent*. Yet all, in their turns, *have been such*, when they were in a ſtate of *political alliance* with the conſtitution of the ſociety, which had ſucceſſively adopted them. Every eſtabliſhed creed is orthodox in the judgment of the impoſers. It is ſo in *Spain* and *Portugal*, as well as in *England* and the *United Provinces*. In the *former*, the *Popiſh system* is ſo orthodox, that no man can become obnoxious to the Inquiſition, with any greater degree of reaſon, than diſſenters in the *latter* are accounted *ſchiſmatics*, and are expoſed to all the diſadvantages of

of nonconformity. Should a creed be as abfurd as the *Musselman's Coran*, it muft be orthodox in the eyes of thofe who believe it; and it muft be fomething more excellent in the enlightened underftandings of thofe, who, inflamed with zeal againft all that oppofe any of its articles, teach them to believe by the irrefiftible *logic* of the HOLY OFFICE.

2. Even *such syllogisms* will be loft on fome. There have been always not a few, who have been either fo *stupid*, or fo *wise*, that they *could* not believe fome articles of the chartered fyftem. Though it was pure, as the folar beam, *the natural man cannot receive the things of the spirit*.* They are the objects of fpiritual difcernment alone. Muft therefore all, who are in the ftate of *corrupt nature*, be ftript of their *natural rights*, and be deprived of their *civil liberties?* Muft none but *saints* poffefs their civil property? Did any of the *apostles* drop a fingle fentence againft the *natural* and *civil rights* of even the moft wicked men? Abfurd!

3. But it is of no confequence in the argument, whether the patent creed is *orthodox*, or the *reverse*. It is not the religious fyftem, as fuch, that can either advantage or injure the rights of mankind in fociety; but it is the *exclusive establishment* of the fyftem in the political conftitution. The popifh fyftem itfelf is as harmlefs as a vulture which hath loft its beak and talons, when it is not enthroned. Civil legiflature, by beftowing on it an exclufive patent, *gives it life and power, that it both can speak, and can cause as many as will not worship the image of the beast to be killed*.† And even the moft unexceptionable creed under heaven, as foon as it is exclufively eftablifhed, becomes an enemy to the rights of mankind. The penal laws, which like its life-

* 1 Cor. xi. 14.   † Rev. xiii. 14, 15.

guard, incircle its awful throne in the political constitution, devour the flesh and eat up the substance of the innocent.

II. It will add no small force to the former reasoning, if it is considered that the eternal law of equity, *whatsoever ye would that men should do to you, do ye also to them*,* calls aloud for the annihilation of religious monopolies.

This comprehensive maxim doubtless implies, that no man, of any character whatever, ought to do that towards others, which, placing himself in their circumstances, he would not wish they should do to him, were they in his circumstances. It must therefore follow, that as those, who sit at the helm in government, would not chuse that any thing should be blended with the civil constitution, which bears hard on any part of their character, whether as *men* or as *christians*, as *members* or as *managers* in civil society; they ought not to permit any objects, (especially such as are foreign to the nature and designs of civil society) which affect the character and consciences of their inferiors, to be consolidated with the constitution. No station whatever can set men above the divine law. As *God hath made of one blood all nations of men that dwell on the earth*; † as all men are equally under moral obligations to the AUTHOR of their existence; and as every man is bound to *love his neighbour* AS *himself*; ‡ every individual of the species is under indissoluble ties to effectuate that for his brother, which SELF-LOVE, under the regulations of reason and of conscience, dictates, that this last ought to do for him, on the supposition of an interchange in their circumstances. Let those, therefore, who have the modelling of the political con-

---

* Luke vi. 31. † Acts xvii. 26. ‡ Matth. xix. 19.

stitutions

stitutions of kingdoms in their power, place themselves in the circumstances, in which many good men have been, and continue to be situated: let them suppose themselves under obligations, by that authority which ought to protect their rights and liberties, to subscribe articles of faith, which they cannot believe; to assent to canons, which they are persuaded are subversive of that liberty with which Christ hath dignified his spiritual kingdom; and to worship God by rites, which they are sure were never instituted by Him, whose authority is both the *reason* and the *rule* of all divine worship: and let them consider themselves as branded with the odious appellation of *heretics*, stigmatized for *schismatics* and ruined by the execution of penal laws enacted against such ugly characters; and all because they cannot believe and subscribe two contradictory systems of faith at one and the same time.—What would they think of their circumstances? Could they be *happy* or even *easy* in them? Would thay not think themselves entitled to speedy and effectual redress?—Let their own feelings dictate to them their duty toward their brethren of mankind. Human nature, in all situations, is endued with *moral* as well as with *natural sensibility*. Even those, who move in the lowest spheres of civil life, are at least as capable of feeling the rigours and miseries of religious imposition, as those, who, being educated in all the softness, dissipation and thoughtless gaiety of courts, are most forward to act in the character of religious dictators. Meanwhile, it is reasonable, that such as are so fond to turn their fellow christians, into the community of cattle, by depriving them of all that is human, but the *erect figure*, should seriously think how uneasily the saddle would fit on their backs, and how ill they would take it, to be *whipped* and *spurred* along by *penal laws*, through

all

all the filth and mire of *oaths, subscriptions* and every other act of conformity to no one knows what, till their humane riders shall have accomplished the tour to the temple of relentless tyranny!

Some may possibly reply, that those who manage the reins of administration cannot alter any thing in the political constitution: that their province is, to govern according to the established laws: that though the divine precepts certainly reach them in their private character, they are answerable to society for their public deportment; and must act according to the statutes and established customs of the realm; and that, on this account, they are under obligations to do many things toward others, which they would not wish any to have in their power to do toward them.

But is not this objection a plain acknowledgment, that the political constitution *stands in need* of a speedy reformation, when it shuts up those, who are legally employed in administration to acts of confessed violence and injustice; and that their *moral principles* are very bad, who assume a character, which obliges them to perpetrate actions, which are acknowledged violations of the laws of nature, as well as of christianity? Astonishing! Does not the law of the supreme Lord of the universe reach men in every sphere? Are the moral precepts made only for those, whose private character incapacitates them for the perpetration of public injuries? Are *these* superior to even *divine controul*, who have it in their power to injure innocence under colour of law? Rather, does not the supreme Lawgiver bind up every man, not only from all acts of injustice, but even from assuming any character, on any consideration whatever, by which he may be laid under a necessity, to treat the divine law with contempt, or his fellow-christians with injury and insult?

Though

Though it be happily true, that political administration cannot overthrow the national constitution at pleasure, the legislature can rectify every thing that is wrong in it as soon as it is pointed out to them. Every society is not only warranted, but is even bound by the law of self-preservation, to remove the known causes of its own woe; and its magistrates ought not only to point out the prolific sources, but to excite and direct it how to remove them in a legal and effectual manner. Though alterations, in the political system of any society, ought not to be attempted on account of *trifling inconveniencies*, which may befal some individuals of society; it has been shewn, that the disadvantages attending exclusive establishments are neither few, nor of small importance to religious as well as civil society. Nor are there any evil consequences to attend the annihilation of these springs of social misery, which can counterbalance the benefit, that would arise from that prudent measure. The only evil, which the most foreboding imagination can suppose to arise from it, is depriving a few men of an opportunity to succeed in some offices, and to enjoy the enormous wealth annexed to them, to which they can pretend no antecedent right. Though some may affect to rank this among the crimes, which Heaven itself cannot forgive, one thing is clear as the meridian beam, that, was this measure to be pursued in *Great Britain*, it would annually add at least one million to her revenue. This will appear with brighter evidence, when it is considered, that—

III. The ADVANTAGES, which would result from a total disengagement of church and state, are *great, universal* and *lasting*.

1. Should

1. Should that measure be approved, the advantages arising from it would be GREAT. Were no other good consequences to attend it, besides the *removal* of so many baneful effects which have been demonstrated to flow from the political alliance of the church and state in one mixed *constitution*, our assertion would be sufficiently just: But a brief enumeration of the positive blessings, which would acrue to society by it, will set this part of the proposition in a clearer point of light.

The natural and religious rights of mankind would be effectually *rescued* from *sacrilegious violation*. Rational creatures would then dare to avow their moral dependence on God; and christians, no longer bound down by penal laws to believe contradictions, would enjoy that liberty in its full extent, by the use of which they approve their subjection and irreproachable loyalty to the KING *of kings*. Their understandings would answer some more important purpose besides that, to which *mere instinct might have directed* them. Raised to the rank of conscious and accountable beings; and elevated above the bestial tribes, to an equality with which the political alliance had forcibly depressed human nature; their elective powers would become of important service to them, in offering up *willing* and *living sacrifices to* GOD; and the use of their consciences, in the regulation of their worship and deportment, would no more be superseded by the arbitrary decisions of those, whom law hath so long authorized to usurp the sovereign direction of the moral arbiter in the human bosom.

The civil rights of citizens, redeemed from unjust forfeiture, would also be enjoyed in their full extent, and with perfect security. Every good subject hath a title to enjoy unmolested his life, liberty and property. His right to these is founded in his having
discharged

discharged his debt to government with steady fidelity. Should his obedience to the commands of government become inconsistent with his more sacred obligations to GOD, through some defect in the constitution, or through any fault in administration; as it is better to obey God than man, his disobedience, in that instance, is not only excusable, but becomes laudable and indispensably necessary. Nor hath he forfeited a full security of life, liberty and property, as a debt due from society, for his steadiness and loyalty in every instance wherein obedience is due, according to the law of God, and the original laws of society. Having fulfilled *his part* of the *virtual contract* between society and him, it would be infinitely unjust to suppose him to be in debt, while nothing remains due. As civil government is not founded on the ruin of GOD's moral government in the world, and on the supersedure of his absolute and incommunicable dominion over the conscience; it has no claim on any subject for more than is due to *civil* society; nor has it any right to demand faith without, or contrary to evidence, and to command obedience in any instance wherein Heaven hath revealed its prohibitions.

Notwithstanding these plain maxims; as every subject, according to the *genius* of the alliance, is legally and *de jure* reckoned a member of the chartered church; these, whose understandings and consciences are not of the same size and complexion with those of administration, and who have fortitude and honesty to avow their superior obligations to GOD, are *ipso facto* deprived of their civil right, and incur a forfeiture of every thing which society is bound to protect. The laws, which should be their guardians, become the inexorable authors of their ruin. How often have the worthiest subjects in *Britain*, been driven from their families, their property and their country, for no other crime, but becaufe they refufed to pay a debt to civil authority, which they neither owed, nor could owe, unlefs they had commenced atheifts, and had renounced their moral dependence on GOD, in order to become ftanch parliamentary chriftians! Even in this age of comparative liberty, and on the fame account, how many of his majefty's beft fubjects, who would cheerfully fpend their laft drop of blood for the proteftant caufe, and for our excellent civil conftitution, are marked out as fchifmatics, as heretics, and as enemies to the political conftitution, and, we are forry to add, are treated accordingly!—The ftiff dignitary deigns to reply,—*They should comply, as in duty bound.*—In the name of common fenfe! For what reafon? Muft they purchafe the character and privileges of conformifts at the expence of their fincerity, their religion, and their allegiance to the eternal God? Are they in duty bound to pay a debt, which government hath no right to demand?—But the creed and ritual, which are blended with the conftitution, are orthodox and pious!—To whom? To government, which impofes them.—And is that a fufficient reafon for demanding conformity? Then it muft be as fufficient in every quarter of the world. It muft be an unanfwerable argument in *Spain*, in *Italy*, at *Petersburgh* and at *Constantinople*, as well as in the *British* dominions!—On the whole, if the civil rights of mankind are valuable; if the fecurity of thefe, in civil life, is juftly accounted one of the greateft bleffings of providence; and if it is matter of fact, that the *genius* of exclufive eftablifhments, unhinges that fecurity;—then a reformation of the political conftitution, by a total *annihilation* of Ecclefiaftical patents, would be one of the *most valuable blessings*, that the *patriotic heart* of a true *Briton* could defire.

Nor

Nor would individuals be the only gainers, a door being opened for every subject indiscriminately to use the endowments of his nature, society in general would reap infinite advantages from an annihilation of religious monopolies.

It hath been shewn already how much the natural rights of mankind have been supplanted by patent creeds and established liturgies. Though it cannot be denied, that many dissenters are possessed of valuable talents, and that they might be of the greatest use to society; the severe statutes, made against them, put them under a *ban*, and oblige them to continue *cyphers* in society, in order to preserve a *conscience void of offence towards God, and towards all men.* Nor must they be blamed for their retreat. No man can hinder the evidence of truth to shine on his understanding; and no good man will ever wish to do it. Having weighed temporal and eternal objects in a just balance, he will never put out the eyes of his understanding, stop the mouth of his conscience, and pierce himself through with many sorrows,—for the uncertain and perishing advantages, which might arise from the exercise of his natural endowments in the *guilty service* of society. He firmly believes, on the best grounds, that God will never hold him a debtor to his scheme of providence in those cases, wherein he cannot act, without overleaping the mounds of morality and religion. And he is no less assured that his temporal loss is more than compensated by *conscious honour,*—an inheritance which the smiles of the mighty cannot bestow, and of which the frowns even of princes cannot rob him.

This has indeed been the deplorable state of society ever since the *æra* of the famous *alliance*. The best of men, rather than that they should plunge their consciences in guilt, and their characters in infamy, have chosen to bury their talents in the obscure walks of private life; and they have quietly beheld, with the grief, of which great minds only are susceptible, *atheists*, *hypocrites* and *novices* raised to the highest spheres of action, and sacrificing the peace of their consciences for an opportunity to prey, like vultures, on the best interest of both civil and religious society. But are individuals the only sufferers? No; society is the principal loser. The nation is injured, while individuals, ignorant of the adequate cause of national misery, sicken under the political disease. The state of *Great Britain*, during the reign of Charles I. together with that of his two royal descendents, is a sufficient comment on the assertion.

Ought not such a grievance to be redressed?—a grievance, which unhinges society, and disappoints its most valuable designs among mankind. Is not every political body bound by the law of self-preservation to attend to its own interests, and especially to take care that none of its useful members either be cut off, or be bound up from exercising the functions, for which the God of nature has qualified them? Shall a nation, which hath hazarded innumerable wars in the vindication of her own honour, and for retrieving or securing the property of a few individuals, refuse to heal a known defect in her own political system, in consequence of which, not only are *individuals* spoiled of their undoubted rights, but even the *whole body politic* is left to languish, through the loss of their important services. The cruel law which authorized the murder of ill-formed infants, and of old men, no longer serviceable to the community, is justly execrated in *Britain* and in every other christian nation. Notwithstanding, had not society some pretext for such a law, while both, had they been suffered to live, must have been burthens on the commonwealth? But is there
the

the least shadow of reason for a political system, which cuts off one half of society, yea, the most valuable part too, from serving their God and their generation, according to the extent of their talents? Those, whom it thus dooms to drag out life in obscurity, when the Author of their beings hath qualified them to shine out in the most important stations, are cruelly numbered among the dead. Life, to a great mind, is only another name for death, when all that is permitted to him to do with a safe conscience and with untarnished honour, is only to breathe.

2. The advantages would be UNIVERSAL as well as *eminent*. All persons, in all spheres, would reap the fruits of such a reformation in civil policy. Subjects, without distinction, would reap a plentiful harvest of civil security, of true honour, and of unallayed felicity; while the prince, beloved of his subjects and dreaded by his enemies, would fill, with unrivalled greatness, a throne established in righteousness,—would be happy in the abundant peace of his dominions, and would derive unmixed pleasure from the increasing prosperity of every quarter of his empire: *atheists* and *hypocrites* could not then have the only chance to thrive in society, to assume the reins of government, or to fill the most important posts in administrations: men of probity and worth, emancipated from all the embarrassments, by which they are forcibly detained in the walks of private life, would be encouraged to step forth for the safety of their country in the time of her distress, would eagerly embrace every opportunity to render the reign of their sovereign illustrious in the annals of time; and would become the authors of countless blessings to their relations, friends and neighbours: as the various classes of subjects could have no jarring interests, nor any temptation to thwart one another,

another, in order to act in concert with the ever jarring parts of an impolitical, inconsistent scheme of police; the important pillars of social happiness would remain unshaken: the constitution, always consistent with itself, uniform in its several branches, and equally auspicious to the civil interests of *good subjects* indiscriminatively, would immoveably fix itself in the affections of all, and would make itself unalterable through the united endeavours of all its willing and interested votaries: no longer would the *peace* of nations be liable to be shaken, either by the *peevish clamour of church-men*, who, as their secular interest lies in opposition to that of other classes in society, are ever under the dominion of capricious jealousy; or by the insurrection of those, who, taught at the expence of the former generations, have learned to dread the interest of an established and dignified clergy, which hath never failed to be at the devotion of an ambitious prince: and as jealousy would naturally subside; and all these party names, which have been the disgrace of Great Britain, would be buried in everlasting forgetfulness; subjects, united in one common design, and enjoying common security, would become happy in mutual and lasting confidence. *The envy of* EPHRAIM *should depart, and the adversaries of* JUDAH *should be cut off*; Ephraim *should not envy* Judah, *and* Judah *should not vex* Ephraim. *

But among all the several ranks of mankind, who would have reason to reckon the annihilation of exclusive establishments one of the greatest of human blessings, there is no one which hath greater reason to wish it, than that class, which we are afraid, would oppose that salutary measure with the most unrelenting obstinacy. We mean the *established*, especially the *dignified clergy*. Our apprehensions

* Isa. xi. 13.

are founded on some late discoveries which their GRACES, belonging to *this class*, have made of *their spirit*, in parliament, when a *bill*, reckoned, by the almost unanimous suffrage of not only the COMMONS, but of the whole nation, one of the most reasonable that was ever brought up to the *House of Lords*, was rejected by the unanimous vote of the episcopal bench, one only excepted, whose name deserves to be inrolled in the records of time with our *Tillotsons*, our *Hoadlys*, and a *very few* more ecclesiastical champions for *British liberty*. An established clergy, in all ages, seem to have acquired an habit of thinking (and plain reasons might be given why such an habit may be easily attained) that the church cannot subsist in the world without an exclusive patent. Hence, they have always acquitted themselves for the church, *tanquam pro aris et focis*, when they thought she was *in danger*. They meant, worthy men! their bishoprics, their revenues and their honours. But in this age, that respectable body begin to open their eyes, to have more refined sentiments, and to give place to more exalted views. Their duty, their honour and their interest conspire to make them the most solicitous advocates for the breaking of that yoke, which has galled their necks, beyond what it has done to any other class of men whatever. Has it not obliged them to overlook all the points of true honour, in order to obtain a livelihood? Can any thing be more disgraceful, than that persons of so sacred a character should trample down common sincerity and every maxim of undisguised honesty, in subscribing articles of faith, which they boldly contradict every time they ascend the pulpit, and in swearing to canons, which they know in their consciences, to be unscriptural, absurd and tyrannical? How shameful, not even to be agreed among themselves, whether the articles, which they subscribe,

scribe, are to be understood in an *Arminian*, or in a *Calvinistical* sense! Where is the *honour* of the *christian ministry?* Is it any wonder, that their *sacred character* should be turned into *jest* among the profane? Can it be surprizing to any, that *deism* should prevail, and that *infidels* should dare to arraign the christian system in so bold a manner, when the *public teachers* of that holy religion have agreed in nothing so much, as in sinking *its credit*, as well as *their own reputation*, by such open contempt of common sincerity, sacred even among pagans? Would clergymen, therefore, retrieve the honour due to the character of christian teachers? Let them conspire with their fellow-subjects, in *legal* efforts, to abolish that system of policy, which must continue to tarnish their reputation, so long as the frailty of human nature is apt to lay open the honour of the best men to temptation from its baneful influence.

The vindication of their honour ought not to be their only motive. A creed and liturgy established with civil penalties, cramp the ministers of JESUS in the discharge of their duty, and force them on measures which they cannot but condemn in their consciences. How many are the disagreeable hardships, to which a chartered clergy are exposed! How great! They must, in one division of *Great Britain, take the childrens bread, and give it to the dogs,*[*] by administering the most sacred mysteries to all who demand the sacrament of the supper, as a qualification for a post in the army or navy, in the customs or excise. They must dispense pardon and absolution authoritatively to all, who barely say, in their last moments, that *they repent*. They must declare, at the funeral of every person within the pale of the church, that " it hath pleased GOD of

---

[*] Matth. vii. 6. xv. 26.

his GREAT MERCY to take to himself the soul of the deceased, and that, therefore, they commit the body to the ground in SURE and CERTAIN hopes of the resurrection to eternal life,"—even though the person has perhaps died for the most enormous crimes, and has used his last breath in bold defiance of all that is sacred! What *good man* would not only *wish*, but *vigourously struggle* to be freed from such hardships!

Nor ought the duties of their sacred function to be overlooked in the present argument. *Set for the defence of the gospel*, they are bound to approve themselves champions for truth together with the original simplicity of evangelical institutions. As it hath been proved already, that exclusive establishments are the *fort-royal* of error, absurdity and superstition; they cannot discharge that part of *their duty* which they owe to the *integrity* and *purity* of the *christian system*, without using their utmost efforts to annihilate that system of policy, which, so long as it remains, must render all their other laudable attempts against infidelity, error and idolatry absolutely fruitless. Vain are their pretensions to a laudable zeal for the doctrines and precepts of christianity, while they are at the same time advocates for a political alliance, in consequence of which, the greatest absurdities and the most idle superstitions may bid bold defiance to all the weapons, which either reason or revelation can furnish.

Wherefore, in fine, if to be freed from legal embarrassments in the discharge of duty,—such duty as nearly concerns the eternal interest of both *pastors* and *people*, can be reckoned an advantage:— If to behold truth *greatly triumphing* over error:— if to see the *honour* of the *gospel ministry* retrieved, and the bold contemners of their sacred ministrations put to everlasting silence;—If to be the much-honoured

honoured inftruments of compleating a reformation in the church, and of reftoring chriftianity to its original fimplicity, and to its primitive fplendour:— If all thefe can give any pleafure to the minifters of Jesus, no rank of men whatever can have more reafon to wifh, and to attempt the total annihilation of all religious monopolies.

3. We fhall only add, that the advantages, which would refult from a total fubtraction of ecclefiaftical affairs from the conftitutions of civil focieties would be LASTING.

That the moft *hopeful reformations* of national churches have not long *survived their authors*, hath always been a fubject of complaint. Hence *Great Britain*, always reforming, yet never reformed, has been fo often a field of confufion and blood. That enterprize hath been like the reformations attempted by the kings of JUDAH, which feldom outlived one generation, *because the* HIGH PLACES, which were the *temptations* to a relapfe, *were not taken away*. The caufes of *Britain*'s relapfes have not been attended to with fufficient accuracy. Our reformers, not content to have the juft objects of their pious refentment removed, have always been ambitious, to obtain an exclufive eftablifhment of their peculiar articles of faith and modes of worfhip. The reformed fyftem, notwithftanding we fhould fuppofe, that it was entirely *apostolical*, could not long continue in that ftate, *because it was established*. This affertion can appear ftrange to none, when it is confidered, that the more evangelical any religious fyftem is, fo foon as it commences the privileged fyftem, it has the lefs chance to be permanent. The reafon is obvious. It is lefs fuitable to the *earthly designs* of political government. And as the principal defign of legiflature, in blending it with the political conftitution, was, that it might become

fubfervient

subservient to these ends, methods will ever be taken to make it *that*, which it was *intended to be*. It will be gradually modelled, by successive adulterations, into a *political fitness* to serve the purposes of the ambitious and aspiring both in *church* and *state*. This is no merely *probable theory*. It hath been confirmed by an uniform series of examples, in every christian nation, ever since the commencement of the *grand alliance*. Let us view the present state of the established church in *North Britain*. The last reformation, which that church underwent, was at the ever memorable *Revolution*, when her clergy were commanded to exchange the *surplice* for the *cloak*. The religious system, which was then blended with the political constitution of the *Scotch* nation, is, by the suffrage of all the protestant churches, not behind any in *apostolical* purity. And the clergy who then filled her pulpits were a venerable, othodox and pious body. But to what deplorable circumstances is that same church reduced in this age! *How is her gold become dim, and her most fine gold changed!* * What hath been the cause of this wonderful falling off? Have the *British* monarchs, since that golden *æra*, done to her as JEROBOAM *the son of* NEBAT, *who* MADE *Israel to sin?* Have they, like these *inglorious monarchs*, who swayed the *British* sceptre before them, and who converted it into the rod of the oppressor, forced her into the present plunge of defection? She dares not affirm it. Except in the case of *lay-patronages*, which queen ANN's *Jacobitish parliament* restored, they stand acquitted of the charge. What then is the mysterious cause? It is no longer a mystery. It is the exclusive establishment, which she obtained at that famous period. Like REUBEN, though she was the *first* in *dignity*

---

* Lament. iv. 1.

among the reformed churches, yet she *hath been unstable as water, and hath not been able to excel, because she went up,* in the claim of right, and took her place in the *constitutional couch,** together with her sister, the church of *England,* and *committed spiritual fornication with the kings of the earth.*† Being established by civil authority, a despotic ecclesiastical administration, secure under the wing of an indulgent government, and pushed forward by an eager desire to merit at the hands of men of influence and power, has brought her to the present state of enormous apostacy.

Subscription to articles of faith is but a feeble defence against innovations, corruptions and spiritual tyranny. It is like the spider's web, which may intangle the feeble fly, but is easily broken and demolished by the robuster insect. Clergymen of *spirit* and *resolution* have often shewn, that they sagely judge a *bishopric,* a *deanery,* a *rectory,* or even a *presbyterian stipend,* a cheap acquisition, at the expence of subscribing articles, which they no more believe than they do the chapters of the *Alcoran,* and of promising that which they never intended to perform. And a celebrated writer hath shewn, that such gentlemen are never at a loss for something to justify their conduct, or at least, to extenuate its enormous guilt.‡

IV. We shall only add to the former reasoning, concerning the *propriety* of abolishing ecclesiastical monopolies, that government, by granting *toleration* to the *protestant dissenters* cannot be consistent with *itself,* or with the *principles,* on which it proceeds, in granting that favour, unless it shall *entirely abolish* exclusive establishments.

* Gen. xlix. 4. † Rev. xvii. 2. ‡ The author of the *Confessional.*

A toleration,

A toleration,* whether it be unlimited or more confined, is a plain and positive *recognizance* of the dissenter's *right* to the enjoyment of his life, liberty and property, *notwithstanding* his dissent from the privileged creed. It is a legal and authoritative declaration, that the exclusive patent is unreasonable; that the penal statutes, by which it is fenced, are unjust and cruel; and that no man's life or property *ought* to be suspended on the *quality* of his faith, or on the *modes* of his worship.

On these principles, toleration is not reasonable or consistent with the grounds on which government grants it, unless it be compleat. For if it is just and equitable to permit protestant dissenters to enjoy *any part* of their civil rights and property; why should they not be allowed to possess these objects in their *full* extent? If it is reasonable to spare their lives; can any good reason be assigned, why their property, to which they have as indisputable a claim, should not be protected? An *imperfect* toleration is a twin-sister to *non-toleration*, which always baptizes its votaries in blood. No government can reasonably stop short. That any good subject should be deprived of his property, on account of the peculiarities in his religious persuasion, by the same authority, which protects his life, when his title to both is founded on the same eternal law of equity,—is

---

* When we speak favourably of *toleration*, we are to be understood as meaning that, which is commonly designed a *negative* toleration. As a *positive* toleration of any sect amounts to a *legal exclusive establishment* of that sect in contradiction from all others; it is besides, one of the greatest *solecisms*, which can be committed in politics as well as in morals. While government, by refusing to grant dissenters a *formal* establishment, plainly declares, that it does not approve of their tenets, it notwithstanding establishes them by a law, and condemns itself as authorizing a creed, which it has prejudged to be *heterodox*.

absurd

absurd as well as iniquitous. if the harmless peculiarities of his creed are a good reason for cashiering the eternal law of equity, by throwing him out of his property, why are they not as sufficient a reason for discarding the same law, by expelling him from the land of the living?

Seeing, therefore, that government, as it vouchsafes a toleration on protestant dissenters, must account it reasonable; and seeing it has been proved, that the same unchangeable law of equity, which makes it reasonable and just, calls upon government to make it *compleat*;—We have all in the present argument at once, that we desire. While we plead for the reasonableness and propriety of abolishing ecclesiastical patents, we plead for no more than a *perfect* and *unconfined* toleration of all his majesty's good subjects. Were all laws fraught with the *negative* as well as the *positive* punishment of protestant dissenters, finally revoked charters of exclusive civil privilege would, in the nature of the thing, become entirely void; society would flourish under the salutary influence of an equitable administration; and government, propitious to all, according to the measure of their civil desert, would no longer bestow *public* encouragement according to any other rule. Indeed, no civil administration can say as that Divine Person in the gospel *Is it not lawful for me to do what I will with my own?* Public encouragements and rewards are not the independent property of any administration, which it may dispense at pleasure! They are in the hands of magistrates as TRUSTEES for society. These are stewards and according to the nature of the thing, ought to be *œconomists*. Their commission implies an obligation, to divide to every man his share of public rewards, when ever he shall make it *his property*, by *deserving* it of civil society. The rewards, which
society

society hath lodged in their hands, are not transferable to any, on any account, which is foreign to the *civil* interests of society. If the contrary was supposed, they would be guilty of purloining, of robbing society of its property, and of squandering away the stock, with which they are intrusted. As no member of society can be entitled to more than he deserves; were the trustees of society to confer more, on any *private* consideration whatever, they would become unfaithful in their trust; would hurt civil society; and would especially injure those, who, on account of their *equal* or *superior* desert, have *similar* or *more extensive* demands on society.

It is clear, as the meridian light, that was government to act consistently with its own approved principles in granting a limited toleration, by making it *compleat*; were none laid under discouragement by penal laws, on any account, that is *foreign* to the real interests of civil society; and were public rewards impartially conferred, according to the degree of civil merit, and without any regard to religious persuasions, which affect not the civil interests of mankind; an inconceivable addition would be made to the happiness, prosperity and peace of the British empire.—In the age of peace,—industry called forth to action by public encouragement; animated with the pleasing hopes of succeeding in every enterprize, according to her activity; and guarded by impartial public justice, as well as cheered by the gentle whispers of a good conscience, her inseparable companion; would walk abroad with courage; would make every city and even every hamlet the place of her auspicious abode; and would fill the treasures of all with her richest stores. No longer should she be obliged, to retire and languish in the dreary wastes of a deserted country, or among the frightful ruins of depopulated cities. Her greatest enemy, voracious avarice, attended by her faithful mate, supple conformity, whose maw, like that of the ostrich, can digest iron, should be no more seen stalking abroad, and robbing the hives of the laborious, to fill the treasures of her ever hungry and slothful votaries.

And in the day of war,—how formidable should *Great Britain* appear to all her enemies! No more should one half of the *British* subjects be legally authorized to tread the other half, equally deserving, under their feet; to disable them from advantaging their country in peace; or to prevent them from stepping forth for her safety in war, by fettering them with sacramental tests, and by obliging them to renounce their moral dependance on the God *of battles*, before they can be allowed to draw a sword in the day of battle. Riches, which are the sinews of war, could never be wanting. As nothing in the political constitution could either alarm the fears of any domination of *loyal* subjects, or throw fetters on their hands, by intangling their consciences; and as every thing in the political system would conspire to defend their rights, to secure their property, and to cherish a modest, enterprising hope; every subject, without distinction, would be ready, either to bleed till he could bleed no more in his country's cause and his own, or to return from war crowned with victory, to sit with safety and pleasure *under his own vine and under his own fig-tree.*

SECT.

The Abolition of Incorporations is necessary.

THOUGH in proving the reasonableness of abolishing incorporations, the necessity of that measure, was in part shewn, yet a few considerations still remain, which will set this matter in a more distinct point of view.

I. The necessity of annihilating incorporations will appear, if it can be shewn, that the measure would greatly contribute to remove those difficulties, by which Great Britain is presently embarrassed, and in danger of being precipitated into the greatest calamities. This will appear from an enumeration of some of these menacing difficulties, and a proof that they originate in ecclesiastical alliances.

1. Great Britain is bowing beneath an enormous load of national guilt. This observation is unquestionably just; and among other causes, incorporations challenge a chief place. Some instances will make this plain.

It cannot be dissembled that immoralities, prevailing among every rank, have signalized Great Britain as a nation not inferior to any in crimes. Nor can it be refused that the incorporations of the British national churches have added very considerably to the score. It is plain from a very long tract of experience, that in proportion as these have been compleat, and of longer duration in any country, ignorance and impiety, a dreadful pair! have prevailed, and have gradually obtained the sanction of custom—a sanction far stronger than that, which any human laws can give the purest system of religion.

gion. The reason is plain, as the fact is notorious. When the public teachers of religion find, that they are absolutely independent of the flocks, which they pretend to feed; that riches and honors, tithes and titles are secured to them by law; and that a species of authority are lodged with them, by the civil legislature, to maltreat " their fellow servants" of other religious denominations, " and to eat and drink with the drunken," * they plunge themselves, and their flocks, by their example, into all the deeps of the most flagitious behaviour.

Nor have incorporations been less instrumental in loading Great Britain with the guilt of atrocious *perjuries*. As they must be fortified with oaths and tests, and as they are, like all sublunary things, in a state of constant vicissitude from the caprice of human nature; that system, which gains the ascendent to-day, and to which authority commands all subjects to swear an unalterable attachment, must be anathematized to-morrow, with the same sacred formalities. Need we, for instance, mention the short period of twenty years, from 1640 to 1660? Did not the English parliament, dispense with all the oaths which clergymen and others had sworn to episcopacy under the reign of Charles I? Did they not prevail with almost all ranks of subjects to bind themselves by the Solemn League and Covenant, to be zealous abettors of another religious system? Did they not oblige the whole nation to renounce this last, and to swear allegiance to a republic, and to a jumble of religious inconsistencies incorporated with it? And, in the end, did they not dispense with all oaths to this last, and command the whole nation to swear inviolable attachment to monarchy, and to renew their homage to old, wrinkled episcopacy,

* Matt. xxiv. 49.

once

once more become young and charming in the eyes of these British demagogues?

During the public confusions of that (and indeed of every other) period, incorporations stand justly charged with having drenched Great Britain in the guilt of all the murders, massacres and inhuman barbarities, which were perpetrated upon the best protestants and most eminent friends of religion, standing in the defence of their natural, civil and religious rights. Yes; at their altars these precious victims bled! Let the bloody annals of the last age, not to mention the seas of blood, which, on a religious account, flowed before that barbarous period, attest the dismal tale!

Incorporations themselves are scandalously immoral! yes; they must plunge that government in guilt that grants them; and that nation in rebellion against the God of heaven which submits to them. They trample down the immutable law of equity; they supersede the authority of God in the consciences of his creatures, and they suspend the right of dominion, which the Redeemer has purchased with his blood, over his own spiritual, free and independent kingdom.

Would Great Britain, therefore, prevent her own ruin, the necessary attendant of accumulated guilt, let her remove the teeming cause of both. Though the abolition of incorporations cannot atone for *past* crimes, it would prevent the filling up of her cup. Were legislature sensible of the national guilt, which hath been contracted by the many tragedies that have been acted on the British stage, in the true *spirit* of incorporations, and would abolish them; the prudent measure would be, in Heaven's eye, the best evidence of a genuine, national repentance. And who knows what a national detestation of such horrid scenes, and of one of their prolific causes,

approved

approved by this measure, may effect towards turning away the Lord's righteous resentment, which seems to hang in doubtful suspence over the British empire?

2. Great Britain is sinking beneath an enormous load of national debt. None will hesitate about the necessity of lessening, and if possible, of annihilating a sum of more than two hundred millions. It is now become an object of government's utmost solicitude. Schemes to this effect, without number, have been offered. One is now publicly adopted. And were the abolition of incorporations adopted too, it would greatly accelerate the execution of so necessary a measure. A great part of those enormous revenues which the nation annually bestows, in furnishing the means of extravagance, in feeding ambition, and in pampering luxury among ecclesiastical dignitaries might not only be saved, but might be employed in rescuing national credit, and in gradually expunging the national score. Besides, it is notorious, that the best lands in England, are in the hands of bishops, deans and chapters, a generation of men who have been frequently compared to the drones in the industrious hive. Were even these alone (at the death of the present incumbents) properly disposed of, they would greatly facilitate the execution of the parliamentary scheme of reduction.

But the tithes are the great source of ecclesiastical wealth. These are such an obstruction to agriculture and rural improvements, that many wise men have thought, that ministry would have more effectually consulted the interest of the treasury, had they even compounded with incumbents and allowed them an equivalent. By that absurd mode of paying the national clergy, the landed gentlemen are discouraged from improving their estates; are kept back from cultivating the commons; and are thereby held fast in the chains of comparative poverty.

Whe

Who will expend some thousands in improvements, when as soon as the lands produce, the rector claims the tithe, which is often more than one half of his profits arising from his industry and expenditure? Is not one tenth of many counties lying waste on this account? What an incredible loss must this be both to private fortunes and public funds! The treasury is virtually robbed of millions, which, were it not for decimation, might be annually collected from rural improvements, without burdening the industrious. As the *jus divinum* of tithes is now generally laughed at; the necessities of the state call aloud upon legislature to revoke its own too indulgent largess: and that his majesty may not lose the benefit of the resumption; nor his subjects be oppressed by so pernicious a mode of taxation, the wisdom of Parliament ought to substitute an equivalent levy, which would neither discourage agriculture, nor any other means of national opulence. By these and similar means, the parliamentary scheme might be rapidly carried into execution; his majesty's revenue would soon rise above national demands; and his subjects would, in a few years, be freed from many heavy taxes, under which they groan, trade languishes, and the nation is ready to sink into a state of insolvency.

II. All those reasons which, in the sixteenth century, made the Reformation necessary, concur to make it necessary to perfect that Reformation, by the abolition of incorporations.

Were we to descend to an enumeration of these reasons, we might shew that they are equally urgent in both cases. Two shall only be mentioned as a proof of the general assertion.

I. The arrogant usurpations of the Roman See afford one sufficient reason. As the Roman pontiff had

had long "fitten in the temple of God, and exalted his throne above the thrones of every monarch," it was high time to wreft both the fceptre of Chrift and the fword of the monarch out of his impious and daring hands. The reformers rightly judged, that as the authority of Chrift is abfolutely incommunicable, they had right to difpoffefs him of a claim to which he had no title.

Meanwhile, it deferves recollection, that all the authority which that proud prieft claimed, and which kindled the indignation of reforming princes, was no other than that fame fovereignty which their own predeceffors once exercifed, and yielded to him; an authority to tyrannife over the confciences of princes and their fubjects; an authority to prefcribe the articles of their faith, the rules of their ignorant devotion, and the canons of their flavifh fuperftition: and that it was the very fame authority, which the European princes refumed when they renounced the Roman pontiff, and fubjected their people to a premunire, in cafe they continued their former connections with him.

Wherefore, as the vindication of Chrift's incommunicable authority was a principle motive with our pious reformers, princes as well as people; the fame generous and pious argument ought to prevail with every proteftant prince to drop all his claims to that fceptre, which without pious emotion, he cannot behold in the hand of the Italian bifhop. The precept is no lefs binding on them than on their fubjects—"Render unto Cæfar the things which are Cæfar's; and unto God the things which are God's." * They have done themfelves juftice; let them do Chrift juftice too. It will not be eafy to juftify royal pretenfions to dictate to the faith of chrif-

* Luke xx. 25.

tians, when pontifical pretenfions are exploded with fo much juftice and propriety.

2. The corrupt ftate, in which our worthy reformers beheld the chriftian fyftem, was another powerful fpring of laudable enterprize.

It hath been already fhewn, we hope with confiderable evidence that the adulterated ftate of the chriftian profeffion, from the fixth, to the fixteenth century, was owing to incorporations. If therefore, in this age, the reformation of thefe corruptions be reckoned an object not below the attention and pious zeal of the wifeft and beft men, in that age;—then the abolition of the acknowledged caufe of the continuation of thefe and fimilar adulterations of the chriftian religion, and of a too general corruption of manners cannot be beneath the notice and moft ferious deliberation of the Britifh Parliament. While the fame caufe continues, it muft ever produce fimilar effects Reformation attempted, without an abolition of ecclefiaftical incorporations, is no more than a well intended, but fruitlefs effort, to lop off fome branches, while the root and trunk remain untouched.

III. When the *great influence*, which incorporations have on the increafe of *infidelity* is maturely confidered, the *necessity* of their abolition will appear in a ftriking light.

All who are friends to chriftianity lament, that deifm is a prevailing evil in this age. Such will acknowledge, that every caufe of fo great a calamity ought to be removed. A fhort detail of fome things, which take their rife from incorporations, will fhew how hurtful they are to all thofe, whofe prejudices and vices have prepared them to liften to the deiftical firen.

1. Thofe

1. Those absurd ceremonies and superstitious rites, which associated with christian institutions, compose the incorporated rituals of Europe, are a stumbling block to many. They wear such a face of absurdity that every sensible deist must laugh at them, and at the devotion which the ignorant and the designing pretend to offer up to the Deity by them. Such men having been accustomed from their earliest years to view these idle rites, as christian institutions, and unwilling to give themselves the trouble to separate the chaff from the wheat, in their own ideas, reject the whole in gross, as if all was absurdity, cheat and imposition. It is not to be expected that such men can see, or will readily acknowledge the excellence of those divine institutions, which are mixed with, and whose glory is obscured by human inventions. Natural reason, especially when it is under a bias, cannot see the first, and it contemns the last. *

2. Nor less hurtful to such men is the horrid abuse of christian institutions in national churches. To instance only in one case,—what must the deist—what must even the unprincipled christian think, when he beholds the most sacred mysteries of the christian religion, converted by the highest national authority, and even at the solicitation, or with the concurring suffrage, of those, who pretend to be the successors of the holy apostles, into a *test* of loyalty to government; and, as such, appointed to be dispensed to every young gentleman, however profane, who hath got a cockade in his hat, and an ensign's commission in his pocket? Must he not conclude, that the nation, which authorizes such profanation of christian institutions,

---

* In the space of only a few years, and since the above Paragraph was written, the whole world has been an astonished Spectator of this melancholy truth, in the extraordinary Transactions of the French nation! *Audiat qui audire velit!*

stitutions, believes the christian system no more than he? Will he not be tempted to look down with sovereign contempt on such christians as the worst of hypocrites? And will he not naturally flatter himself and his infidel brethren as deserving the character of honest men, who dare not profess to believe, what pretended believers dare so openly to profane.

3. Promiscous admission to the sacraments, unavoidable in all incorporated churches, serves to confirm deists in their prejudices. Every subject, let his christian character be ever so exceptionable, provided he offend not against the laws of the state, is a good constitutional christian; and, as such, the national clergy are legally authorized, yea even bound to admit him to the most august mysteries. Infidels demand proofs of the exclusive title of the christian religion to inspiration and a divine origin from the superior sanctity of its professors. Yet it is notorious, that in national churches, which are the only churches allowed by law, and in which a public exhibition is made of the power of the christian religion, their legal members generally are not to be easily distinguished, either in piety or in the discharge of the social duties, from the votaries of Zoroaster, of Confucius, or of Mahumed. Must not, therefore, the deist felicitate himself in the impious inference, "that the claims of the christian religion, by being carried so high, defeat themselves, seeing the lies of these impostors seem to have an equal claim, if the morals of London, Paris or Petersburgh be compared with those of Persia, Pekin, or Constantinople?"

It is true, in no age hath God left the christian religion without a great cloud of witnesses to its exclusive claims! But where must they be looked for? Do not incorporations ordinarily shut them up in corners? Are they not ordinarily driven into separate communions; and reprefented, even to the enemies of chriftianity, as the worft of men? Thus, their practical teftimony to the truth and power of chriftianity is defeated, and even turned againft it. If they have continued in the communion of the allied church, like the feven thoufand, in Elijah's age, they have been chafed into the obfcure avenues of private life; and have there remained invifible to the friends, and unknown to the enemies of the chriftian religion.

4. All know that inconfiftencies, real or imagined, in the clerical character, furnifh a delicious morfel to every deift. Incorporations are one prolific caufe of thefe fcandalous inconfiftencies. They hold out riches and preferments to the incorporated clergy, as powerful lures to contradict by their practice thofe rules of chriftian behaviour, which their official character obliges them to teach their flocks. Deifts fee as well as others the national clergy breaking over all the laws of chriftianity, in order to become the public teachers of it: and they, who catch at every thing to confirm their prejudices naturally throw the odium of a practice, fo impious, upon revelation itfelf. All know and lament the triumph of deifm, during the flagitious reign of Charles II. And the judicious afcribe it to the fudden leaps, and the fcandalous compliances which the national clergy made at and after his acceffion to the throne. Livings, preferments and riches were only to be obtained by taking and breaking alternately the moft folemn engagements!

5. Incorporations confirm deifts in a perfuafion that the profeffion of the chriftian religion is nothing more than a political engine. Deifts can prove from facts, that all the national churches, and all

all their several creeds and liturgies have been incorporated with an express and avowed intention to serve the good or the bad purposes of government. If history can vouch any thing, it authenticates this fact. How natural, though very unjust, is the conclusion which infidels draw!

To all that has been alledged on this head, some may object "that since deism is only of a modern date, incorporations, which have existed these thirteen centuries, cannot be ranked among its causes. Why did they not produce it sooner? Why not all along?"

We answer; Deism, like some weeds, cannot grow in the shade. In order to form and finish the character of an infidel, knowledge and common sense must have first broken in upon his understanding, and put an end to the reign of gross ignorance and sportive superstition. Before the invention of printing and the Reformation which followed, many circumstances conspired to keep men in the impenetrable thickets of ignorance. The public exhibition of christianity, in the national churches, was exactly suited to that state of things. Gaudy ceremonies were invented to amuse the ignorant, great and small. Unmeaning meanings were affixed to them, to catch the attention of the superstitious. The gloomy doctrine of purgatory was invented to alarm their fears; while the senseless tales of all-powerful merit soothed their ignorant expectations. In short, in these dreary ages, men were thrown headlong into the deeps of ignorance, superstition and profaneness; and they long continued the fettered slaves and willing votaries of these gloomy deities, in consequence of the incorporation of a system, which was admirably well adjusted to prolong their reign, and to procure them a succession of worshippers. At length, however, light and liberty

liberty brake in upon their kingdom at once! What was the consequence?—Men saw that there is nothing in superstition but what is only calculated to give superficial pleasure or real pain to a warm and ungoverned fancy; and to alarm or sooth the passions, ordinarily under the immediate influence of that faculty. They therefore, either have attempted to separate the chaff from the wheat, by restoring christianity to its original purity, as was the case with the venerable reformers; or, having formed their ideas of christianity from the superstitions and absurdities, formerly or at present, mixed with the profession of it in national churches, they have been prejudiced against it, and have rashly enlisted themselves under the proud banners of deism. The history of infidelity shews, that the transition from the grossest superstition to the wildest scepticism is short and easy. No more is requisite to ripen the credulous dunce into the smart deist, but only a few beams of intellectual light, bursting in upon the unsanctified mind of a person who is a slave to the corrupt passions of his heart. During the long winter of popish darkness, the seeds of deism lay only under the clod, secure from harm, in the dry husk of monkish devotions, established by law. The approach of the sun of science, the diffusion of intellectual light, and the warmth accompanying the return of civil liberty, burst the brittle husk, and infidelity, like a tree, began to grow and flourish in the luxuriant soil of corrupt human affections.

IV. Incorporations, having such powerful influence on the increase of deism in christian nations, must be of very great obstruction to the propagation of christianity in Pagan countries. If this be true, it is another powerful argument for their abolition. It is superfluous to prove that the ruling powers of
christian

christian nations ought to make every lawful effort to propagate the gospel among the nations which know not " the true God and Jesus Christ whom he hath sent." The proof, therefore, of the assertion will be attempted and comprised in the two following observations.

1. Incorporations have been one of the chief reasons, why christianity has been losing ground, during these last twelve hundred years, in all countries and in all climes, to which the good hand of God, by the zealous efforts of the first christians, had triumphantly carried it.

This is a mournful fact, which, when the history of the sixth, seventh and eighth centuries is duly considered, cannot be denied. The author of the Revelations* proclaims it loudly. To what was the revolt of Asia and Africa from the christian faith owing? Was it not to the incorporation of christianity with the constitutions of the Eastern and Western empires? Did not the extinction of christianity attend or soon follow the revolt of the provinces, and the dismemberment of these empires?

2. Incorporations have been a principal reason why christianity has gained so little ground, among the Pagan nations, during these thirteen centuries.

It is in virtue of incorporations that *European* and *Christian* are words of the same signification with Africans, Asiatics and Americans. Now, such are the exhibitions of christianity by Europeans to these nations, that, incapable of knowing its spirit any other way, they naturally both curse them, and execrate their religion. How can it be otherwise? Can ever robbery, peculation, murder and every abomination recommend christianity to the approbation of even the most savage nations? Until the

* Rev. xi. and xii.

lives of chriſtians preach to the eyes of infidels, they will have no patience to lend their ears to the moſt forcible arguments, that may be offered in defence of chriſtianity. Nor is this ever to be expected till incorporations ceaſe, and chriſtianity be exhibited in the lives of its profeſſors ſuch as it is in the holy oracles of the living God. It is no proper recommendation of that holy religion to Indians and others to perpetrate the greateſt cruelties upon them in order to bring them over to worſhip two croſs-ſticks, a ruſty nail, or the putrified bones of ſome animal which they call a ſaint.

Nor are infidels ignorant, that the eſtabliſhed ſyſtems of chriſtianity are adjuſted for *extending* empire. Experience has taught them, that the zeal of thoſe charitable nations, who ſend miſſions among them, and pretend to pant for their ſalvation, is inflamed chiefly by a deſire of peculation and ſubjecting them to a foreign yoke. The ſagacious Chineſe well knew, that theſe were the pious deſigns of the Romiſh miſſions among them. The Aſiatics *know* the *diſintereſtedneſs* of our viſits to their country. Nor have Africans and Americans leſs reaſon to tremble at the name of chriſtian. Were incorporations aboliſhed, Pagans might then feel, that they might take Chriſt's yoke upon them, without having their necks galled with the yoke of any foreign potentate. But in the preſent ſtate of things, this is impoſſible!

In fine, we cannot help thinking, that ever ſince the chriſtian religion was corrupted by incorporations, and blended with the political conſtitutions of nations, in that corrupt ſtate, divine providence hath wiſely provided, that it ſhall *not* be propagated among the reſidue of the nations in a condition ſo much adulterated. We believe on the beſt grounds, that "all the ends of the earth ſhall ſee the ſalvation of of God;" but having reserved his best blessings for the last ages of the christian church; and foreseeing what the experience of Europe can too well attest, "that it is much easier to establish the christian religion in the most uncultivated nations, than to supplant an adulterated state of that religion when it hath been incorporated; he hath hitherto rendered abortive those efforts, which some of the protestant nations, with even the most disinterested intentions, have made, and are still making for the conversion of the savage nations.

V. With all, who sincerely pray for the conversion of the JEWS, it will be a weighty reason for abolishing incorporations, "that they are a principal obstruction to that much-desired event."

Should this be the truth, it is dangerous for any christian legislature to permit their continuance, on any political consideration whatever, lest they should incur the punishment of *Edom* by "standing in the crossway," and preventing their return to DAVID their PRINCE. The following considerations will set this assertion in a just light.

1. The Jews, in common with all other infidels, baptized, unbaptized or circumcised, having those grounds of prejudice, enumerated above, are not likely to join the christian standard, as long as incorporations, which have been shewn to be the causes of these prejudices, continue in christian nations. Besides, through their itinerant state of life, and by their general acquaintance with all nations, they behold, with growing contempt and hatred, the many hurtful consequences of political alliances between church and state. Nor are the lives of christians in national churches formed to confute their rooted prepossessions.

2. They behold *idolatry* incorporated with the
political

political conftitutions of many European nations; efpecially in thofe which arrogate the names *catholic* and *chriftian*. Idolatry is their juft abhorence: wherefore, as that is efteemed by all thofe nations, in which it is incorporated, to be the very *marrow* and *essence* of the chriftian religion, their infidelity is lefs wonderful than the obftinate attachment of pretended chriftians to that which they muft know to be the caufe of their infidelity. And as thofe churches, in which idolatry is eftablifhed, are of the greateft *eclat*, and pretend to be the only churches of Chrift upon earth; it is no wonder that they entertain unconquerable prejudices againft the chriftian fyftem, according to the exhibition which is made of it in thefe focieties.

Befides, they have felt the fiery breath of incorporated fects and fyftems. The *auto de fes* of Spain and Portugal are not calculated to cure them of their infidelity. If there were no other chriftianity befides that which is profeffed and breathes in incorporated churches, they would have too good reafon obftinately to maintain, that the perfecuting fpirit of incorporated fects is the true fpirit of chriftianity.

3. It is in confequence of incorporations, that the national *Shibboleths* are kept up with much fcandalous animofity among thofe kingdoms which are refpectively attached to thofe political engines of national malevolence. The Jews difperfed over the chriftian world, are fagacious enough to obferve this; and they afk with a Jewifh grin, to what fcheme of the chriftian religion they ought to attach themfelves, while the chriftians of every nation and of every incorporated fect are anathematizing one another without mercy, in every corner of the earth?

Befides, they know that, were they to defert Mo-
fes,

fies, and so acknowledge the advent of the Messiah, incorporations would oblige them in every country where they might chance to reside, to profess the national creed and use the established liturgy. Thus the Jews in Russia would be obliged by law to curse the christian Hebrews in Italy; and both would be obliged to anathematize the christian descendants of Abraham in England! The Jews are too strictly connected, ever to embrace christianity on these terms; and are too sagacious not to see, that it would be morally impossible for them to continue any longer a separate people.

Were they indeed, to embrace christianity, according to its present corrupt state, in the many jarring systems of Europe, over which they are scattered, they would not only become aliens and enemies to one another, as the several christian nations have been, and still continue to be; but they would be obliged to incorporate themselves with the several nations, in the political constitutions of which those religious systems which they are supposed to embrace, are effectually blended. Thus, they would be under a necessity of renouncing all *national expectations*, as a peculiar people, whom God, for some wise purpose, for so many ages, and under so many temptations, has miraculously preserved from mingling with the nations; and they would consent unto their final dissolution;—an event this, which is not to be expected; yea, we know not if it ought to be desired.

Were incorporations abolished; and were the kingdom of Christ to stand on its own basis, detached from all political connection with the nations of Europe;—the insuperable hinderances in the way of the conversion of the Jews would be removed at once; and with them, whatever obstructs many other grand events, which prophecy warrants us to expect. But as long as these continue the idols of christian nations, and an engine of policy to their rulers, it is hypocrisy and solemn mockery of the Majesty of heaven, when they pray for the conversion of that extraordinary people. It is an event, which, in such circumstances, is not an object of rational expectation; and therefore ought never to be made the matter of devout supplication at the throne of grace.

SECT. III.

The Abolition of Incorporations is both possible and safe.

THOUGH the reader should acknowledge that the two preceding sections amount to a proof of the *propriety* and the *necessity* of abolishing incorporations; yet he will hesitate still, unless the measure can be shewn to be both *practicable* and *safe*. This shall be attempted in this section.

I. The abolition of incorporations is *practicable*.

The proof of this proposition shall be attempted, by stating a comparison between the situation of affairs in Europe, both in church and state, at the Reformation, and the condition in which they appear at present. A just contrast will shew, that the Reformation in the sixteenth century was an undertaking much less hopeful than an abolition of incorporations can be in the eighteenth. An enumeration will set this matter in the best light.

1. As the proposed abolition, were it attempted, would strike at the pecuniary interest of the national clergy, it is no more than reasonable to fear, that they would exert all their influence, both to mar its success,

success, and to make its authors to repent the rashness of their enterprize.

But did not the same discouragement present itself, with additional circumstances of dismay, to the first reformers. Clergymen, then, had much more to lose than now. The reformers knew the extent of their riches; and how much the fear of losing them tends to rouse all the other passions. But churchmen now, have not the *sovereignty* and the riches of a whole country to lose by so necessary a reformation.

Besides, in the sixteenth century, the canonical obedience, which churchmen swore to the See of Rome, and the superstitious attachment they had to its religion, made them enemies to the sovereignty of their lawful princes. It became therefore necessary to degrade them, as well as to seize their enormous benefices. This stung them to the quick. This kindled their indignation. This suggested to them all those resentful measures which threw whole nations into confusion, rebellion and civil wars. But this is not the case now. Were government to abolish incorporations, there is no reason why it should degrade the present incorporated clergy, or deprive them of their revenues during their lives.

Nor ought it to be forgotten, that churchmen, in this age, pretend not to an equal degree of authority and influence, either in courts or among the populace, as at the Reformation. They cannot now lead their princes, nor controul their consciences. They cannot dictate to them at their council tables. The church then considered herself, as superior to the state, and wholly independent of the secular power. Now, she is become a subordinate branch in the political constitution, in the same manner as any of his majesty's courts. On account of the

clamours

clamours of a few interested individuals, shall the supreme authority of the nation not dare to amend any part of the political constitution, when it is found inconsistent with other parts, and hurtful to the rights and liberties of the subject? Was not the *Star Chamber* once a branch of the English constitution? Did not the Supreme power wisely and justly abolish it, because it was inconsistent with the rights and liberties of British subjects? Were the clamours of a few interested lawyers, the noise of some dignified clergymen, or even the strong reluctance of majesty itself against so salutary a measure, regarded in the smallest degree? just as little ought the vociferations of a few dignified clergymen be dreaded in the abolition of ecclesiastical incorporations.

2. It is probable that the annihilation of incorporations would be attended with a considerable degree of dissatisfaction among those, who, being zealous of ancient traditions and of the high claims of church-authority, would lose the power of trampling upon better christians than themselves. Those also who make religion an engine to monopolize places of honour and profit, would be certainly disappointed; and would as certainly grumble, that such sources of wealth should be laid open to those aliens of the British commonwealth, the dissenters.

But the same discouraging objects presented themselves to our reformers with aggravating circumstances. Incorporations are not so close and compact, as when the profession of popery was the only way to preferment both in church and state; and when no man could literally either buy or sell unless he had the mark of a beast in his forehead. Then, superstition and ignorance had made men brutal, cruel and ferocious. Now, true religion and sound learning have taught them to see objects in a very different light. Then, the incorporated system, being

ing properly a carnal scheme of wild superstition, and a mere political contrivance, was well adjusted to the political constitutions of the European nations. Now, the reformed systems are not so. Being much more agreeable to revelation, the connections which they have with political constitutions are forced, unnatural, and with the slightest touch dissoluble. In fine, the popish system taught its blind votaries to perpetrate the most inhuman cruelties on all, who should dare to attempt the smallest innovation, however necessary. These our worthy reformers had good reason to dread;—yet they attempted, persevered and prospered. Now, persecution is justly fallen into discredit in all protestant and even in some popish countries. All affect to hold it as a first principle, that persecution is irreconcilable with the spirit and maxims of the christian religion. Reformation, therefore, in so necessary an affair as that of incorporations, the never failing sources of persecution, hath nothing to fear from that discouraging object.

II. The abolition of incorporations is safe.

The truth of this proposition will best appear by stating a contrast between the inviting advantages which protestants now enjoy, and the forbidding difficulties, with which the reformers bravely struggled and at last overcame.

1. The advances which learning hath made, since the sixteenth century, deserve to be first considered.

Intellectual light hath now chased away that gross darkness, which during the middle ages, held all Europe in sleep and slavery. Religious objects are now seen in a very different light from that in which politicians beheld them, when all useful learning was shut up with the gloomy sons of darkness in the cloisters and their cells. Our reformers were not
only

only obliged to undergo the labour of cleanfing the Augæn ftable; but, at the fame time, were expofed to all the inconveniences and dangers which neceffarily attend an attack upon cloiftered ignorance and interefted bigotry. In this age, we enjoy what thefe men only beheld in idea, and in hope; and that for which they ftruggled hard, that we, their children, might inherit. We now have entered into their labours. Sitting under our vine, the rights of human nature are both underftood and efteemed. The right of private judgment is now no longer afferted only in corners. The immediate dependence of the human underftanding and confcience on God alone is generally confeffed. The diftinction between the kingdom of Chrift, and the nations of this world, is almoft univerfally acknowledged. And the defence of perfecution is abandoned by all; a few only excepted, who, permitted of God, through the force of ignorance, prejudice or intereft, to employ their mouths and pens in the fervice of the old murderer, ferve to fhew the neceffity of removing from political conftitutions every thing, which men of fuch a temper might lay hold of, in any future period, for kindling the flames of perfecution in the European kingdoms.

2. At the Reformation, the incorporated fyftem was fo clofely connected with the *titles*, which chriftian princes had to their crowns, that the champions of reformation had too good reafon to fear that their refpective fovereigns would view their attempt in the light of a rebellion. Facts afterward fhewed that they were not miftaken. But, in this age, no fuch object of difcouragement can prefent itfelf to any European legiflature. Every fovereign knows, that his royal titles are not fo clofely connected with any religious fyftem, that he fhould have any thing to fear from the legal abolition of incorporations,

incorporations. Happy is it for Great Britain, that her monarchs, continuing proteftants, are not beholden to any religious fyftem, for their right to fway the Britifh fceptre.

3. Nor is the fad experience which all nations, at one time or other, have had of the pernicious confequences of incorporations, a lefs encouraging motive to proteftant legiflatures to attempt their abolition. Though, before the Reformation, the nations of Europe had been grievoufly galled with that yoke; yet, being accuftomed to flavery, they were infenfible of the grievance, and couched down with fo much filly patience between the two burdens of civil and ecclefiaftical tyranny, that it became a hard tafk to convince them that they were flaves. But now, liberal fentiment flourifhes in every nation, popifh as well as proteftant. Civil liberty hath had a rapid progrefs. Men of all ranks and of all denominations have tafted its delicious fweets; and therefore has their eyes open on every object which has even the remoteft tendency either to enlarge or abridge it. It has been fhewn, that abolifhing incorporations is a meafure both *just* and *necessary*; and therefore, as mankind are now awake to their own intereft, it is more than probable, that, would legiflatures fet about it in good earneft, it would be crowned with every degree of fuccefs.

4. We fhall only add, that liberty to think, fpeak and write is now the acknowledged privilege of chriftians; a privilege denied at the reformation. Then, to have fpoken againft the moft abfurd trick of wild fuperftition was ordinarily punifhed with a ftake. To have heard, even the neareft relation do it, and not immediately to become informer was the fure way to fhare the fame cruel fate. To have given houfe-room to the oracles of God was the unpardonable fin. Now, men are allowed to fpeak and

and write. Freed from the galling yoke of arbitrary power in the state, and from the no less grievous burden of priestly imposition, in the church, they *may* safely suffer themselves to be instructed, *may* yield to the evidence of truth, and *may* listen to the dictates of their own consciences, without any to make them afraid.

If this be a just state of affairs throughout Europe, and especially in Great Britain; a neglect to attempt the abolition of incorporations, and thereby to perfect the reformation, will betray a coolness in the cause of religion, only equalled by its own ingratitude. This age seems to be marked out by the providence of God as most proper for annihilating every relict of antichristian slavery, especially in protestant countries. That work was ever *reasonable*, and always *necessary*; now, it appears to be *practicable* and altogether *expedient*.

At the Reformation, all things could not be accomplished at once. The Lord did not see it proper to finish it in one generation. He is the God of order and not of confusion. As he made the world in the succession of six days, and even " worketh hitherto;" so he restores his church to her primitive purity by slow degrees, and in the course of ages. Like a wise œconomist, he hath assigned work for all his servants; and he " opens a great door and effectual" for some eminent pieces of service, which he expects they should accomplish, in those ages, in which he calls them into being by his power, and unto action by his providence. Such a door was opened to the reformers; and they bravely did their work, even in the heat of the day. They were not warranted to attempt the work of succeeding generations. While an unerring providence set them their task, it shut the door against their interfering with that which was reserved for their sons unborn,

unborn, and for their childrens children. The political state of Europe forbad their enterprizing the abolition of incorporations. She was not ripe for it, without the interpofition of a miracle. The minds of mankind were fo much under the influence of prejudice in favour of the old channel, in which things both facred and civil had run, during more than a thoufand years, that they could not, in one age, be fully difengaged from the objects of their miftaken attachment. The miftrefs experience behoved firft to have performed her tafk, before they could either think juftly or act wifely in regard of incorporations.

But in this age, fhe feems to have finifhed all her lectures upon that fubject. Thofe centuries, which have elapfed fince the reformation, have exhibited fuch fcenes, as ferve to demonftrate the noxious nature and fatal confequences of incorporations. The fame infinitely wife God, who called our anceftors to attack the papal *supremacy*, is now directing and encouraging men of authority, by fimilar providential incidents, to affert the *spirituality, freedom* and *independence* of Chrift's kingdom; to bear witnefs to his title to fway his own fceptre; and to endeavour, in their feveral fpheres of action, to fettle the church on her own foundations.

May God, who hath already laid the foundation of the glorious Reformation, fpeedily animate thofe inftruments for whom the honour is referved, to bring forth the copftone in triumph, crying, Grace! Grace! unto it: Amen;

CHAP. VIII.

Answers to the most considerable Objections against the Abolition of Incorporations.

THE imperfect state of human knowledge, and of the means of communicating it, render it impossible to lay down any subject in such a manner as to anticipate all objections against it. Besides, it is with the human mind in reasoning, as it is with the natural eye in the act of vision. An object may appear regular and beautiful from one station, while to another, yea even to the same eye, placed in a different point, it may seem to be an unshapen block. In like manner, any object of knowledge may seem to be congruous to reason, at the same time that others, contemplating the same object in a disadvantageous situation, may imagine that it is inconsistent with reason. In the present case, it is not doubted but some, prepossessed in favour of incorporations, have piled up an heap of objections against their abolition. The author, however, after having viewed the subject in every possible light; after having supposed himself to be—a designing politician,—a church dignitary,—a beneficed clergyman,—a furious bigot,—a zealot for uniformity, —an advocate for the tradition of the elders,—and fifty other characters of similar importance; and after having felt his pulse in each of them;—is more confirmed concerning the *utility*, *necessity* and *practicability* of the measure. Some slight inconveniences might follow. This is no more than what necessarily attends the present imperfect state of things. But if these should be less and fewer than such as attend incorporations ordinarily; and should the

the advantages to the church and fociety counterbalance them (both which have been proved) no cowardly apprehenfions ought to ftand one moment in the way of executing fo neceffary,—fo falutary a fcheme. But that nothing may appear to be defignedly wanting, we fhall attempt anfwers to the moft plaufible objections againft it.

SECT. I.

"*That the Abolition of Incorporations would abridge Royal Prerogative, and endanger the Safety of Religion,*"—*Anfwered.*

THOSE who imagine, in the fpirit of falfe patriotifm, that the conftitutional prerogatives of the prince are unfriendly to the liberty of the fubject, deferve contempt. Thofe who attempt to perfuade mankind that it is fo, merit the refentment of both the prince and his people. Juft prerogative is effentially neceffary for the protection of right, and the execution of juftice. The rights of the fovereign and of the fubject muft rife or fall together. We may therefore fuppofe, that not only the devoted flaves of prerogative, but even the fober friends of the rights, both of princes and their people will be jealous of the meafure propofed, as tending to abridge that power, *circa sacra*, which the European nations, ever fince their erection, have tamely yielded to their fovereigns. Such will object " that the abolition of incorporations would leffen that power and influence which princes have always claimed over ecclefiaftical perfons; and that, befides, sides, it would abridge, if not annihilate their authority in all ecclesiastical causes."

Nor are those deserving of less contempt, who in the spirit of deism and modern latitudinarianism affect to think that all princes ought to be the sons of Gallio; that the legislative and executive powers ought to act with the most perfect indifference towards all religion, true as well as false; and that they ought to give no preference, even to that profession of religion, which, according to their best lights, they approve for themselves, and account to be most deserving the choice of every good man. Persons who esteem religion, and account it of the last importance to themselves; who have studied and known the exclusive right which christanity has to be accounted, received, and professed as the only true religion; and who are alarmed at the growth of deism in Europe;—may fear, that the abolition proposed would gratify the wishes of a certain description of men, who, if the tendency of their writings be a just commentary on the *penchant* of their hearts, give reason to think that the restoration of Paganism and the revival of the Julian age would be very agreeable to them. Such pious characters may object " that the abolition of incorporations would put christianity, which alone has a right to be professed and patronized, on a level with every false religion; that it would tie up the hands of both the legislative and executive powers, in christian nations, from positively patronizing the cause of christianity; and that it would contradict the doctrine of all the protestant churches, in their articles and confessions concerning the authority of the ruling powers about ecclesiastical objects."

As a satisfactory answer to these several objections cannot be made without ascertaining the nature of that establishment of christain churches for which

the

the writer has declared himself an advocate, he begs the candour as well as the patience of the reader, while he lays open his thoughts upon the subject at some length.

I. While the abolition of incorporations would both *fully* make, and peaceably leave, every prince the common father and guardian angel of all his subjects, according to the degree of their political and civil merit, " there is no branch of prerogative" which any prince *ought* to claim, which could suffer by that necessary measure. That influence which princes claim, and ever since the Reformation, have claimed over the clergy, beyond what they have a just right unto over all other classes of subjects, is no other besides what the court of Rome claimed, in the ages of papal tyranny and triumph over the nations of Europe. It is that power, which the christian emperors claimed before papal usurpations had come to their height. It is that same influence, which the bishop of Rome appropriated, upon the dissolution of the empire, and its division among the *ten kings*. It is, in fine, that same papal power, which the protestant princes severally resumed, when they wrested their sceptres out of the hands of Rome's proud pontiff, at the Reformation. Seeing the uses he had put it unto, and falsely imagining that it would be of the same advantage to them, they claimed it as a prerogative of their respective crowns. During the dreary ages of pontifical encroachments, the pall and the crosier were the gift of Rome. The right of investitures was claimed by the popes, and yielded by many of the princes. In consequence, the mitred clergy were dependent on the pope, and, at any time were ready to abet his cause against their own sovereigns. At the Reformation, therefore, the princes, who had long,

with

with indignation, beheld this foreign dependence, and its *uses*, made the mitred clergy immediately dependent on themselves, by reserving to the crown the nomination to bishoprics; and made the inferior ecclesiastics mediately their dependents, by retaining and confirming the right of patronage to bishops, chapters and lay patrons.

But though some princes have availed themselves of this universal and servile dependence of the incorporated clergy upon themselves, to carry forward measures hostile to the peace and prosperity of the nation, subversive of public liberty, and eventually ruinous, as well as scandalous to the church; yet no wise, no virtuous prince ever used so mischievous a tool of government. He who has ever dared to do it, has always made himself suspected to his subjects; rendered his measures contemptible; and hastened the decline, and sometimes the fall, of his own greatness.

No wonder! Such a dependence is founded on injustice; and every fabric, so founded, will sooner or later fall upon, and bury in its ruins the man who imprudently seeks for shelter under it. No monarch can have a right to bribe one part of his subjects, by bestowing upon them the spoils of private or public property, to become the tools of court intrigue. Yet, this is done in all incorporated churches. Their revenues are often paid their clergy by those who never employed them, and against whose liberties they sell themselves, in order to purchase that reward of unrighteousness. It follows, therefore, that were incorporations abolished, princes would only lose what never was of any real use and advantage to them. Yea, they would be gainers. While the *undue* influence of the crown would cease, they would be no more tempted by that object, to hurt themselves, tarnish the glory of their
crowns,

crowns, and injure their subjects, by employing the pretended ministers of heaven to enslave their subjects on earth.

But it does not hence follow that they would lose any degree of *due* influence over the ministers of Christ in their dominions. No: they would reap services from them much more important than ever were, or could be performed by an incorporated clergy. These being bound to abet indifferently the tyrannic intrigues, as well as the patriotic plans of the court; and being seldom needed or employed, but in the former; are, when called upon, always justly suspected by all the other description of subjects, in the nation. The public takes the alarm; and the consequence ordinarily is,—even the best schemes, instead of being promoted, are retarded, and often ruined, through their interference. But were incorporations at an end, ministers, being wholly independent of undue influence, and being bound by all the ties of patriotism, loyalty and religion, would act with vigour, and without suspicion, in the cause of their prince and of their country. Being the ministers of peace and the public teachers of christianity, they would pray for the peace of their country; they would preach peace and practise it. They would demonstrate by their lives, as well as by their doctrine, that christianity inspires loyalty, and that the honour due to the image of God's authority, on earth, is strictly connected with the fear of God himself, in heaven, and with an entire and conscientious subjection to the authority of the Redeemer at his right-hand. They would be always true patriots. Actuated by the love of God, they could not but love his vicegerent, and zealously abet all his acts of government for the good of their fellow subjects, and for the interest of those flocks " over which the Holy Ghost," not the civil magistrate, giftrate, "hath made them bishops." Devoted to their service, they would be conscientiously attached to every measure of political administration, which has a tendency to make them secure, easy and prosperous in society, in order that, without distraction, they may attend to the important concerns of religion. No more would the clergy of one sect only be the devoted friends of the prince. As every description of christians would have their natural, civil and religious rights fully secured to them; and further, would meet with public encouragement, in proportion as they should excel, in realizing christianity, by performing all the substantial duties of religion and patriotism; their ministers would vie with one another in acts of public, as well as of private utility; and, by their instructions and example, would excite and animate their flocks to do the same.

In the present state of things, the case is far otherwise. The rewards of rapacity and unrighteousness are rigidly exacted of the subject without distinction, and paid to the clergy of the incorporated sect, in order that they may insultingly crow over every other religious denomination. Is it in the power of human nature to be sincerely attached to the service of a government, whose administration is so marked with partiality? Thank God! Even in these circumstances, protestant dissenters have always approved themselves faithful,—often, the most faithful to virtuous administrations, even in the most trying cases. But what would these sons of liberty and righteous zeal not do,—what indeed would not all do, were liberty and right properly secured to them, without these provoking discriminations!

II. By the abolishing of incorporations, the "SUPREMACY of the prince, over all causes ecclesiastical," would indeed cease. But what then?

1. Would

1. Would he lose any dignity which he, of *right*, ought to claim? in this age of liberty and common-sense, it cannot be said. No potentate has a right to dictate to the understanding and to controul the conscience of one man, in things of pure revelation. How much less of a whole nation, or of a whole empire! can he answer for his subjects at the dread tribunal of God? Can he endure eternal punishment for them, in case he dictate falsehood for truth, and force them into the paths of rebellion against their Maker and their Redeemer? Can he find security to ten or twelve millions of souls, that they shall be indemnified, and kept altogether without harm, in case he abuse his high claim? has he a right to consider himself as the only rational and accountable creature in his dominions; and to treat all mankind, within the reach of his sceptre, as beasts, which have no understanding?

2. Would he lose any thing which he may *honourably* claim? This can be affirmed with as little consistency and respect for majesty. The pope claims to be supreme head over all causes ecclesiastical, or to have all such causes ultimately referred to him for decision, as supreme judge. This very claim is allowed, by all protestants, to mark him out as the "man of sin," who, while claiming a right to controul the consciences of Christendom, "sitteth in the temple of God, and exalteth himself above all that is called God, or is worshipped." Now, shall it be reckoned a prerogative, worthy of protestant princes,—of British princes, to succeed that old friar in all the arrogance of his pride, and in all the blasphemy of his fastidious claims? Do their interested flatterers consult their honour or their safety, when they confer upon them one of the incommunicable prerogatives of the Deity himself? Do they know what they are doing, when they

make their own princes, whom God has mercifully delivered from papal usurpations, sharers with the court of Rome, in the guilt of similar usurpations? Can they be ignorant, that for such incroachments on the prerogative of the Most High, Heaven's heavy wrath hath already fallen on the church of Rome, and will never cease to pursue her, till all the earth hear the angelic voice crying,—" Babylon the Great is fallen, is fallen, and is become the habitation of devils!"*

3. Would majesty lose any thing which it may *wisely* claim? History forbids this also to be affirmed. Ever since that prerogative was rashly assumed by Henry VIII. no British prince ever claimed it, and availed himself of it, without fixing an indelible stain upon his memory, which even his best and wisest actions could never efface. What is blame-worthy in the long, auspicious reign of the celebrated Elizabeth, besides her claiming this branch of prerogative; and her acting, too much like her royal father, up unto the tyrannic spirit of it? Did it not make James I. ridiculous to foreigners, and the Merry-Andrew of his own subjects? Did it not bring Charles I. to the block? did it not render the reign of the second Charles dishonourable to himself, and superlatively inauspicious to the worthiest part of all his subjects? Did it not chace the second James from the throne, and send the royal family of Stuart into ignominious exile? And, in fine, has the illustrious race of princes which now so auspiciously sways the British sceptre, and has been always too much attached to the honour of God, and too attentive to the welfare of their subjects, ever to avail themselves of that claim, been, on that account, less illustrious, less sovereign princes than those of the former tyrannic race?

* Rev. xviii. 2.

Were

Were incorporations juſt now aboliſhed, the proteſtant ſovereigns in Europe would ſtill inherit every thing that is ſubſtantial and worthy of their royalty, in that branch of their prerogative. That coſtly gem, freed from an inglorious ſpeck, would ſhine with much more radiance and true beauty. At the Reformation, they found it neceſſary, to aſſert their right to be the ſovereigns of eccleſiaſtics as well as of every other deſcription of their ſubjects; and as theſe had very often greatly diſturbed ſociety, by appealing eccleſiaſtical cauſes to Rome, they laudably put a ſtop to that abſurd and rebellious practice, by providing that theſe cauſes ſhould in future be finally decided at home. Now, the abolition of incorporations ſtill leaves that right with princes. Though ſovereigns cannot, without uſurping upon the authority of God and the rights of conſcience, be the ultimate judges in things purely eccleſiaſtical, or bring them for deciſion to their tribunals; yet they can do every thing which wiſe, political and pious princes will do, and ought to do. They will provide that theſe cauſes be finally determined among the parties concerned in them. They will prevent diſorders, tumults and every act of injuſtice among the parties. And they will, with an impartial hand, puniſh every act of delinquency againſt the order and laws of ſociety.

Indeed, were incorporations removed, eccleſiaſtical cauſes, however important they may be in themſelves, and to the parties concerned in them, in regard to another world, would become perfectly innocent, as far as civil ſociety is connected with them. On that account, they would become as unworthy of royal interference as any of thoſe harmleſs controverſies, which are daily ſtarting up, and with much decency agitated among the different ſects of the literati in the philoſophical world. Nor would

would majesty suffer any more from its ceasing to act as sovereign umpire in the former, than it does in the latter case. Incorporations alone, making these causes first dangerous to society, and formidable to its civil rulers, by engaging the secular interests and the inflamed passions of mankind in them, swells them into that degree of importance, which ranks them with objects, worthy the monarch's attention and officious interference. How impolitic in the extreme must it be, to make even the most innocent and harmless things, the most hurtful, merely that the executive part of government may find employment! How absurd to raise a political storm, only that royalty may display its authority in vainly attempting to smooth those swelling billows, which its own improper interference had raised? And how unreasonable to object to the abolition of that which has been proved to be so eminently hurtful, both to civil and religious society, merely because it would ease sovereigns of the trouble of extinguishing those flames which it necessarily kindles among their subjects!

III. The serious christian, whose heart sympathetically trembles for the ark of God, has no reason to be alarmed for the safety of christianity. He need not fear, that, were incorporations abolished, infidelity would triumph, and deists obtain their wishes. There is no reason to object, " that christianity, which alone, on account of its divine character, has a right to political patronage, would be put, or left on a level with imposture and superstition."

No! Christianity can never be on a level with any false religion. Her own intrinsic worth raises her infinitely above all,—even the most specious and the best guarded system of imposture. The HIGH-
EST

est himself has always guarded her rich treasures, and ever will preserve her sacred foundations. Legions of devils, pouring from the gates of hell, cannot prevail against her. Craft, aided by cruelty, cannot move her from her foundation; nor detach a single stone from her superstructure. Her weapons, it is true, are not carnal, but spiritual; but they are always, and in every conflict, greatly triumphant. No daring foe could ever pluck the laurel from her brow; or snatch the palm from her hand. Her greatest enemies cannot endure the effulgence of her shield; nor cease from trembling at the shaking of her spear. She beholds them flying her approaches with precipitate steps; and, at a safe distance collecting their scattered remains. These her friends always find, either deeply entrenched in the howling desert of ignorance and error, behind a strong breast-work of political arrangements and penal statutes; or sneaking away into the fortress of prejudice, which, with unavailing pains, they labour to render impregnable by all the contemptible arts of sophistry, and by all the mock artillery of profane wit and sarcastic raillery.

But the anxious friends of incorporations will think that they have still reason to object, " that if these were abolished, christianity would be left upon a level with every false religion that might dare to shew its hideous form among the ambitious demagogues, or the mad enthusiasts of a nation."

We answer,—No: and the reasons will be assigned, with more propriety under the next article.

Meanwhile, there is, it is presumed, reason to alledge, that incorporations are the only things that sink, or can sink christianity to a level with any false religion.

Imposture is destitute of a firm foundation of its own to stand upon. However specious it may appear

pear to be, it cannot abide the eye of the examiner. Reason revolts at it; and revelation condemns it. Its only dependence, therefore, is upon something adventitious. It naturally turns its eye to political authority, and the power of the sword. Destitute of arguments, it can only force its way by sanguinary laws. These it procures, by all its own arts of fallacy and fraud, to be enacted against recusants and dissenters. Cruel laws and preposterous measures are ever in its suit. Injustice is the foundation of its throne. Ruthless tyranny is its sceptre. Incapable of subsisting but by plunder and rapine, it robs mankind of all their rights. At its tribunals, even the rights of conscience cannot be redeemed at a less ransom than that of mens lives.

In all these respects incorporations level christianity with base imposture. Though the religion of JESUS be the only revealed religion on earth, and is entitled to build her throne on the ruins of imposture in every possible shape; yet let it not be once said, that she ever claimed, or ever permitted any of her friends to claim, to build her kingdom on the ruins of natural justice, and the wreck of mankind's inviolable rights! Let none of either her mistaken friends or her designing foes dare to affirm, that she authorizes any description of christians to build even their purest profession of attachment to her doctrines and institutions, on the supersedure of the rights of one individual, whether he be her devoted friend, or her determined foe! NEMINI NOCEAS is her device armorial. " Thou shalt not kill."—" Thou shalt not steal."—" Thou shalt not even covet" are her laws. But wherever christianity is incorporated with the political constitution of any nation, and the national profession of the established system is enforced by penal laws, which provide that every subject, whether he be
convinced

convinced or not of its orthodoxy, shall profess himself a believer in it, under pain of forfeiting life, or even the least considerable part of his property;—she is instantly metamorphosed into a public robber, and, as such, is exposed to the hatred of heathens and the execrations of all their enemies. She is no more that last and best gift of God to Man;—that true christianity, which in the scriptures, her only glass, smiles with benignity upon all the rights of mankind. No! 'Tis a dragon, called by her sacred name. Let it even be admitted, that the incorporated system is the most orthodox exhibition of christianity; yet, being thus incorporated, it ceases, *ipso facto*, to be any longer pure and unadulterated. Yes; genuine christianity lifteth up her voice, and crieth—Do not kill,—do not rob,—do not even covet. But incorporated christianity, if the avowed principles and practices of its votaries can ascertain its nature, allows them to profess before the world, and to write it with the blood of all its enemies, that it authorizes them to commit every act of injustice and cruelty in order to propagate its tenets, perpetuate its reign, and enrich its friends!

But, after all, may we not ask, When and where, since the famous edict of Constantine, was christianity established in any of the European nations? That holy religion is not confined to any one sect of christians, nor exhausted by its creed. Yet that which has been the object of all the European incorporations, these thousand years, has been the peculiar creed only, of one particular description of christians. Now, these pretended incorporations of christianity have not only authorized christians to commit violence upon the rights of mankind, who were enemies to, or ignorant of christianity, but also upon the lives or liberties of even its best friends, who, though they dissented from the incorporated

creed

creed in some of its articles, were notwithstanding, much nearer the true, scriptural idea of that divine religion than their privileged persecutors. Thus, christianity is sunk even *below* the level of the very worst religions, which ever disgraced mankind. What false religion ever turned about and devoured its own children? Did even the many-headed monsters of ancient Paganism devour its own offspring? Did it command the votaries of Jove to murder the worshippers of Apollo? Did ever any of the heathen themselves so far forget the reverence they had for it, as to affirm that it did? But incorporations make christianity turn indiscriminately upon her best friends and her worst enemies; yea, to commit violence upon herself, as professed and exhibited by her best friends, and to devour them, together with the flesh of her own arm!

But we confess, that we have spoken improperly, when, in compliance with vulgar prejudice, we have talked of the establishment of *christianity*. That holy religion is naturally incapable of any establishment, beside that which the Divine Spirit always gives it by the irresistible force of its own evidence, both external and internal, in the understandings and consciences of christians. It is the PROFESSION of christianity alone, which is capable of an incorporation. Now, the profession of the christian religion may either be *general* or *particular*. It is *general* when christians make profession of it, as it is exhibited in the holy scriptures, without any regard to the particular creed of any particular church, or description of christians. It is particular, when any church makes profession of christianity, according to their own idea of it, as that is exhibited in their own particular and characterizing symbol, or confession of faith.—This necessary distinction being

premised,

premised, we shall join the two following observations.

1. The general profession of christianity never was incorporated in any empire or nation since the first edicts of Constantine. The edicts in the latter years of his reign, and in the reigns of his sons and successors were not general, but particular incorporations of certain sects, who disputed by turns for them, in order to kill and devour one another.

Wherefore, had Constantine's general edicts not been preclusive, and armed with penal sanctions against the persons and just rights of those, who could not at first, with the concurrence of their understandings and consciences, become converts to christianity, they would have been unquestionably right. Much was in his power to do for the profession and the professors of that holy religion, without disgracing it, by making them robbers of others rights. Much he might have done for rendering the profession of it both safe and even honourable, without converting it into a false and lying profession, importing that christianity licences its friends to fatten on the spoils of its enemies.

Christianity indeed, on account of its divine original, has an exclusive right to be both professed and patronized? But by whom? By none surely but those who know and acknowledge that right. With contempt, that holy religion rejects the fictitious right, for which some of its pretended friends so warmly contend, to be professed and openly avowed by those who are blind to its evidence. It pronounces all such professors, hypocrites; and all who forcibly extort such a profession, persecutors and murderers. Constantine, therefore, acted laudably, both when, from conviction, he embraced and professed christianity himself; and when he patronized the profession of it by others, by every possible encouragement,

couragement, which he could hold up, confiftent with private right, the laws of civil fociety, and the genius of the chriftian religion itfelf. But that fame religion bound his hand from afferting and fupporting a right which it reprobates,—a right to be profeffed by thofe, who faw not its evidence, and could only be dragged to its altars by the chains of violence.

It is no lefs true, that no falfe religion can have a right to be profeffed or patronized. No lie can have a right to be patronized by the delegated powers of the God of eternal truth. A religion muft be right, before it can have a right to be profeffed or encouraged. Conftantine, therefore, acted virtuoufly, when he renounced the profeffion of paganifm himfelf; and when he availed himfelf of every mean, which the gofpel allows, and which truth and juftice confecrate, to perfuade others to abandon it. But if he proceeded to violence; if he invaded the rights of human nature in the cafe of any, who did not fee the evidence of chriftianity, and were, on that account, morally incapable of making a profeffion of it, as *true*, and the *only* true religion, without lying to both God and man; or if he invaded private right, by penal laws, fufpending the enjoyment of civil property and privileges upon the condition of embracing chriftianity;—if he did any, or all of thefe, he went beyond the line which chriftianity had marked out to him; and his profeffion of it became a lie upon it. It nowhere authorizes fallible mortals, of any rank whatever, and however much convinced in their own minds, to intrude upon the feat of God's moral government in the bofoms of other men; to fnatch the reins of moral controul out of his hands; and by fanguinary laws, to force accountable beings to lie to the Holy Ghoft. It no where warrants any to violate the laws

of

of justice, by depriving any of the sons of Adam of their property or their lives, merely because, not having yet perceived the wisdom of christianity, they are morally incapable of making a *true* profession of her right to universal empire; and, yet, are too honest to make a *false* one. But all persecutors say, that christianity allows all this; and that it is their godly zeal for its rights, which prompts them to perpetrate all this. They lie. Their profession of christianity is therefore a lie against it.

2. All the incorporations of modern Europe are particular establishments.—It is not the profession of christianity, according to the idea given of it in the New Testament, which is incorporated with the political constitution in any country of Europe; but it is the profession of that holy religion, according to the view given of it in some particular system, symbol, or confession of faith.

Upon the slightest view of these, it is plain, that the exhibition of that holy religion in some symbols, differs essentially, in some articles, from that in others. Is christianity, therefore, vague and various? God forbid! All this variety and contrariety arise from the different views, which different men, under the influence of different prejudices and passions (chiefly, indeed, occasioned by incorporations) have gotten of it. It is, therefore, certain, that no one profession of christianity, in the eyes of those of other professions, is compleat; and that no one professional symbol so far monopolizes the whole of christianity, so as to leave no share of it to others.

It is hence plain, that a particular incorporation is not an establishment of christianity. It is only an incorporation of a particular creed, which is reputed by all other descriptions of christians, adhering to opposite symbols, to be a defective exhibition of christianity. Besides, admitting the compleatness of the exhibition; one defcription of chriftians can never exclufively poffefs themfelves of all the chriftianity in the world, leaving no fhare of that treafure to other denominations. They alfo, doubtlefs, poffefs lefs or more of it, proportionably as their profeffional creeds are more or lefs conformable to the idea of it in revelation. If this be juft, it follows, that the incorporation of one creed, however compleat, is no eftablifhment of chriftianity, or of the profeffion of it. Not of chriftianity, becaufe, though it were allowed that the religion of the incorporated fect is eftablifhed, the very act of incorporation puts chriftianity under a public, parliamentary interdiction, as fhe is found in the creeds of other denominations.—Not of the profeffion of it, becaufe, notwithftanding one particular profeffion be patronized, every other profeffion, even of the fame articles, becaufe they are prefented in a different form, is put under the ban of national authority, and prohibited under certain penalties. Befides, the fuppofed compleat exhibition of chriftianity, which is honoured with an incorporation, by that very incorporation ceafes to be compleat! Yes; it lies againft chriftianity, by avowing that fhe allows her friends to turn their backs, even upon herfelf, if fhe be in any inftance profeffed defectively by others, and to murder their perfons or rob their treafures, becaufe they confcientioufly do fo!

IV. The abolition of incorporations by no means infers the annihilation of all civil eftablifhments and legal fecurities in favour of religious profeffions. None have any reafon to object, " that the meafure propofed would bind up the hands of the legiflative and executive powers, in chriftian nations, from
publicly

publicly and positively patronizing the profession of christianity among their christian subjects."

The very reverse is the case. We avow, "That christianity being the only and true religion of revelation on earth, hath an inherent and exclusive right to be professed by all the sons of Adam; that every profession of it ought to be patronized and established by the ruling powers of every christian nation, in exact proportion, as these powers, judging for themselves only, view these professions more or less perfect and agreeable to the idea of it, given in the oracles of revelation; and that were incorporations abolished, the civil powers, instead of having their authority and influence abridged, would find themselves more at liberty to serve the interests of religion effectually, than ever they have done since the age of Constantine."

1. "Christianity being the only true religion of revelation, hath an inherent and exclusive right to be professed by every son of Adam."

The truth of this proposition cannot be doubted by any, who without prejudice, and an unworthy attachment to some speculative scheme, or practical course of libertinism, has read and duly considered the many judicious productions of this age, in defence of christianity, against the repeated illiberal attacks of pretended freethinkers and infidels. No religion, falsely boasting of a revelation from the Father of lights, can have a right to be professed. Who ever dared to affirm that a lie hath a right to be told and avowed? The teller had indeed a right to have examined into the truth or falsehood of it, before he told it; but having affirmed it, he hath transgressed the laws of justice as well as truth. His ignorance and precipitation could never confer a *right* to lie; and his sin is proportioned to the means he had of being ascertained of the truth, and
his

his diligence in the use of these means. As truth alone hath an inherent right to be told; so the true religion alone possesseth an exclusive title to be professed and publicly avowed.

But ought every son of Adam to profess christianity, whether he apprehend its evidence, or not? We answer,—The question implies an absurdity. What is it for any to profess the christian religion? Is it not to avow that he believes that it is true upon evidence? And can he do so, in consistency with veracity, before he perceive its evidence? Can any man be in duty bound to make a lie? Yet every man is bound, by the open and avowed pretensions, which christianity itself makes of its being the only true religion, to examine with attention, candour and impartiality, its evidence and the grounds of its high claim. If, after examination, he embrace and make profession of it, he acts in a manner worthy of that religion which he now believes. It is all light,—all evidence; and condemns the man who professes himself its votary upon grounds inferior to full conviction. If he be blind to its evidence; and if, rejecting that holy religion, he embrace and make profession of one, falsely professing itself to be divine; he avows a couplet of lies. He says, that christianity, after examination of its evidence is false: and a false religion is true. His guilt therefore, before the God of truth, is proportionate to the means he had of discovering truth and avoiding mistakes; and to the degree of his own diligence in the due use of these means. He may be sincere; but as the matter of his profession is falsehood; and the reasons of his making it are ignorance, prejudice and precipitation; the sincerity of his heart cannot wholly excuse his crime, much less justify his profession, and entitle him to affirm falsehoods in the presence of the God of truth.

2. " Every

2. "Every profession of christianity ought to be patronized and established by the ruling powers of every christian nation, in exact proportion as these powers, judging for themselves only, view these professions more or less perfect, and agreeable to the idea given of it in the oracles of revelation."

Were it not for prejudice, arising from early ideas, and early attachments to incorporated sects and systems, this proposition would appear evident at first view. It is even capable of proof from the only principle, upon which the advocates of incorporations dare to stand forth in their defence. "The incorporated system, say they, is a true and genuine exhibition of christianity. The ruling powers therefore, ought to do every thing, consistent with justice, for the truth; but nothing against her." Perfectly just! But is truth wholly confined to the incorporated exhibition of christianity? Is there no particle of truth, no beam of that soul-cheering luminary to be found in the avowed creeds of other denominations? Can the ruling powers discharge their duty to truth, by cherishing her only in one creed, and crushing her in all others? Is this to do every thing for the truth and nothing against her? Or, is she only truth when she figures in national articles, is enthroned in an act of incorporation, and is surrounded by a body-guard of penal laws? No! She is not a creature of law! She is not conjured into existence by votes and established by statutes! She is immutable; and claims, in her own right, the honour of being both generally professed and publicly patronized. As therefore every profession of christianity is truth, as far as the *matter* of it agrees with its scriptural architype; it has an indisputable claim upon the ruling and influencing powers, for protection and patronage, as far as the coincidence of its matter with the original idea of christianity extends. And as even those professions,

professions, which in their matter, are defective, are, notwithstanding, declarations of the truth of christianity in general; and avowals, that the denominations, who make these professions, believe christianity to be the only true religion, they are, in that respect, true; and as such, they claim protection and patronage.

It therefore follows, that if truth have an intrinsic worth, and on that account, an inherent right to be told and avowed; and if men, in every character, are bound to abet, and to the utmost of their power to patronize truth; the legislative, executive and influencing powers of every christian nation, as far as they apprehend that the Bible idea of christianity is maintained and professed by any society, are under the strictest obligations to encourage and establish that society, and to protect and patronize its profession. Instead of establishing one description of christians by an incorporation of it with the political constitution of the nation, thereby giving it horns to push, and talons to tear all other religious societies of fellow-christians, by disfranchisements, disqualifications, and other engines of injustice, to the utter ruin of a christian profession in them; truth, justice, obligations to the christian religion, and love to the souls of mankind, call upon them to cherish that portion of truth, which, upon examination, they find to belong unto, and to constitute the several distinct professions of the christian religion in the nation.

It is true, the same powerful advocates call upon them, not to patronize, but to discourage that portion of falsehood or mistake, which we suppose to be, in these several professions. But how? Not, surely, by acts of cruelty and injustice; for no powers whatever have right in any case to commit them. Not by dictating to the consciences of mankind, and flinging themselves into the throne of God!

God! *Civil* rulers can only sit on *civil* tribunals. They sustain no official character in the kingdom of Christ, nor in the court of the conscience. Not by arming the reputed orthodox to kill and devour all whom prejudice, ignorance or interest may dare to pronounce heretics. Would the virtuous and sound profession of the ruling powers themselves,* be no check upon error in the professions of others? Would the public countenance and patronage given to truth be no check to falsehood? Would the public encouragement given to learned defences of the truth be of small use in rectifying mistakes, suppressing error, and recovering even heretics from the error of their way?

But, will some say, Does not this chain of reasoning tend to make the ruling powers in civil society the public judges of orthodoxy; and to establish it as a rule, that soundness in the faith, as judged of by them, is a rule of dispensing civil rewards and punishments.

We answer, No, not in the least degree! The civil powers, like all other men, must judge for themselves what is truth, and what is falsehood, in order to regulate their own profession of christianity; and like all other men of public character and influence, they must examine what their character, both as christians and as men of influence, binds them to protect and patronize in the professions of others. But this does not infer, that reputed orthodoxy is the rule of dispensing civil rewards and punishments. Orthodoxy, as judged of by them, for themselves, is indeed that which is to regulate their conduct toward the professions of others. But in doing so, they consider themselves only as men of *influence*, in common with all other men of influ-

---

* *Mobile mutatur semper cum principe vulgus.*   CLAUDIAN.

ence; not as men of *office*. In the latter character alone, they difpenfe civil rewards and punifhments; and their rule is ONE. It is not *orthodoxy*, but the unchangeable *law* of equity, more or lefs diftinctly engraved on the hearts of all men. In the former character alone, they, in common with all other perfons of influence, whether great or fmall, judge of, patronize or difcountenance the religious profeffions of other men. They have a right to reward the pious chriftian, the laborious minifter, or the learned defenders of chriftianity with all the liberality of the generous patron; but the *patron* has no right to put the *prince's* hand into the pockets of thofe, whofe profeffion he even juftly difcountenances, in order to furnifh the reward.

Analogy ferves to illuftrate abftrufe points.— Learning in no country was ever made a rule of difpenfing civil rewards and punifhments. To be ignorant of mathematics was never reckoned a crime, and made matter of an indictment in any of his majefty's courts of law. To encourage learning and to reward learned men, legiflature never dreamed that it was neceffary, to incorporate the Ariftotelian, Cartefian, or Newtonian philofophy, with the political conftitution of Great Britain; to make it criminal to teach or believe but according to the incorporated fyftem; and to give all its teachers revenues and livings out of the eftates of thofe, who believe in other fyftems. Such a wild fcheme of policy, inftead of cherifhing literature, would recal all the darknefs of the twelfth century. By encouraging the literati of every fyftem, or of no fyftem, according to their different degrees of literary merit, learning is fully patronized; and none have reafon to arraign the ruling powers of tyranny, in dictating to the underftandings of philofophers; or of injuftice, in amercing other members of fociety, in order

order to reward thofe, who believe and write according to the eftablifhed tafte. Sir Ifaac Newton was juftly rewarded for his great learning and ufeful difcoveries. But though he tafted the royal bounty, it was the hand of the *patron*, not of the *prince*, which conferred the reward.

3. " Were incorporations abolifhed, the civil powers, inftead of having their authority and influence abridged, would find themfelves more at liberty to ferve effectually the interefts of true religion, than ever they have done fince the days of Conftantine."

The truth of this propofition, from what has been already faid, is almoft felf-evident. All the *juft* authority, which the ruling powers ever had, would continue with them; and a great acceffion of lawful power and influence would reward them for the lofs of a power only to injure and tyrannize over the heritage of the Lord. Yes; the only thing they would lofe is a legal right to injure chriftians of other defcriptions, by aiding, abetting and authorizing the incorporated fect to devour, like Egypt's lean kine, all the better fed and more fightly of their kind in the paftures of the church. A happy lofs, this! Good princes and patriotic legiflatures would account it a chief bleffing. Pious and confcientious magiftrates, now excufed from the intolerable hardfhip of abetting injuftice, by punifhing the beft men and the moft induftrious citizens, and of patronizing abfurdity and fuperftition, by heaping national wealth on the pampered clergy of the incorporated fyftem; would ever have it in their power to act ultroneoufly and confcientioufly in the difcharge of their duty, by cherifhing or difcouraging religious profeffions, according to their conformity or difconformity to the original idea of chriftianity in the

infpired

inspired oracles; and according to their benign or malign aspect toward the interests of society.

Of what power would the abolition of incorporations deprive the ruling powers?—Is it of a power to cherish useful learning? This cannot be alledged. Indeed the reverse is the case. In England, in the present state of things, one half of his majesty's subjects are shut out from these sources of learning, the universities. Incorporations have poisoned them; and, at the same time, shut their doors against all of every liberal profession, unless they first pollute their consciences by swearing these absurd oaths required at matriculation, and declare themselves members of the incorporated sect.

Is it of a power to patronize true piety?—Their power and influence would be greatly enlarged. Now, the executive powers are often, against their consciences, legally obliged to cherish impiety and scandalous wickedness. For example; a profane wretch has friends. They procure him a living, levied out of the estates of those who never employed him. He drinks to excess, w—res, games, &c. yet the ruling powers protect him officially in these edifying practices, and patronize him with the wages of unrighteousness. But were incorporations abolished, they would protect the pious man, and make the impious wretch to feel the effects of their virtuous displeasure. For example; a minister has the charge of a flock by their own choice and consent, from whom he receives a legal security for a competent maintenance, during his good behaviour. He is guilty of some gross immorality, scandalous to his flock, and unworthy of his own character. His flock refuse to support him. He sues his bond. The cause is civil, and is tried in a court of law. The jury finds the fact proved and the bond forfeited. Thus, the guilty is summarily punished; and society

is

is delivered at once from a pecuniary burden and a poisonous example.

Is it of a power to propagate the knowledge and profession of christianity?—A great accession also would be made to this power, were incorporations abolished. In the present state of things, the ruling powers have their hands bound up from propagating christianity, or any profession of it but that of the incorporated sect. Perhaps, this is a defective exhibition of christianity; and accounted such by the ruling powers themselves. Yet, in spite of their convictions, they are legally bound to propagate it, or none at all. But more frequently it happens, that persons of *influence* in a nation, who are piously disposed to propagate christianity, pure and unadulterated, are greatly discouraged by incorporations. Subjects, themselves, of a certain nation, they must propagate, under pain of being suspected of heresy and rebellion, the incorporated exhibition of christianity in that nation, even while they are persuaded, on the best grounds, of its falsehood and absurdity. Suppose a subject of France, a gentleman of property, and seriously devoted to religion, to reside in China. He wishes to do all he can to propagate the knowledge of the true God, and of the only Saviour among the idolatrous votaries of Confucius. But he wishes in vain! The incorporation of the popish system in France precludes him. For, if he attempt to teach the popish exhibition of christianity, and talk of the pope being the universal father and head of all christians, he risks expulsion or death. If he presume to tell them, agreeably to the protestant system, that they may be good christians, and may be saved, even though they never be within the pale of the Roman-catholic church, he is both a heretic and a rebel in the eyes of his own country,

and

and muſt never return to it, leſt he ſhould be treated as ſuch.

In fine, is it of a power to confer peculiar marks of royal favour on that profeſſion of chriſtianity, which they themſelves moſt approve; and which they feel themſelves obliged both to profeſs and to patronize?—Of this very power incorporations deprive them! They make princes mere ſtate puppets, who muſt act a part in ſociety, reſpecting the moſt important of all things, religion, without conſidering themſelves to be moral agents, who act ultroneouſly; or to be accountable beings, who muſt be judged for all their actions, public and official as well as private and perſonal. King William III. no doubt gave the ſyſtem of preſbytery and of Calvin the preference in his own judgment. Yet, if at any time, he threw but one favourable glance at thoſe who approved that ſyſtem, all England was inſtantly alarmed; every pulpit reſounded—The church is in danger! King George III. it is probable, moſt approves the ſyſtem of epiſcopacy. Yet the friends of that mode of eccleſiaſtical government, in his dominions, on the north ſide of the Tweed, are under a ban; and royalty itſelf cannot relieve them.—The truth is, were incorporations removed, good princes, who will always give the preference to the beſt profeſſion of chriſtianity, would always have it in their power to give it all that patronage, which is competent even to royalty itſelf, without encroaching upon the rights of peaceable diſſenters from it: and bad princes, who naturally hate religion, would have their hands bound up from either greatly tempting, or forcibly obliging any to follow their example.

V. After what has been ſaid, it is plain, "That in ſo far as the doctrine of the reformed churches, concerning the civil magiſtrate's power *circa sacra* is confistent with scripture, reason, and the principles of civil and religious liberty, the abolition of incorporations would be, in no respect hostile to it."

It has been shewn, that the measure proposed would cancel no one right of any prince. It would deprive him of no power to do good;—of no power *at all*, but that of encroaching upon the religious rights and liberties of his subjects. If therefore any of the protestant churches, in ages when the principles of liberty were not duly studied, nor fully understood by any, taught, in their articles, that christian princes are invested with, and may lawfully exercise such a power; who will stand forth in their defence? Who now of all the protestant churches themselves will openly avow the consistency of such a power?

It cannot be dissembled indeed that SOME of these churches, at the Reformation, ascribed to their princes very extravagant powers—powers of ultimately judging in all ecclesiastical causes;—powers as extensive as those of the typical sceptre of David! But what can be inferred from hence? Nothing! But that incorporated churches very naturally assign to their sovereigns all that power, which is necessary to maintain, defend and render effectual the worldly designs of their incorporations. To incorporations alone it is owing that such articles, were at first inserted in the creeds of some reformed churches; and to them alone we owe it, that they cannot be altered, even when protestants have been generally convinced of their futility. Yes: had it not been that they belong to the political constitution, which political prudence forbids any rashly to touch, the doctrine of liberty, as taught by a *Locke* and others, would have long since produced a change of such articles, as it has already effected a total

change

change of sentiment concerning them, in all the nations of Europe.

But when we said SOME of the protestant churches flattered their princes with extravagant powers *circa sacra*; we meant to except others. The church of France ascribes no undue powers to christian princes. She only asserts that they are the guardians of the *first*, as well as of the second table of the divine law. The churches of Bohemia and Saxony, in their confessions presented at the council of Trent, ascribe to princes no Erastian powers. And the Helvetic and Augustan confessions assign, even to imperial dignity, no more than the patronage of the church in the posession of her own unalienable rights.

Upon the whole, let incorporations be abolished, which give national churches, and the European princes at their heads, a power of violating the rights of conscience, and of rifling the treasures of private property, in order to support an incorporated clergy, and no christian prince can ever exceed in his interference with religion and the public profession of christianity.

SECT. II.

The Abolition of Incorporations would supersede the Use *of Articles, or Confessions of Faith in Churches.—Answered.*

THE nature of the present disquisition, together with the noise which is still made, concerning *subscription*, makes it necessary to return an answer to another objection which the friends of truth will readily make to the abolition of incorporations. " As all obligation arising from public authority to subscribe articles of faith would cease, all such articles would be rendered useless; all terms of ministerial connections would be abolished; every thing respecting christian communion would be thrown loose; and as teachers might disseminate the greatest absurdities, people would be at liberty, without any check, to make open profession of them."

It is not doubted, that this objection will appear so formidable to many, that they would rather wish incorporations to continue, notwithstanding their inconveniencies, than that the purity to which the reformed churches have attained in their respective confessions, should run any risk by their annihilation. But should we even grant that these consequences might follow, may we not modestly ask— Do not these evils already exist in national churches, notwithstanding their incorporations? Is not the Jesuitical trick of subscribing Calvinian articles in an Arminian sense openly avowed? Are there no Socinians in the churches of Britain? In such a case, what avail articles, as terms of either ministerial or of christian communion?

But we hope to shew, that though the abolition we plead for would supersede all obligations to subscription arising from penal disfranchisements and disqualifications, neither would the use nor even the necessity of confessions cease; nor would the moral obligations to subscription be dissolved; nor, in fine, would these consequences, enumerated in the objection follow.—In order to this, a proof of the following proposition shall be attempted.

I. The true principle, on which the necessity and use of articles of faith are built, would still remain, notwithstanding the proposed abolition of incorporations.

II. That incorporations furnish matter for all those objections against confessions of faith, by which they have fallen into contempt. And,

III. That all the valuable ends of articles, would be more effectually gained without the interposition of penalties enforcing subscriptions, than ever they have been, even by the most rigorous execution of penal statutes.

I. The true principle on which the necessity and use of confessions are built would still remain. That principle is no other beside that RIGHT which all the churches of Christ, as free societies, have, to demand both from their public teachers, and from candidates for membership, an explicit declaration of their faith, in order that the labours of the former, and the communion of the latter may answer their several designs.—The evidence of this will appear from the following considerations.

1. Liberty is the unquestionable birth-right of all mankind. Wherefore, any number of person, provided

vided their design hurt not others, may unite themselves in society, for such purposes, and under such regulations as appear to themselves to be most useful. No stranger can pretend a right to usurp the management of its affairs; or to thrust himself upon it, as a member. To do so, would violate the law of equity, and overthrow the liberty of others, independent of him.

2. It has been proved already, that the churches of Christ are such societies. They are founded on the free consent of their members. These, united in one faith, join in their respective assemblies, for the purposes of worshipping their one Lord, and maintaining communion with one another as his people. That such societies should exist, even the light of nature gives its suffrage. It testifieth that religion is the glory of human nature; that it is the most important business of every reasonable creature; and that as men are *accountable* as well as *social* creatures, it is equally inconsistent with the constitution of human nature to live without social worship, as it is to live alone. But it is revelation only, which institutes these societies; presents their divine plan; and furnishes that body of laws, by which they must be governed. From it we are taught, to form exalted ideas of that union, which subsists among all christians; and to have enlarged views of that communion, which ought to be cultivated among all Christian churches. Animated by one spirit, governed by the same laws, and conspiring in the same important pursuits, they, though dispersed over the whole world, compose but one body, one catholic church, visibly united to Christ, their one common Lord.

3. As every man hath a natural right of private judgment; so any number of men, united in church society, must be allowed to enjoy the same privilege.

Every church, as a free society, hath a right to judge for herself, what articles of faith she ought to profess, what rites of worship she should observe; and what doctrine she chuses to be preached in her assemblies, in order to her advancing in the knowledge of Christ. None can lawfully assume an authority over her, to oblige her to hear doctrines which she cannot believe, or to receive members, with whom she can have no communion.

4. As the most plain and momentous truths of revelation are too often denied by those, who own the scriptures to be the word of God; any church, as a free society, and bound to take care of her own interests, may demand from those who ask admission, either in a public or private character, an *explicit declaration* of their religious sentiments, in such words as have the greatest possible tendency to satisfy her members of the sameness of their faith with that of the church, in order that they may have communion together as brethren: or, which is the same thing, she may require a subscription to her public articles, which are supposed to contain those expressions, which are best adapted to give her members that satisfaction.

Nor is this inconsistent with the leading principle of the Reformation, "that the scriptures are a *full* and *clear* revelation of the will of God." They are, indeed, made up of phrases, well chosen for the purpose of a revelation; and without ambiguity in the mouth of the God of truth; but who knows not that they *may* have, yea, that they often have a very doubtful meaning in the mouths of some men? The question is not,—Are such phrases a plain revelation of the mind of God to men?—But are such phrases a determinate signification of men's minds concerning the matter of God's revelation? Is a repeating over and over again these phrases, a sufficient answer to the question—What are your
sentiments

sentiments concerning the meaning of these phrases? Articles of faith are not intended to give an account of what the Spirit of God *says*. He hath done this himself in the scriptures, But they are designed to *ascertain* what a society believes to be the *meaning* of what God hath already said, many ages ago. Hence they ought to be conceived in such words and phrases, as are best calculated to answer that end in society.

Some may probably exclaim—Is any church infallible? Is the creed of any fallible society to be reckoned a standard of truth? We answer,—No! The Bible, the Bible alone is the religion of protestants—of christians! Yet, the public confession of any church is the public standard to her own members, of that *sense* in which she understands the scriptures. Her articles declare, that she believes the scriptures to be the infallible standard of revealed truth; at the same time, that they ascertain in what precise sense, she understands that infallible standard. True, she is fallible! what then? Must she profess a moral certainty in nothing, because infallibility in every thing, is the incommunicable excellency of God alone? Must protestants become sceptics to avoid being papists? If a church err, she errs for herself; and she must follow her own light. It is absurd to suppose, that her members, after having informed their own understandings from the word of God, concerning any article of the christian faith, should forsake their own judgment, because it is fallible, and follow that of others, which is at no greater remove from a possibility of erring than their own.

5. As there is nothing in reason or in revelation that determines the numbers who may unite in sacred society; there seems to be as little in either to forbid any number of less societies, to form them-

felves into a larger body, for their common advantage. Nay—every thing in both declares it to be a reasonable service to their common Lord and eminently conducive to their common interests. Christ commands them " to speak the same things, and that there be no division among them."* The authority of God, their intimate union, and their joint interests conspire to oblige them to cultivate communion. If, therefore, the greatest part of professed christians in a province, in a nation, or a continent, or even in the whole world, were so happy as to agree in the same articles of faith and mode of worship; would it not be highly reasonable that such a society should make public profession of her faith; and should take care, in the admission of candidates either for office or membership, that her faith remain with herself unadulterated?

In such a case, no person, when denied admission for refusing to profess, by his subscription, the same faith with the society, could, with reason, complain of injury. It can be no injury to any to shut the gates of a city against a declared enemy. It is the unquestionable design of such supposed candidates to overthrow the faith, or to corrupt the worship of the society. Indeed, they have no right to ask admission. Their demand implies prevarication. It supposes a desire to be built up in the faith of the society, while they refuse their assent to it; and shews, that, being deceitful workers, they can have no fellowship with the children of sincerity and truth.

These are a few of the plain and easy maxims of common sense. They are principles, sufficient to bear the weight of a practice, to which all religious societies in all ages, have uniformly given their suffrage and their sanction. They are principles, which

* 1 Cor. i. 10.

derive

derive not their strength from statute or canon law. They have no dependence upon, or relation to, incorporations. They are reason! When, therefore, all that authority which articles of faith have received from the kingdoms of this world, and by which they have been cruelly crammed down the throats of conscientious christians, shall be removed;—that foundation which God himself hath laid in Zion will remain unshaken. As long as there is a church of Christ upon earth, she will find herself under a necessity of having recourse to articles of faith; and she will never find herself at a loss for a firm ground to build her practice upon, while these principles remain.

II. " Incorporations have furnished matter for all those prejudices against confessions of faith, in consequence of which they have fallen into disgrace with many, in all the protestant churches."

It cannot be denied, that there are many specious arguments against the use of public creeds; arguments which recommend themselves to many, by that spirit of liberty which seems to glow in them. Yet upon due examination, it will be found, that they are not hostile to those principles on which we have built the DUE use of articles. These are the first principles of liberty, which can never be inconsistent with themselves. These arguments, and the prejudices arising from them, are founded wholly on the ABUSE of confessions. Having been armed with force by incorporations, they have been converted into political engines, for overturning the liberties of mankind, for violating the rights of private judgment and conscience, and for supplanting the authority of the holy scriptures. These objections, therefore, are not so much against confessions of faith, as against engines of injustice and cruelty;

ty; and those who make them, inadvertently lay the churches of Christ open to every inconvenience, while, because an ordinance of God for preserving their purity is abused, they attempt to lay it aside, not only as useless, but as hurtful to their liberty.

The objection against articles of faith, which appears to have the greatest force, and which, indeed, is a summary of all that can be alledged against them, is, "that they are an arbitrary invasion of the rights of mankind; while they supersede the title which every christian has to judge for himself, concerning religious objects: and that they are founded on the maxims of popery; maxims, directly opposite to the spirit of the gospel, to christian liberty, and to the leading principle of the Reformation,—" That the scriptures are the only rule, by which we are to try opinions and to determine controversies."

Upon a review of the principles already laid down, it appears, that the objection, though too just when applied to the tyrannic abuse of articles, is wholly inadequate to overturn the *due* use of them.

Creeds are not " an invasion on the rights of mankind." No! They are themselves the *necessary exertions* of these very rights. Every free society hath a right to use their own understandings, in chusing what they shall believe and profess for themselves. They impose not upon others, independent of the society; no, nor even on their own members. Every member retains his natural right to leave it, whenever he cannot conscientiously concur with the society, either in its faith, its worship, or its practice, without incurring the loss of any thing to which he hath a title independent of the society. Were free societies precluded the right of declaring what they reckon worthy of all acceptation; and of taking

care

care that their public teachers and members be of one and the same faith, in order to answer the purposes of communion, they would cease to be free. They themselves, without invading the rights of any, would become the prey of the worst kind of invasion. Every heretic, every novice, every enthusiast might demand access to their communion; and usurp upon their unquestionable right to chuse by *whom*, and in *what* they shall be instructed.

Nor is the *due* use of creeds " contrary to the leading principle of the Reformation!" They are not *standards* of truth. But they contain those articles by which free societies express their *sense* of the only standard of truth. Instead of being engines to thrust the scriptures down from the honour of being the supreme judge in all religious controversies, they are *formal appeals* to the tribunal of truth in the sacred oracles; and are explicit *declarations* of that sense in which every church, for herself, understands them.

III. " That all the valuable ends of articles would be more effectually gained without the interposition of civil authority enforcing subscriptions, than ever they have been, even by the most rigorous execution of penal laws."

We cannot proceed to a proof of this assertion, without enumerating the chief designs, which churches have lawfully had in their view, in publishing their several creeds, or confessions of faith.

1. One of the first occasions of creeds has been the necessity, which churches are ever under, of giving a fair and candid account of the doctrines they maintain. They reckon themselves debtors to the world, to sister churches, and to themselves, to give a just idea of their tenets. This was one of the principal designs of the first creeds, and of all the

several confessions published at the time of the Reformation. None can question the lawfulness of this design. Every religious society is under obligations to religion, to truth, and to honour, to put defamation to the blush, by a plain declaration of its faith, when its soundness is suspected or arraigned.

And may not all this be done, without employing penal laws against, and violating the consciences of others? Besides, incorporated creeds are not fair and true declarations to the world of the faith of the incorporated church. Composed under the influence of secular authority, they may serve to ascertain the faith of the court, or of the convocation who composed them: but they are not the faith of those who were never consulted about the business. They, possibly may contain the faith of these societies; but they do not ascertain the fact. Being imposed under the lash of certain penalties, they ascertain only one fact, that these churches are treated as if they were literally folds of sheep. It is, therefore, plain, that incorporations overthrow the primary design of creeds. The enemies of churches, notwithstanding such creeds, may still alledge, and even *prove*, that the faith of such societies is diametrically opposed to the articles of their confessions. Some churches might be named, whose incorporated articles are strictly Calvinian: yet, the man who would say, that either the body of the laity, or even the majority of the public teachers are Calvinists, would expose himself to general laughter. Had the apologies and creeds of the ancient churches, or of the reformed churches at the æra of the Reformation, been as far from expressing their real religious principles, they would have been deservedly treated as nests of prevarication and hypocrisy.

2. A

2. A church-state is an institution of God, for the express purpose of exhibiting christianity, in all its branches, both to its friends and its enemies. Every particular church is a "pillar and ground (buttress) of truth." A confession of faith therefore, is essential to the idea of a christian church. Churches have ever understood it so; and accordingly, have always, in proportion to their zeal for the truth, avowed with a firm tone, their attachment to it. By their confessions, they have shewed, that instead of being ashamed of the gospel, opposed by many, and despised by the most of mankind, they gloried in it, as the dearest of heaven's gifts to them, and their richest possession on earth.

And why may not christians still glory in a religion, hated and despised, without being hired to it by those rich emoluments, arising from incorporations, which are often, in their use, not less scandalous to that holy religion, than they are burdensome and injurious to society? Besides the glory and credit of their testimony are much abated. Courted by riches and honours; or frightened by disqualifications and disfranchisements; are they not exposed to suspicion in their profession of atachment to the incorporated system? It may be sincere before God, who knoweth the heart; but it can neither edify the friends, nor convince the enemies of christianity.

3. Articles of faith serve to shew to other churches how far, and in how many momentous things the members of that society, which publicly and voluntarily homologates them, are agreed both with one another, and with other churches on the common faith of christians. Upon this ground, christian churches maintain a profitable correspondence with other churches, cultivate mutual love, and severally

contribute to build up one another in their moſt holy faith.

But it is plain, that this end may be gained much more effectually without, than with incorporations. Creeds allied to the political conſtitution of a nation, and enforced by civil pains, are incapable of aſcertaining what is the faith of the national church. Should a chriſtian of Geneva read the doctrinal articles of the church of England, and compare them with the modern ſermons of the biſhops, and the greater part of eccleſiaſtics in that church, would he not be tempted to form ſentiments very diſadvantageous to their honeſty and uprightneſs?—We ſhall only add,

4. Another deſign of confeſſions. It is their ſubſerviency to the maintenance of the purity of chriſtianity. They ſerve to diſtinguiſh thoſe who are infected with hereſy from thoſe who perſevere in the uncorrupted faith of the goſpel. They diſcover who ought to be admitted to communion with the churches; and who, with ſafety may be ordained unto, or continued in the office of the holy miniſtry. That articles of faith may be, yea, ought to be uſed for this important end, we have already ſhewn; nor do churches need the aid of penal laws in order to obtain it.

While churches are protected by authority, in the exerciſe of their own proper rights, in common with any other voluntary aſſociation, it is impoſſible that they can ſuffer any injury from the admiſſion of either infected members or heretical teachers; unleſs they be wanting to themſelves, in the exerciſe of thoſe rights, which are competent to every free ſociety. But churches loſe their freedom, when they are incorporated; and their confeſſions ceaſe to be any longer diſcriminating teſts. Though they ſhould be unexceptionably found, theſe churches cannot
uſe

use them any farther than government permits them. It is therefore natural to suppose, what indeed has always taken place, that every member of the body political, Arians, Socinians, Arminians, Calvinians; profane swearers, sabbath contemners, &c. will be legally authorized to claim the communion of saints; and that whoever hath interest enough to obtain a *conge d'elire*, or a presentation, will be consecrated a bishop or instituted a public teacher in these churches.

Besides, though a church should be convinced of the falshood of any doctrine, or of the superstition of any rite, in the incorporated system, she cannot reform either, without the consent of the legislature. This cannot be granted, without unsettling the mixed, political constitution. Hence she must continue in the practice of the vilest prevarication in her subscriptions, and in the daily use of modes and forms of worship, which the consciences of her ministers and members loudly condemn.

From the whole, it is plain, that incorporated creeds fall infinitely short of the laudable ends for which they are intended and ought to be used. They are insufficient to keep the Heathen and the Christian, the Socinian and the Calvinist, the openly profane and the devoutly pious from jointly profaning the most sacred institutions of the christian religion.

SECT. III.

The Abolition of Incorporations would overthrow Uniformity.—Answered.

AMONGST all, who, in order to gain and prosecute their own designs, effect a flaming zeal for public decorum, the objection against the abolition

abolition of incorporations will be of great weight,—" That as good order in society is of the last importance to its happiness; no government can maintain it, unless uniformity of religious sentiment and practices be enforced by an incorporation of one creed and liturgy, as the fixed standards of thinking and of worshipping for all in the nation."

As this objection appears plausible to some, we shall attempt a particular answer to it.

Though uniformity in religious sentiment and worship hath been much desired, and vigorously attempted, in almost every age; yet even its greatest advocates have not been uniform in their ideas of it. Few of them have taken that uniformity, which is described and enjoined, in the inspired books, for that model. Should any fear that the measure proposed would prevent *primitive* uniformity from resuming her throne in christian churches; we hope, in the subsequent section, to prove that the reverse would be the case. Meanwhile, that species of uniformity, after which partisans in all ages, have so vehemently thirsted, is very different from that voluntary, unconstrained agreement of churches, " to walk by the same rule, and to mind the same things," which was their primitive glory. " It is a forced concurrence of a whole nation or empire, in the professed belief of that creed, which the legislature pronounces orthodox and national; and in the use of those religious rites, which government lays, as a yoke, on the necks of all to whom it extends the sanction of its authority." Concerning this species of uniformity, which we shall distinguish by the epithet *political*, as opposed to that which is *apostolical*, we beg leave to make the following observations.

I. Unless

I. Unlefs violence be offered to human nature, political uniformity is impoffible. As men are fo different from one another in the complexion of their imaginations, in the clearnefs or cloudinefs of their underftandings, in the modes of their education, in the ftrength and kinds of their prejudices, and in a thoufand other circumftances; it is abfurd to expect that a whole nation, or a whole great empire, confifting of many millions of rational creatures, can ever be brought to this fpecies of uniformity, as long as they are allowed the ufe of their own underftandings and the liberty of a rational choice. As long as human nature and human imperfection are fo clofely united, it never can obtain in any nation whatever. Violence muft be ufed. Political uniformity always eftablifhes her throne on blood, or on the fuperfedure of all that is *human* in man. Her votaries have always treated human nature, as the cruel Philiftines handled the Herculean Ifraelite. They have put out her eyes. They have found it neceffary to take away the key of knowledge from mankind; and to throw them into a ftate of profound ignorance of God, of themfelves, and of all their moral relations. They have not only denied them the ufe of revelation; but have made ftrange efforts (in many inftances, too fuccefsful!) to unteach them all that even natural religion teacheth the favage of the wildernefs. Thefe are the only meafures by which political uniformity hath eftablifhed her throne, and maintained her dominion in all ages;—meafures, equally rational and humane as thofe of the celebrated prince, who ufed the ax and the rack to reduce all his good fubjects to an uniformity of ftature. No doubt, that *merciful* and *wife* prince intended this ftroke of policy, as a great bleffing to fociety, without which he could neither maintain order in the ftate, nor preferve peace among

among its members! At any rate, he prevented them from disturbing public tranquillity, by writing satires against one another, on account of any criminal diversity in their size!

II. Harmony and peace are never promoted by political uniformity. Can violence, cruelty and injustice ever produce harmony? Is it among freemen, or among slaves that this species of uniformity obtains? When did it most prevail in Europe? Was it not in those barbarous ages, when human nature was most ingloriously debased by blood-thirsty popes, and by royal bigots? It is indeed, the shortest road to one kind of tranquillity,—that which is effected among galley-slaves, who, condemned to the oar, exert the remains of a miserable life, in profound silence, under the lash of their brutish master!

III. Harmony, peace and social happiness are destroyed by political uniformity. Can harmony, with her amiable attendants, reside in that society, which denies equal security to the rights and liberties of all its deserving members? No; when men are put in a state, wherein they hourly ly at the mercy of their fellow-creatures, interested in their ruin, only because they claim to see with their own eyes; human nature will rouse itself in them to a vindication of their moral dignity, and will irresistibly prompt them to appeal from the tribunal of the tyrant to the throne of the Lord of hosts. Mutual confidence, which is the foundation of harmony in society, is destroyed by political uniformity. It converts the most populous nation into a wilderness, fruitful in nothing but the entangling briar, and the injurious thorn.

IV. It

IV. It is no presumption to affirm, that public tranquillity, instead of depending on political uniformity, can never be enjoyed in its perfection, but in consequence of its utter abolition. Yes; it is wished for in vain, as long as every member of society, approving himself strictly obedient to the laws of society, enjoys not the unmolested possession of his life, liberty, and property. Facts are unanswerable proofs. In nations where civil merit is the standard of civil administration, public peace and mutual confidence reign; and these nations thereby become objects of terror and of envy to their less happy neighbours. But as soon as any nation hath departed from that maxim, and hath suspended the lives or property of peaceful subjects, on conditions foreign to the genius and ends of civil society, her peace and prosperity have been instantly eclipsed, and have given place to discord, desolation, and public woe.

V. The very means by which political uniformity must be effected are infinitely repugnant to the idea of religion. Their very names grate the ear and shock the imagination. Prisons and chains, racks and stakes, gibbets and gallies, make a strange apparatus for promoting uniformity in the profession of a religion, whose Author came not to destroy men's lives but to save them!

The ideas of coercion and violence are inconsistent with religious sentiment and devotion.

Sentiment, in general, must be the result of a man's own conviction and choice. Religious sentiment is the effect of faith, apprehending the sense of revelation, and captivating the understanding to a perfect acquiescence in the infallible testimony of God in it. It is therefore plain, that political compulsion

compulsion and religious sentiment are incompatible.

Nor is coercion more consistent with devotion. Religious worship is that homage, which the rational creature performs to God, and which arises from a full persuasion of, and a willing compliance with, his authority, at once ascertaining its matter, and prescribing its manner to the conscience. If this be a just account of religious devotion, the means necessary to effect political uniformity destroy its very essence. Besides, that worship which is prompted by these means, though it be externally addressed to God, is really offered up to that authority, which the enslaved devotee formally acknowledged to be *supreme* in this case; and thus, it becomes a species of idolatry, no less dishonouring to God than that of *Jeroboam's* too supple and complaisant subjects.

Upon the whole, it is plain, that uniformity, founded on penal laws, tends to banish religious sentiment, and acceptable worship out of the christian world; and introduces, in their place, three of the greatest plagues with which it can be cursed! Yes; it introduces hypocrisy, rebellion, and persecution. Cowards, whose servile meanness unfits them from attempting any enterprize, worthy of their erect figure, will always wear the mask of the vile hypocrite: the brave whose souls are always superior to base submissions, will bid defiance to oppression, and nobly rebel against the arrogant pretensions of its authors: and the sons of violence, whose secular interests, or tyrannical dispositions engage them on the side of political uniformity, will be, as they have always been, like so many tigers, let loose by authority, on conscientious dissenters, to fill whole nations with murder, massacre, and every desolating calamity.

SECT.

The Abolition of Incorporations would introduce Anarchy.—Answered.

THOSE, who are acquainted with the sources of those prejudices, which govern the greatest part of mankind, can see, that the influence of CUSTOM is universal and almost irresistible. While it reconciles many to the most palpable absurdities; it prepossesses them, at the same time, against the plainest maxims of common sense. If the objects of human policy have run for some ages in even the most absurd channel; mankind contract an habit of thinking, that they could glide along in no other. This is true in the case of incorporations. Many are at a loss to conceive how order should be maintained in christian nations, were these abolished; and many, who are sincerely attached to the interests of true religion, will, perhaps, find themselves under the powerful influence of this prejudice, in regard to national churches.

We may conceive their objection stated in the following manner. "Were incorporations abolished, churches would be thrown into a state of anarchy: every religious party would then perk up, and assume airs of importance: there would be no end of *sectaries* and *subdivisions* among christians: and, amidst all these religious differences there would be no umpire, to whom they could be referred, and who should have authority to bind the wrangling parties to an acquiescence in his decision." We beg leave to make the following observations on the several articles of the objection.

I. That

I. That the abolition of incorporations would throw churches into anarchy is a surmise, without any foundation; is contrary to facts; and implies a rash impeachment of the wisdom and goodness of God in the institution of the christian church.

1. It is without any foundation.—Rather, were incorporations annihilated, religious fury would subside; and religious controversies would be both fewer in number, and would be conducted with more moderation. Ever since that fatal age, which connected secular interest with creeds and liturgies, the zeal of religious partisans hath been often nothing but a complicated passion, made up of hatred, malice and envy, inflamed by ambition, pride, and covetousness. Designing men, finding, or hoping to find their account in the established system, have sworn and drunk, or have prayed and fasted, according to the prevailing humour of the incorporated sect; and, in the end, have plunged whole nations, as well as churches into a state of anarchy indeed! Why is the christian zeal of the eighteenth century so different in its character from that of the first century? Alas, good souls! The primitive christians had nothing to prompt their zeal, but what served equally to enflame their love to God and their neighbour. There were no modern bishopricks, no ecclesiastical revenues of a thousand per annum, much less twenty thousand! no tithes, and even no titles to blow the flame of ambition, pride and emulation. Let these be removed by the abolition of incorporations; and the tide of zeal will subside, and flow in its first channel, purged from all those muddy impurities, which have kept that celestial stream in such a turbid state, during a space of more than a thousand years.

These passions are the true springs of dreaded anarchy; and these would soon languish and expire,

were

were incorporations, which inflame them, abolished in the nations of Europe. Were worldly advantages, those inflammatory causes of the basest passions, removed in common from all christian sects; or were they indiscriminatively, moderately, and judiciously bestowed upon all who deserve them; it would quickly appear, that *dissention*, that infamous brand, which precluding establishments have fixed on the forehead of christianity, would soon cease; that the religion of Jesus, ever supremely benevolent and peaceable, would retrieve its honour and shine out in all its native beauties; and that it would become superlatively amiable in the eyes of even those, whom the barbarous consequences of incorporations have tempted to despise and blaspheme it.

2. Notorious facts prove that the objection is groundless. How could the measure proposed introduce anarchy, when it has been proved that incorporations have been the cause, or guilty occasion of the most dangerous and hurtful controversies by which christianity has been disgraced? The attention which government, in consequence of incorporations, must pay to religious opinions gives them all their importance and all their malignity. Besides, many controversies, of the most rueful consequences, would never have been heard of, had not precluding establishments found a place in European policy.—Examples are the best illustrations.

A controversy hath long subsisted between the church on the south and that on the north of Tweed. The superiority of a bishop above a preaching presbyter hath been fiercely asserted by the former; and hath been as firmly denied by the latter. In vain hath political authority attempted to end it. The question is still undecided, and will remain so till incorporations are abolished. They alone give occasion for it. Take away from the diocesan bishop

bishop all that incorporations give him,—his title, his extravagant revenue, his secular authority, and his consequence as a peer of the realm, none of all which the christian religion gives him; and he will be left so naked, so like one of his own presbyters, that even the most snarling advocate for parity will not bark at him. It is civil authority only, which bestows upon him all that raises him above the apostolical bishop, whom Paul also calls by the less dignified title of presbyter.*

Another question hath been long agitated among even the advocates for equality of order and office among the teachers of christianity. It is—Whether courts of appeal in the church possess a jurisdictional, or only a consultative power of decision?"—A question this, which hath fixed party names on men who have been always great ornaments to the christian profession in Britain; hath divided them into distinct communions; and hath made too many, on both sides, unattentive to the laws of christian charity towards one another.—But were incorporations abolished, together with that secular authority which synods derive from them, the controversy would be instantly decided. As that authority, by which incorporated courts of appeal enforce their decisions, is purely civil; as the exercise of that authority has given many of their decrees the appearance of secular jurisdiction; and as some imprudent men have gloried in that authority as the chief excellency of presbytery;—it has become a stumbling-block to Independents; it has converted the regular gradation of ecclesiastical courts into an engine of tyranny; and hath often tempted christians of every description to contemn that spiritual authority, with which Christ has invested those synods which are regularly convened in his name.

* Acts xx. 17—28. 1 Tim. iii. Philip. i. 1.

Such

Such synods possess authority indeed;—but it is wholly spiritual. It seems to consist in their diligently searching into the nature and circumstances of those causes, which are referred or appealed for decision; in their harmonious agreement concerning the quality of these causes; and in their declaring, in the name and by the authority of the supreme Lawgiver and Judge, the final result of their deliberations. Synods are certainly *authorized* to act, in this manner, in virtue of their institution; they are *qualified* to act thus, in consequence of the gifts bestowed on their members, and the office-power with which they are invested; and they are *encouraged* to act in this way by the promise of the divine presence with them, in all their deliberations and judicial decisions.

From this short account of synodical authority, it is plain, that in so far as it is the authority of Christ himself, exercised in the way of his own institution, it is strictly *juridical*; but when it is viewed as office-power, committed to creatures, invested with sacred offices, it is wholly *ministerial*. Were due attention paid to this obvious distinction, the controversy would be at an end. Presbyterians cannot reasonably claim any other authority besides a power of deliberating concerning what judgment Christ himself, in his oracles, hath already passed upon the cause, under judicial discussion; and a right of announcing that sentence, with all the solemnity, which the nature of the thing makes necessary. They will not pretend to an authority to oblige persons to acquiesce in their decisions, whether they apprehend them to be agreeable to the sentence of Christ in the scriptures or not. On the other hand, Independents cannot modestly put the question,—Is Christ's authority, in his own spiritual kingdom, a juridical power? Seeing all power in heaven and

in

in earth is given to him; and since the Father judges no man, but hath committed all judgment to the Son. And no man who has deliberately considered the nature of the present œconomy of Chrift's kingdom, will doubt, that he exercifes that juridical authority, in the prefent ftate of that kingdom, by the inftituted miniftrations of his fervants, as a prelude to the more fplendid exercife of that authority, in the future and final judgment.

3. The objection implies a rafh impeachment of the wifdom and goodnefs of God in his drawing the plan of the chriftian church. Had her incorporation with the kingdoms of this world been fo eflentially neceffary to prevent anarchy, the wifdom and goodnefs of an infinitely lefs prudent and kind Lawgiver would not have been fo far wanting to her, as to have neglected its pofitive and exprefs inftitution. Yet, he, who is all wifdom and goodnefs, hath not once mentioned it, in the roll of divine inftitutions. Was this an overfight? Is it true, that, were it not for the exertions of human policy, rectifying divine plans, the church, whofe model divine wifdom contrived, would fall into anarchy! Let arrogance fpeak and not blufh—Canft thou mend what God hath made? Canft thou perfect his plans? Canft thou add to the number of Chrift's inftitutions, and not fin? Was not Uzzah's rafh attempt feverely punifhed as an affront to the power, wifdom, and goodnefs of God, whoever challenges the undivided honour of protecting the fymbols of his own prefence?

II. The want of an umpire can alarm none but thofe who know no other means of terminating religious controverfies but the halter or the ftake. All who think like proteftants will affign to TRUTH that honour. Yes; great is truth; and when permitted to fight her own battles fairly, fhe will always

merit

merit the palm. She is the effulgence of the Father of lights. Who, on the question, does the sun shine? asks an umpire? Does not the Father of day himself decide the controversy by his own natural radiance? Yet, should the disputants be shut up in a dark cell, they might sit an age over the question, and at last leave it undecided. In like manner, as long as incorporations guard the ebon throne of intellectual night, men may dispute away all the ages of old time about truth, without becoming one whit wiser men, or better christians. The truth of this observation appears from the present state of theological controversies, even after the decisions and counterdecisions of more than one thousand years. Is the world one whit wiser or better for them? All men know, that the tenet which was condemned and cursed with every requisite solemnity, eight, ten, or twelve centuries ago, is as impudent and as orthodox as ever it was, as soon as it gets footing at court, and obtains an incorporation.

In fine, truth must always decide for herself, in the human understanding. No human decision can beget conviction in the minds of others. Councils may deliberate, and may decree; but it is the evidence alone, which they hold up, as the foundation of their decrees, that can determine the mind to an acquiescence. Were incorporations therefore abolished; were none authorized to impose their decisions upon whole nations; truth would not only retrieve the honour of being her own evidence; but would be acknowledged by all parties, as the universal umpire in all controversies. No longer should we behold ignorance, error, and superstition, standing behind the ramparts of an incorporation, and securely laughing at the shaking of truth's victorious spear.

SECT. V.

That the Annihilation of Exclusive Incorporations would deprive the PUBLIC TEACHERS *of a* LEGAL *Maintenance—Answered.*

OBVIOUS reasons might be assigned why some gentlemen of the most revered character will object to the measure, " That, was legislature to execute such a scheme, the public teachers of christianity would be deprived of a legal maintenance: that men of learning, discouraged by the prospect of indigence and dependence, would refuse to enter upon the work of the holy ministry: and that therefore the people would be in danger of being again plunged into ignorance and barbarism."

To the several branches of this objection, we shall attempt as concise, and as satisfactory an answer as the nature of the thing may admit.

I. Though the present state of incorporations secure the public teachers of a *particular sect* in a *legal*, and often in an affluent living, yet it deprives *many* of the *public teachers* of *christianity*, and sometimes even those who are most deserving, of a legal provision adequate to their literary and official desert. How many thousand of protestant dissenting ministers are thus deprived in the dominions of the British monarch! These, though the tried and approved friends of the protestant cause, and of the illustrious prince who sways the British sceptre, are contented to live on the voluntary contributions of their respective congregations. Were exclusive establishments abolished; and were the objection admitted

admitted in its utmost extent;—the teachers of christianity in general, and *as such*, would not be in a *worse* condition than that in which many are fixed by the absurd policy of Europe. Though custom, joined to the splendour of enormous revenues, has fixed the eyes of the undiscerning multitude on the established clergy; they are not the *only* teachers of christianity. They are only the demagogues of the established sect, viewed as the national clergy. These livings, therefore, if they be a debt due to the public ministers of christianity, belong not to them *alone*, but are due, on the foundations of eternal right, to others, who merit equally of the christian religion, and of their fellow subjects, by a diligent discharge of their duty, under all the discouragements arising from the want of civil patronage.

II. There is no connection between the *abolition* of preclusive establishments, and the *denial* of a *legal right* to a competent maintenance, *voluntarily* stipulated by the Church, and accepted by the Pastor. Where is the inconsistency between renouncing all parliamentary partiality to one sect of christians, and *appointing*, or at least *enacting the legality* of a salary, not below the acceptance of men of learning, provided it be *ultroneously* given by the Flock, and voluntarily accepted by the minister, and provided no levy be made upon the property of others, unconcerned in the mutual agreement? Though government pays not the wages of servants belonging to one denomination of subjects, and much less levies their hire on other masters, yet it follows not, that it hath made no provision for servants. It gives them a right to their wages, and to sue for them, by an action against their employers, when they are injuriously withheld. The case is similar with respect to a gospel ministry. That " the labourer is worthy of his hire," is a maxim in the law of nature, which is the foundation of all civil policy, as well as a *first* principle which the writers of the New Testament have laid down respecting those who have sequestered themselves to the service of the church. All ministers, therefore, have a right to a competent provision; a right founded in the law of nature, * and recognized by the authority of the christian Lawgiver himself. Government, founded in the law of nature and bound to execute its sovereign dictates, by applying it to particular cases, is under the strictest obligation to make their maintenance legal, by recognizing their natural right to it, in the laws of their country.

III. We shall only add, that, by this regulation, an ordinance of divine institution, which, during many centuries hath gone into desuetude, would be revived in the christian world. To CHUSE and to MAINTAIN such ecclesiastical officers as Christ hath appointed and approved, seems to be as much an ordinance of the christian church as *baptism* or the *Lord's supper*. There is an express, unequivocal institution of it. " Who goeth a warfare at any time on his own charges, &c.? Do ye not know, that they who minister about holy things, live of the things of the temple? And they who wait at the altar are partakers with the altar? EVEN so hath the Lord ORDAINED, that they who preach the gospel should live of the gospel."† This last expression evidently implies, that ministers have a right, founded both on natural equity, and upon christian institution, to be respectably maintained, as a fruit of love to the GREAT SHEPHERD, and of gratitude for his pastoral care. But how absurd is it to pretend a right to eat the milk of

---

* Blackstone's Commentaries, Vol. II. p. 25. Dub. Edit.

† Cor. ix. 7—14. ῟ΟΤΤΩ καὶ ὁ Κύριος ΔΙΕΤΑΞΕ.

those

those whom they never fed! This is not to live of the gospel as the Lord hath *ordained*; but to live, like the vulture, on the vitals of common sense and eternal equity, as the civil magistrate hath ordained.

And here we cannot help animadverting on the inconsistency of many professed zealots for christian liberty. They are loud in their clamours for, and positive asserters of, a divine right to *chuse* their own pastors, while there is not a whisper heard from them of their divine right to *maintain* them. In both cases, the right is indeed divine, and in both equal. To suffer either to be violated is base pusillanimity; and to permit either to be done by proxy is a flagrant violation of the divine law. The duty is the same in both. " It is a demonstration of love to the Divine Author of the christian dispensation, exerting itself in active care about the interests of his spiritual kingdom; especially, about HAVING and honourably MAINTAINING a gospel ministry in the church, in order to gain the important designs of her erection in the world."

IV. From what hath been said, it appears, that the *last* part of the objection is entirely groundless. Though gentlemen should not have the prospect of bishoprics, and of ten, fifteen or twenty thousand pounds *per annum* to quicken their zeal for the holy ministry; no man of true piety, probity and learning, could meet with any discouragement from the abolition of an exclusive incorporation of a particular sect. The reverse would instantly obtain. Gentlemen of character would meet with encouragement, proportioned to their worth. A blessing this, rarely seen in established churches! How often may the man of learning and of acknowledged merit be found starving in a curacy on twenty or thirty pounds *per annum*, while the dissipated fop

or

or the half-learned pedant has had the addrefs to obtain a plurality or a deanery—perhaps, a bifhopric! Comparifons are ever odious; yet, it can give no juft offence to obferve, that if fome incorporated churches can juftly glory in the name of a Tillotfon, a Sherlock, or a Secker, diffenters are at no lofs to mention *others* of their communion, who have not been lefs learned, and lefs ufeful to the interefts of real religion and chriftian morality.

Should any be charitably afraid that the abolition of an exclufive incorporation of one fect would introduce a cloud of ignorance among the common people,—we would only beg fuch to inform themfelves from thofe to whom they are difpofed to give the greateft credit,—Whether the lower claffes of his majefty's fubjects, in the communions of the Britifh eftablifhed churches,—or thofe in the communion of proteftant diffenters, are *generally* beft inftructed in the principles of the chriftian religion, and are moft capable of defending them againft the cavils of heretics and infidels?

Thus, an anfwer has been attempted to the principal objections againft the annihilation of exclufive eftablifhments.—

May GOD, in whofe hands are the hearts of all men, fpeedily remove their prejudices in favour of that baneful fource of focial woe; and effectually incline them, in their different fpheres, to concur in its final extermination. *Amen.*

F I N I S.

www.ingramcontent.com/pod-product-compliance
Lightning Source LLC
Chambersburg PA
CBHW032051230426
43672CB00009B/1552